G000244584

Essential tables

INCOME TAX RATES

(ITA 2007, Pt 2, Ch 2)

Taxable income £	Rate %	Tax £	Cumulative £
2021/22			
Savings: 0–5,000	0	Nil	Nil
0–37,700	20	7,540.00	7,540.00
37,701–150,000	40	44,920.00	52,460.00
Over 150,000	45	–	–
2020/21			
Savings: 0–5,000	0	Nil	Nil
0–37,500	20	7,500.00	7,500.00
37,501–150,000	40	45,000.00	52,500.00
Over 150,000	45	–	–
2019/20			
Savings: 0–5,000	0	Nil	Nil
0–37,500	20	7,500.00	7,500.00
37,501–150,000	40	45,000.00	52,500.00
Over 150,000	45	–	–
2018/19			
Savings: 0–5,000	0	Nil	Nil
0–34,500	20	6,900.00	6,900.00
34,501–150,000	40	46,200.00	53,100.00
Over 150,000	45	–	–
2017/18			
Savings: 0–5,000	0	Nil	Nil
0–33,500	20	6,700.00	6,700.00
33,501–150,000	40	46,600.00	53,300.00
Over 150,000	45	–	–

continued

Taxable income £	Rate %	Tax £	Cumulative £
2016/17			
Savings: 0–5,000	0	Nil	Nil
0–32,000	20	6,400.00	6,400.00
32,001–150,000	40	47,200.00	53,600.00
Over 150,000	45	–	–
2015/16			
Savings: 0–5,000	0	Nil	Nil
0–31,785	20	6,357.00	6,357.00
31,786–150,000	40	47,286.00	53,643.00
Over 150,000	45	–	–
2014/15			
Savings: 0–2,880	10	288.00	288.00
0–31,865	20	6,373.00	6,373.00
31,866–150,000	40	47,254.00	53,627.00
Over 150,000	45	–	–

See further **Personal Taxation**, p 1 and **Scottish Taxes** p 224.

PERSONAL ALLOWANCES AND RELIEFS

(*ITA 2007, Pt 3*)

	2021/22 £	2020/21 £	2019/20 £	2018/19 £	2017/18 £	2016/17 £
Personal allowance						
Born after 5 April 1948	12,570	12,500	12,500	11,850	11,500	11,000
Income limit for personal allowance	100,000	100,000	100,000	100,000	100,000	100,000
Married allowances						
Marriage (born on/after 6 April 1935)	1,260	1,250	1,250	1,190	1,150	1,100
Minimum (born before 6 April 1935)	3,530	3,510	3,450	3,360	3,260	3,220
Maximum (born before 6 April 1935)	9,125	9,075	8,915	8,695	8,445	8,355
Income limit for married couples' allowance, born before 6 April 1935	30,400	30,200	29,600	28,900	28,000	27,700
Blind person's allowance	2,520	2,500	2,450	2,390	2,320	2,290
Rent-a-room relief	7,500	7,500	7,500	7,500	7,500	7,500

	2021/22 £	2020/21 £	2019/20 £	2018/19 £	2017/18 £	2016/17 £
Trading income allowance	1,000	1,000	1,000	1,000	1,000	–
Property income allowance	1,000	1,000	1,000	1,000	1,000	–
Savings allowance – basic rate	1,000	1,000	1,000	1,000	1,000	1,000
Savings allowance – higher rate	500	500	500	500	500	500

See further **Personal Taxation**, p 5.

CORPORATION TAX RATES

(CTA 2010, Pt 2, Ch 2, 3; Pt 3)

Year from 1 April	2022	2021	2020	2019	2018
Main rate	19%	19%	19%	19%	19%
Year from 1 April	**2017**	**2016**	**2015**	**2014**	**2013**
Main rate	19%	20%	20%	21%	23%
Small Profits Rate		–	–	20%	20%
Small Profits Rate can be claimed by qualifying companies with profits not exceeding		–	–	£300,000	£300,000
Marginal Relief Lower Limit		–	–	£300,000	£300,000
Marginal Relief Upper Limit		–	–	£1,500,000	£1,500,000
Standard fraction		–	–	1/400	3/400

See further **Taxation of Companies**, p 84.

CGT RATES AND ANNUAL EXEMPTIONS

(TCGA 1992, ss 3, 4, Sch 1)

Tax Year	Annual exempt amount		Tax rate paid by		
	Individuals, personal representatives (PRs) and trusts for disabled	**General trusts**	**Individuals within:**		**Trustees and PRs**
			Basic rate band	**Higher tax bands**	
	£	£	%	%	%
2021/22	12,300	6,150	10	20	20
residential property & carried interest			18	28	28

continued

Tax Year	Annual exempt amount		Tax rate paid by		
	Individuals, personal representatives (PRs) and trusts for disabled	General trusts	Individuals within:		Trustees and PRs
			Basic rate band	Higher tax bands	
	£	£	%	%	%
2020/21	12,300	6,150	10	20	20
residential property & carried interest			18	28	28
2019/20	12,000	6,000	10	20	20
residential property & carried interest			18	28	28
2018/19	11,700	5,850	10	20	20
residential property & carried interest			18	28	28
2017/18	11,300	5,650	10	20	20
residential property & carried interest			18	28	28
2016/17	11,100	5,550	10	20	20
residential property & carried interest			18	28	28

See further **Capital Gains Tax**, p 97.

NIC RATES AND THRESHOLDS

NIC: Class 1 monthly thresholds

(SSCBA 1992, ss 5(1), 8, 19(4); SI 2001/1004, regs 10, 131; Pension Schemes Act 1993, ss 41, 42A; SI 2006/1009, art 3)

Employee (primary)	2021/22 £	2020/21 £	2019/20 £	2018/19 £	2017/18 £	2016/17 £	2015/16 £
Lower earnings limit (LEL)	520	520	512	503	490	486	486
Primary threshold (PT)	797	792	719	702	680	672	672
Upper accrual point (UAP)	N/A	N/A	N/A	N/A	N/A	N/A	3,337

Employee (primary)	2021/22 £	2020/21 £	2019/20 £	2018/19 £	2017/18 £	2016/17 £	2015/16 £
Upper earnings limit (UEL) and Upper secondary threshold (UST)	4,189	4,167	4,167	3,863	3,750	3,583	3,532
Employer (secondary threshold)	737	732	719	702	680	676	676

See further **National Insurance Contributions**, p 174.

NIC: Class 2 rates and exception

(SSCBA 1992, ss 11(1), (4), 117(1); SI 2001/1004, regs 46(a), 125(c), 152(b))

Tax year	Flat rate per week £	Share fishermen per week £	Volunteer development workers per week £	Small earnings exception/profit threshold £
2021/22	3.05	3.70	6.00	6,515
2020/21	3.05	3.70	6.00	6,475
2019/20	3.00	3.65	5.90	6,365
2018/19	2.95	3.60	5.80	6,205
2017/18	2.85	3.50	5.65	6,025
2016/17	2.80	3.45	5.60	5,965
2015/16	2.80	3.45	5.60	5,965

See further **National Insurance Contributions**, p 180.

NIC: Class 3 rates

(SSCBA 1992, s 13)

Tax Year	Weekly Rate £
2021/22	15.40
2020/21	15.30
2019/20	15.00
2018/19	14.65
2017/18	14.25
2016/17	14.10
2015/16	14.10

See further **National Insurance Contributions**, p 180.

NIC: Class 4 rates and thresholds

(SSCBA 1992, s 15(3), (3ZA))

Tax Year	Main rate %	Additional rate %	Lower profits limit £	Upper profits limit £
2021/22	9	2	9,568	50,270
2020/21	9	2	9,500	50,000
2019/20	9	2	8,632	50,000
2018/19	9	2	8,424	46,350
2017/18	9	2	8,164	45,000
2016/17	9	2	8,060	43,000
2015/16	9	2	8,060	42,385

See further **National Insurance Contributions**, p 181.

Key Tax Dates

Monthly

- 19th – Non-electronic payments of PAYE, Class 1 NIC and CIS deductions for tax month to 5th should reach HMRC's Accounts Office (*SI 2003/2682, reg 69(1)(b); SI 2005/2045, reg 7(1)(b); SI 2001/1004, Sch 4, reg 10(1)*).

- 22nd – Electronic payments of PAYE, Class 1 NIC and CIS deductions for tax month ended 5th should clear into HMRC's bank account (*SI 2003/2682, reg 69(1)(a); SI 2001/1004, Sch 4, reg 10(1); SI 2005/2045, reg 7(1)(a)*).

3 May 2021

- Employers must submit Form P46 (Car) to report new cars provided during the quarter to 5 April 2021.

5 May 2021

- Last day for a 2021/22 tax credits claim to be back dated to 6 April 2021.

31 May 2021

- Employers must provide a 2020/21 form P60 to employees who they employed at 5 April 2021 (*SI 2003/2682, reg 67*).

- FATCA returns due for year to 31 December 2020.

- Returns under the Crown Dependencies and Overseas Territories reporting rules due for year to 31 December 2020.

1 June 2021

- Claims for the fourth SEISS grant must be submitted by midnight (*SEISS 4 Direction: https://tinyurl.com/SEISS4dir*).

5 July 2021

- PAYE Settlement Agreements (PSAs) for 2020/21 must be agreed with HMRC (*SI 2003/2682, reg 112*).

- Letting agents acting for non-resident landlords must make return of the rents paid to landlords and tax deducted in 2020/21 (form NRLY). If no letting agent is acting the tenant must make the return.

6 July 2021

- Employers to submit forms P11D and returns of Class 1A NICs (forms P11D(b)) to HMRC for 2020/21 (*SI 2003/2682, reg 85; SI 2001/1004, reg 80*).

- Employers must supply relevant employees with P11D(b) and P11D information for 2020/21 (*SI 2003/2682, reg 94*).

- Annual returns for reporting events relating to all employee share schemes in 2020/21 must be submitted through ERS (*ITEPA 2003, s 421J*).

- Employee share schemes put in place in 2020/21 must be registered by this date.

- File report of termination payments and benefits where non-cash benefits included in the package, where total value of settlement is £30,000 or more.

- Directors and employees to make good cost of the following provided in 2020/21: cars, vans, road-fuel, non-cash vouchers, accommodation, credit token and benefits treated as earnings, to avoid being taxed on those items.

- Where a close company has provided beneficial loans to a director, must elect by this date for all loans to be treated as a single loan to calculate benefits in kind (*ITEPA 2003, s 187*).

7 July 2021

- Return must be made of non-cash benefits provided in 2020/21 to retired employees under employer-financed retirement benefits scheme (*FA 2004, s 251(2); SI 2005/3453*).

19 July 2021

- Employer non-electronic payments of Class 1A NICs for 2020/21 on benefits returned on a declaration of expenses and benefits (form P11D(b)) must reach HMRC. The due date is 22 July for payments made by an approved electronic payment method (*SI 2001/1004, reg 71*).

31 July 2021

- Second payment on account of self-assessed income tax and Class 4 NIC for 2020/21 due.

- Tax credit claims for 2020/21 must be confirmed and renewed for 2021/22 if required.

- Where a pension scheme annual allowance charge of over £2,000 is due for 2020/21 the pension scheme member must inform the scheme administrator if they want the scheme to pay that charge from their pension benefits.

1 August 2021

- Individual taxpayers who have not paid their remaining tax liabilities for 2019/20 face a further 5% penalty, in addition to the 5% penalty suffered on amounts outstanding at 1 March 2021 (*FA 2009, Sch 56, para 3; SI 2011/702, art 3*).

2 August 2021

- Employers must submit Form P46 (Car) if appropriate to report new cars provided during the quarter to 5 July 2021.

31 August 2021

- If HMRC have not issued a notice to file a 2020/21 income tax self-assessment return by now, the normal submission deadline of 31 October 2021 is extended to two months after the date on which the notice to file the tax return is issued (*TMA 1970, s 9(2)(b)*).

1 October 2021

- Reduced rate VAT at 12.5% applies to supplies of hotels and holiday accommodation, food served in restaurants and cafes and hot takeaways, and entrance fees for tourist attractions and events (VAT Notice 709/1, VAT Notice 701/14).

5 October 2021

- Any person chargeable to income tax or CGT for 2020/21 who has not received a notice to file a self-assessment return must notify HMRC by this date that they are so chargeable (*TMA 1970, s 7(1)*).

19 October 2021

- Deadline for non-electronic payments of tax and NI due under PAYE settlement agreements (PSAs) for 2020/21 to reach HMRC Accounts Office (*SI 2003/2682, reg 109(2); SI 2001/1004, Sch 4, reg 13(1)*). The due date is extended to 22 October 2021 for payments made by an approved electronic payment method.

31 October 2021

- Paper income tax self-assessment returns for 2020/21 must be filed for individuals (*TMA 1970, s 8(1D)–(1F)*), trustees (*TMA 1970, s 8A(1B)–(1D)*) and partnerships which include one or more individuals, if the taxpayer's circumstances do not fall within one of the exclusions (*TMA 1970, s 12AA(4A)–(4D)*).

- If HMRC have not already issued a notice to file a 2020/21 self-assessment income tax return, the return must be filed within three months from the date of the notice, whether the return is electronic or paper (*TMA 1970, ss 8(1G), 8A(1E), 12AA(4E)*).

- An individual who submits a paper self-assessment return for 2020/21 must do so by 31 October 2021 if they wish HMRC to collect the tax due through their future PAYE code (*ITEPA 2003, s 684(3A); SI 2003/2682, reg 186(4)*).

2 November 2021

- Employers must submit Form P46 (Car) to report cars first provided during the quarter to 5 October 2021.

15 December 2021

- Last day for person to submit a US tax return for 2020 if they have obtained a filing extension.

30 December 2021

- Last day for person to submit an electronic self-assessment return for 2020/21 if they wish HMRC to collect the tax due through their future PAYE code where possible (*ITEPA 2003, s 684(3A); SI 2003/2682, reg 186(4)*).

31 January 2022

- Electronic income tax self-assessment returns, and any paper returns or self-assessment returns which are excluded from online filing, for 2020/21 must be filed by this date (*TMA 1970, ss 8(1D)(b), (1G), 8A(1B)(b), (1E), 12AA(4B), 12AA(4E)*).

- All outstanding self-assessment income tax, and class 4 NIC, plus any residue of capital gains tax for 2020/21 must be paid. Where notice to file was issued after

31 October 2021, the payable date is extended to three months after the date on which the notice to file was issued (*TMA 1970, s 59B(3), (4)*).

- Where a first payment on account is required for the tax year 2021/22, the tax and class 4 NIC, if applicable, must reach HMRC (*TMA 1970, s 59A(2)(a)*).

- Deadline to file an outstanding 2017/18 self-assessment return to displace a determination.

- Deadline to amend 2019/20 self-assessment tax return.

- Last day to provide final income figures for tax credits claim for 2020/21, if renewal done by 31 July 2021 used an estimated figure.

1 February 2022

- Individual taxpayers who have not paid their remaining tax and NI liabilities for 2019/20 by this date face a further 5% penalty, in addition to the 5% penalties suffered on amounts outstanding at 1 March 2021 and 1 August 2021 (*FA 2009, Sch 56, para 3; SI 2011/702, art 3*).

2 February 2022

- Employers must submit Form P46 (Car) to report new cars provided during the quarter to 5 January 2022.

14 February 2022

- Last day for employees to apply for deferment of primary class 1 NIC for 2021/22.

2 March 2022

- Individual taxpayers who have not paid their tax and NI liabilities for 2020/21 by this date face a 5% penalty (*FA 2009, Sch 56, para 3; SI 2011/702, art 3*).

1 April 2022

- MTD for VAT: All VAT registered businesses must enter the MTD regime for VAT return periods starting on and after this date.

- VAT on supplies in the hospitality and tourist sectors reverts to standard rate of 20%.

5 April 2022

- Last opportunity to utilise income tax personal allowances, annual ISA allowances and exemptions for CGT and IHT for 2021/22.

- Last day to pay voluntary Class 2 or Class 3 NIC for 2015/16, or claim exemption from Class 4 NIC for 2021/22 where earnings also subject to Class 1 NIC.

- Final day for claims for 2017/18 relating to: personal allowances, remittance basis, terminal loss relief, overlap relief, carry-forward of trading losses and capital losses (see **Chapter 6**).

- Deadline to claim an asset became of negligible value or loan to a trader became unrecoverable in 2019/20 (*TCGA 1992, ss 24(2), 253*).

19 April 2022

- Employers must make final RTI payroll report for 2021/22 using FPS or EPS.

30 April 2022

- Daily £10 late filing penalties start to apply to outstanding 2020/21 self-assessment returns.

- Payment of IHT on lifetime transfers between 6 April and 30 September 2021 is due by this date (*IHTA 1984, s 226(1)*).

- ATED returns and ATED relief declarations must be filed for 2022/23. The ATED charge must be paid for 2022/23. Deadline for amending ATED returns for 2021/22.

Note

The above list is for general information purposes only, and is not exhaustive.

Bloomsbury's Tax Rates and Tables 2021/22

Budget Edition

Compiled by:

Rebecca Cave FCA CTA MBA

Welcome to *Tax Rates and Tables 2021/22 (Budget Edition)*, published by Bloomsbury Professional.

This edition of *Tax Rates and Tables 2021/22* been updated to reflect measures announced in the Spring Budget on 3 March 2021 and changes proposed in the *Finance Bill 2021*.

Adjustments to the VAT rules effective from 1 January 2021 due to the UK leaving the EU Single Market and Customs Union have been included in **Chapter 12**.

The temporary increases in the zero rate bands for SDLT, LTT and LBTT are detailed in **Chapter 11** and **Chapter 18**.

This edition also includes brief summaries of the Coronavirus Job Retention Scheme (CJRS) and the Self-Employment Income Support Scheme (SEISS) at the end of **Chapters 3** and **6**.

I am very grateful for the help provided by Lucy Webb and Neil Warren in compiling this edition, as well as the editorial team at Bloomsbury Professional, particularly Jane Bradford for her patience and considerable skill in bringing all the material together.

I hope that you find *Tax Rates and Tables 2021/22 (Budget Edition)* useful and practical. I would welcome your constructive comments or suggestions for future editions.

Rebecca Cave FCA CTA
Rebecca@taxwriter.co.uk
April 2021

Bloomsbury Professional

LONDON · DUBLIN · EDINBURGH · NEW YORK · NEW DELHI · SYDNEY

BLOOMSBURY PROFESSIONAL

Bloomsbury Publishing Plc

50 Bedford Square, London, WC1B 3DP, UK

1385 Broadway, New York, NY 10018, USA

29 Earlsfort Terrace, Dublin 2, Ireland

BLOOMSBURY and the Diana logo are trademarks of Bloomsbury Publishing Plc

First published in Great Britain 2021

Copyright © Bloomsbury Professional, 2021

British Library Cataloguing-in-Publication Data

A catalogue record for this book is available from the British Library.

ISBN: PB: 978 1 52652 011 1
       ePDF: 978 1 52652 013 5
       ePub: 978 1 52652 012 8

Typeset by Compuscript Ltd, Shannon
Printed and bound by CPI Group (UK) Ltd, Croydon, CR0 4YY

To find out more about our authors and books visit
www.bloomsburyprofessional.com. Here you will find extracts, author information,
details of forthcoming events and the option to sign up for our newsletters

Personal taxation

RATES OF INCOME TAX

(ITA 2007, Pt 2, Ch 2)

Taxable income £	Rate %	Tax £	Cumulative £
2021/22			
Savings: 0–5,000	0	Nil	Nil
0–37,700	20	7,540.00	7,540.00
37,701–150,000	40	44,920.00	52,460.00
Over 150,000	45	–	–
2020/21			
Savings: 0–5,000	0	Nil	Nil
0–37,500	20	7,500.00	7,500.00
37,501–150,000	40	45,000.00	52,500.00
Over 150,000	45	–	–
2019/20			
Savings: 0–5,000	0	Nil	Nil
0–37,500	20	7,500.00	7,500.00
37,501–150,000	40	45,000.00	52,500.00
Over 150,000	45	–	–
2018/19			
Savings: 0–5,000	0	Nil	Nil
0–34,500	20	6,900.00	6,900.00
34,501–150,000	40	46,200.00	53,100.00
Over 150,000	45	–	–
2017/18			
Savings: 0–5,000	0	Nil	Nil
0–33,500	20	6,700.00	6,700.00
33,501–150,000	40	46,600.00	53,300.00
Over 150,000	45	–	–
2016/17			
Savings: 0–5,000	0	Nil	Nil
0–32,000	20	6,400.00	6,400.00
32,001–150,000	40	47,200.00	53,600.00
Over 150,000	45	–	–

continued

Taxable income £	Rate %	Tax £	Cumulative £
2015/16			
Savings: 0–5,000	0	Nil	Nil
0–31,785	20	6,357.00	6,357.00
31,786–150,000	40	47,286.00	53,643.00
Over 150,000	45	–	–
2014/15			
Savings: 0–2,880	10	288.00	288.00
0–31,865	20	6,373.00	6,373.00
31,866–150,000	40	47,254.00	53,627.00
Over 150,000	45	–	–

Notes

(1) *Scottish tax bands and rates* – From 6 April 2017 Scottish taxpayers pay Scottish rates of income tax (SIT) in different tax bands in respect of income which is not savings or dividend income, see **Chapter 18**.

(2) *Welsh rate of income tax* – From 6 April 2019 Welsh taxpayers pay the Welsh rate of income tax (WRIT) on 10% of income in each band, see **Chapter 18**.

(3) *Order of taxation* – Income is deemed to be taxed in this order (*ITA 2007, s 16*):

- Non-savings income: net rent, profits and earned income

- Savings income

- Dividend income

(4) *Savings rate band* – Where non-savings income exceeds this band, the savings rate band does not apply (*FA 2014, s 3*). 'Non-savings income' does not include dividend income.

(5) *Savings rates* – See Tax rates for savings income.

(6) *Dividend rates* – See Tax rates for dividend income.

(7) *Non-residents* – Pay savings rates on savings income, dividend rates on dividend income, and the default rates on all other income (*ITA 2007, s 9A*).

TAX RATES FOR SAVINGS INCOME

(ITA 2007, ss 7–18)

Savings within:	2021/22	2020/21	2019/20	2018/19	2017/18	2016/17
Savings rate band	0%	0%	0%	0%	0%	0%
Basic rate band	20%	20%	20%	20%	20%	20%
PSA: £1,000 (note 1)	0%	0%	0%	0%	0%	0%
Higher rate band	40%	40%	40%	40%	40%	40%
PSA: £500 (note 1)	0%	0%	0%	0%	0%	0%
Additional rate band	45%	45%	45%	45%	45%	45%

Notes

(1) *Personal savings allowance (PSA)* – All individual taxpayers, including Scottish taxpayers, are entitled to a PSA of either £1,000 (basic rate taxpayers), £500 (higher rate taxpayers), or nil (additional rate taxpayers) (*ITA 2007, s 12B(2), (3)*).

(2) *Net income* – The income measured for the PSA determination is the result of step 3 of *ITA 2007, s 23*; total income less reliefs.

(3) *Thresholds* – The higher and additional rate band thresholds can be expanded by making personal pension contributions or gift aid donations. These thresholds also apply to Scottish taxpayers for the purpose of deciding the level of PSA.

(4) *Tax rate* – Savings income (defined in *ITA 2007, s 18*) not within the savings rate band which is covered by the PSA is taxed at the savings nil rate (*ITA 2007, ss 12A, 12B*). Savings income in excess of the savings allowance is taxed at the income tax rate for the tax band, if it is not covered by the personal allowance.

(5) *Interest received* – From 6 April 2016 deposit takers (banks, building societies and other institutions including NS&I) are not required to deduct income tax from yearly interest paid in respect of relevant investments (*ITA 2007, Pt 15, Ch 2*).

(6) *Reclaim tax* – Companies which are not deposit takers, who pay yearly interest are required to deduct 20% tax from the interest paid. Where tax has been deducted, but the interest is taxed at the nil rate, the taxpayer can reclaim the tax deducted at source (*ITA 2007, s 17*).

TAX RATES FOR DIVIDEND INCOME

(*ITA 2007, ss 10–19*)

Dividends within:	2021/22	2020/21	2019/20	2018/19	2017/18	2016/17
Basic rate band	7.5%	7.5%	7.5%	7.5%	7.5%	7.5%
Dividend allowance	£2,000	£2,000	£2,000	£2,000	£5,000	£5,000
Higher rate band	32.5%	32.5%	32.5%	32.5%	32.5%	32.5%
Dividend allowance	£2,000	£2,000	£2,000	£2,000	£5,000	£5,000
Additional rate band	38.1%	38.1%	38.1%	38.1%	38.1%	38.1%
Dividend allowance	£2,000	£2,000	£2,000	£2,000	£5,000	£5,000

Notes

(1) *Dividend allowance* – Dividend income covered by this allowance is taxed at 0%, but it does use up the tax band it falls into. Only available for UK-resident individuals, trustees and PRs do not have a dividend allowance (*ITA 2007, s 13A*).

(2) *Tax credit* – The 10% non-repayable dividend tax credit was abolished on 6 April 2016. Before that date dividend income received was grossed-up by applying a fraction of 1/9th to the net amount (*ITTOIA 2005, ss 397–397C*).

(3) *Dividend income* – Before 6 April 2016 where gross dividend income did not exceed the basic rate threshold, the income tax was charged at 10%, and the tax due was covered by the dividend tax credit.

(4) *Requirement to notify* – The taxpayer doesn't have to notify HMRC of receipt of dividend income if there is no lability to tax on that income (*TMA 1970, s 7*).

TRUST RATES

(ITA 2007, s 9)

Income within:	2021/22	2020/21	2019/20	2018/19	2017/18	2016/17
Standard rate band: up to £1,000 (note 1)	default basic rates apply see note 2					
Dividend income	38.1%	38.1%	38.1%	38.1%	38.1%	38.1%
Other income	45%	45%	45%	45%	45%	45%

Notes

(1) *Standard rate band* – In the case of trusts made by the same settlor, the standard rate band is divided by the number of such trusts, subject to a minimum starting rate band of £200 (*ITA 2007, ss 491, 492*).

(2) *Default rates* – Income within the standard rate band is generally taxable at the (non-trust) rates applicable to the particular source of income (see tables above). From 6 April 2016 dividends within this band are taxed at the dividend ordinary rate (7.5%), savings and other income is taxed at the default basic rate (20%) (*ITA 2007, s 9A*).

(3) *No allowances* – Trustees and estates of deceased persons are not entitled to the personal savings allowance or dividend allowance.

(4) *Notification* – From 2016/17, where the only income of a trust, or estate in administration, is savings interest and the tax liability is below £100, the trustees and personal representatives are not required to notify HMRC (*HMRC Trusts & Estates newsletter* August 2019).

(5) *Discretionary trusts* – The above trust rates broadly apply to accumulated or discretionary trust income (*ITA 2007, s 479*).

(6) *Interest in possession trusts* – These trusts are generally liable to income tax at the rates applicable within the basic rate band for individuals (see Tax rates for savings income and Tax rates for dividend income), although certain capital receipts for trust law purposes are liable at the above trust rates (*ITA 2007, ss 481, 482*).

(7) *Trust Registration Service (TRS)* – All UK express trusts and non-UK trusts which receive income from a UK source and pay UK taxes have to be registered on the online TRS (see Bloomsbury Professional *Trusts and Estates 2020/21* Chapter 3).

PERSONAL ALLOWANCES AND RELIEFS

(ITA 2007, Pt 3; ITTOIA 2005, Pt 7, Ch1)

	2021/22 £	2020/21 £	2019/20 £	2018/19 £	2017/18 £	2016/17 £
Personal allowance	12,570	12,500	12,500	11,850	11,500	11,000
Income limit for personal allowance	100,000	100,000	100,000	100,000	100,000	100,000
Allowances for couples						
Marriage Allowance (notes 4 & 5)	1,260	1,250	1,250	1,190	1,150	1,100
Married couple's: min	3,530	3,510	3,450	3,360	3,260	3,220
Married couple's: max (note 3)	9,125	9,075	8,915	8,695	8,445	8,355
Income limit for age-related and married allowances	30,400	30,200	29,600	28,900	28,000	27,700
Blind person's allowance	2,520	2,500	2,450	2,390	2,320	2,290
Rent-a-room relief (note 5)	7,500	7500	7,500	7,500	7,500	7,500
Trading allowance (note 6)	1,000	1,000	1,000	1,000	1,000	N/A
Property allowance (note 7)	1,000	1,000	1,000	1,000	1,000	N/A

Notes

(1) *Abatement of personal allowance* – Personal and age allowances are reduced by £1 for every £2 above the £100,000 threshold, where the taxpayer's adjusted net income (see *ITA 2007, s 58*) exceeds £100,000 (*ITA 2007, s 35*).

(2) *Married couple's allowance* – The rate of tax relief for the married couple's allowance is 10%. At least one party to the marriage or civil partnership must have been born before 6 April 1935 (*ITA 2007, s 45*).

(3) *Marriage allowance election* – Married couples and civil partners can elect to transfer 10% of their personal allowance (rounded up to the nearest £10) to their spouse or civil partner, if the conditions in note (5) apply. This election can be made on behalf of a deceased spouse or civil partner (*ITA 2007, Pt 3, Ch 3A*).

(4) *Recipient of marriage allowance* – Must be taxed at no more than the basic rate (20%) or the Scottish intermediate rate (21%). The recipient is given a tax reduction of 20% x marriage allowance (£252 for 2021/22), whatever their marginal tax rate actually is for the year (*ITA 2007, s 55B(2)*).

(5) *Rent-a-room* – Where more than one person is receiving rent from the property the relief per person is half the total (*ITTOIA 2005, s 789*).

(6) *Trading allowance* – Miscellaneous or trading income, as well as income from providing assets and services within this limit is treated as nil. It cannot apply to income from a partnership or property (*ITTOIA 2005, s 783A*).

(7) *Property allowance* – Income from property that does not qualify for rent-a-room relief, and which is within this limit, is treated as nil (*ITTOIA 2005, s 783B*).

HIGH INCOME CHILD BENEFIT CHARGE (HICBC)

(ITEPA 2003, ss 681B–681H)

The amount of the high income child benefit charge is the appropriate percentage of child benefit. The 'appropriate percentage' is the lower of:

(a) 100%; or

(b) $\dfrac{ANI - L}{X}\%$

Where: ANI = adjusted net income;

L = £50,000;

X = £100.

Notes

(1) *Applies where* – The taxpayer or their partner receives child benefit on or after 7 January 2013, and the taxpayer's 'adjusted net income' exceeds £50,000. If both partners have adjusted net income over £50,000, the charge is levied on the partner with the highest income (*ITEPA 2003, s 681D*).

(2) *Effect* – The HICBC is 1% of child benefit for every £100 of adjusted net income above £50,000. The HICBC claws back 100% of child benefit where adjusted net income exceeds £60,000. The amounts and percentages used in the formula are rounded down if not whole numbers.

(3) *Election* – A claimant may elect to stop receiving child benefit payments to avoid the HICBC, but the child benefit claim is maintained to protect NI credits (note 5). This election can be revoked with retrospective effect for up to two years (*SSAA 1992, s 13A; SSA(NI)A 1992, s 11*).

(4) *Declaration* – Taxpayers who are subject to the HICBC must declare the child benefit received by themselves or their partner on their self-assessment tax return for the relevant tax year.

(5) *Claim benefit* – Parents should claim child benefit at the earliest opportunity to protect the claimant's rights to NI credits, and to ensure the child is allocated an NI number before they reach age 16.

(6) *Further information* – For rates of child benefit see **Chapter 15: State Benefits**. For HMRC guidance see: https://www.gov.uk/child-benefit-tax-charge.

STATUTORY RESIDENCE TEST (SRT)

(FA 2013, Sch 45, paras 3–15)

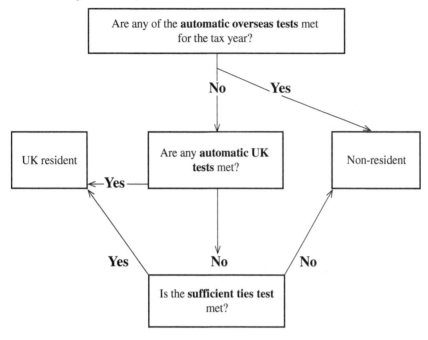

Notes

(1) *Order of tests* – To establish whether an individual is resident in the UK or not in a tax year, follow the diagram above. Start with the automatic overseas tests. If any of these tests are met the individual will be automatically non-UK resident for the tax year, and no further tests are required.

(2) *Automatic overseas tests* – The automatic overseas tests for living taxpayers are summarised as:

    (a) fewer than16 days in the UK – for those individuals who are resident in the UK for one or more of the three preceding tax years;

    (b) fewer than 46 days in the UK – for those individuals who are resident in the UK for none of the three preceding tax years;

    (c) fewer than 91 days in the UK – for individuals who work full-time overseas with no significant breaks.

(3) *Automatic UK tests* – The automatic UK tests for living taxpayers are summarised as:

    (a) 183 days or more in the UK;

    (b) has a home in the UK and spends sufficient time there;

    (c) works full-time in the UK.

Sufficient ties test

(FA 2013, Sch 45, paras 17–20, 31–38)

Notes

(1) *Scope* – If the individual has 'sufficient UK ties' for that tax year he will be UK resident.

(2) *UK ties* – these are summarised as:

    (a) family tie;

    (b) accommodation tie;

    (c) work tie;

    (d) 90-day tie; and

    (e) country tie (only considered if the individual was UK resident in one or more of the preceding three tax years).

(3) *Sufficient UK ties* – The number of UK ties needed for an individual to be UK resident is based on the number of days spent in the UK, in accordance with the tables below:

    (a) If individual was UK resident for one or more of the three tax years before the tax year under consideration:

Days in the UK in tax year	Number of UK ties sufficient for residence
16–45	At least 4
46–90	At least 3
91–120	At least 2
Over 120	At least 1

    (b) If individual was UK resident for none of the three tax years before the tax year under consideration:

Days in the UK in the tax year	Number of UK ties sufficient for residence
46–90	All 4
91–120	At least 3
Over 120	At least 2

SRT – General points

(FA 2013, s 218, Sch 45)

Notes

(1) *Commencement* – The SRT has effect from 6 April 2013 *(FA 2013, Sch 45, para 153)*.

(2) *Scope* – The SRT applies to individuals for income tax, CGT and IHT purposes to the extent that an individual's residence status is relevant to those taxes.

(3) *Temporary non-residence* – There are separate rules for temporary non-residence, which apply for departures from the UK on and after 6 April 2013, in respect of distributions to participators in close companies (*ITTOIA 2005, s 401C*), and for CGT purposes (*TCGA 1992, s 10A*).

(4) *Days in the UK* – An individual is present in the UK if he is there at midnight at the end of a day, with limited exceptions. However, the taxpayer may be deemed to be in the UK, when he was not physically present, if certain conditions are satisfied. Days in the UK may also be ignored if exceptional circumstances apply, such as due to the coronavirus, see HMRC's Residence Domicile and Remittance Basis manual RDRM11005 (*FA 2013, Sch 45, paras 22, 23*).

(5) *Deceased persons* – There are different automatic tests where the individual dies in the tax year. The 'sufficient UK ties' tests also apply to individuals who die during the tax year, but subject to specified modifications in some cases (*FA 2013, Sch 45, para 20*).

(6) *Split year treatment* – An individual is generally either UK resident or non-UK resident for a full tax year. However, the tax year may be split into two parts (ie a UK part and an overseas part) in eight specified circumstances (*FA 2013, Sch 45, Pt 3*).

(7) *Transitional provisions* – These apply if an individual is considering residence status for any of the tax years 2013/14 to 2017/18, or the application of the split-year rules to those years, and it is necessary to determine the individual's residence status for a tax year before 2013/14 (*FA 2013, Sch 45, para 154*).

(8) *Further guidance* – See HMRC guides: RDR1, RDR3, and RDR4. For detailed guidance, see *Booth and Schwarz: Residence, Domicile and UK Taxation* (20th edition, Bloomsbury Professional).

REMITTANCE BASIS CHARGE (RBC)

(*ITA 2007, s 809H*)

Resident in the UK in at least:	2021/22 £	2020/21 £	2019/20 £	2018/19 £	2017/18 £	2016/17 £
7 of last 9 tax years	30,000	30,000	30,000	30,000	30,000	30,000
12 of last 14 tax years	60,000	60,000	60,000	60,000	60,000	60,000
17 of last 20 tax years (note 3)	N/A	N/A	N/A	N/A	N/A	90,000

Notes

(1) *Payable by* – Individuals who are not domiciled in the UK, but who are tax resident in the UK and who make a claim to use the remittance basis. The charge is in addition to any tax payable in the UK on remitted income or gains (*ITA 2007, Pt 14, Ch A1*).

(2) *Nominated income* – The taxpayer must nominate a source of offshore income or gains against which the RBC is levied and must be very careful not to remit that income or gains to the UK.

(3)   *Deemed domicile* – From 6 April 2017 non-domiciled individuals who have been resident in the UK for at least 15 out of the preceding 20 tax years are deemed to be domiciled in the UK for income tax and CGT purposes. Individuals with UK domicile of origin are not eligible to claim non-domiciled status while resident in the UK (*F(No 2)A 2017, s 29, Sch 8*).

CAP ON INCOME TAX RELIEFS

(FA 2013, s 16, Sch 3)

Title and description of relief	Legislation
Trade loss relief against general income (aka 'sideways loss relief')	*ITA 2007, s 64*
Early years trade losses relief – available in the first four years of the trade, profession or vocation	*ITA 2007, s 72*
Post-cessation trade relief – for qualifying payments/events within seven years of the permanent cessation of the trade.	*ITA 2007, s 96*
Property loss relief against general income – property business losses arising from capital allowances or agricultural expenses	*ITA 2007, s 120*
Post-cessation property relief – for qualifying payments/events within seven years of the permanent cessation of the UK property business	*ITA 2007, s 125*
Employment loss relief	*ITA 2007, s 128*
Former employees deduction for liabilities	*ITEPA 2003, s 555*
Share loss relief (see note 3)	*ITA 2007, s 131*
Losses on deeply discounted securities – only for losses on gilt strips and listed securities held since 26 March 2003	*ITTOIA 2005, ss 446–488, 453–456*
Qualifying loan interest – on loans to buy an interest in certain types of company, or in a partnership	*ITA 2007, Pt 8, Ch 1*

Notes

(1)   *Commencement* – The cap is applied in respect of the above income tax reliefs claimed by individuals for 2013/14 and subsequent years.

(2)   *Application* – Where the individual seeks to claim more than £50,000 in reliefs, the cap is set at the greater of £50,000 and 25% of adjusted total income (*ITA 2007, s 24A*).

(3)   *Exclusions for venture capital* – The cap does not apply to share loss relief where the shares are qualifying EIS, SEIS or SITR shares (*ITA 2007, s 24A(7)(d)*).

(4)   *Overlap relief* – The cap does not apply to overlap relief allowed under *ITTOIA 2005, s 205 or 220.*

(5)   *Business premises renovation* – The cap does not apply to the business premises renovation allowance, which was abolished in 2017, see **Chapter 10** (*CAA 2001, Pt 3A*).

(6)   *Same trade* – The cap does not apply to deductions for trade or property loss relief or post-cessation trade or property relief made from profits of the same trade or property business (*ITA 2007, s 24A(7)(b)*).

SELF-ASSESSMENT TAX RETURNS

Filing dates: individuals and trustees

(TMA 1970, ss 8, 8A)

Type of tax return	Filing date
Paper returns (non-electronic)	31 October following the end of the tax year unless an exclusion applies *(TMA 1970, ss 8(1D)(a), 8A(1B)(a))*.
Electronic returns	31 January following the end of the tax year *(TMA 1970, ss 8(1D)(b), 8A(1B)(b))*.
Return (or notice to file) issued after 31 July but before 31 October following the end of the tax year	3 months from the date of the return/notice for paper returns, or 31 January for electronic returns *(TMA 1970, ss 8(1F), 8A(1D))*.
Return (or notice to file) issued after 31 October following the end of the tax year	3 months from the date of the return/notice (whether paper or electronic) *(TMA 1970, ss 8(1G), 8A(1E))*.

Notes

(1) *PAYE coding* – Individuals who wish to have their tax coded-out through their PAYE code for the following year must file their tax return by 30 December at the latest, instead of 31 January.

(2) *Partnerships* – The above filing dates also apply to partnerships with individual members *(TMA 1970, s 12AA(4)–(4E))*. Separate provisions apply in the case of partnerships involving one or more companies *(TMA 1970, s 12AA(5)–(5E))*.

(3) *Must be paper* – The following tax returns cannot be submitted online and must be submitted in paper form by 31 January following the tax year end:

- SA970 – Trustees of Registered Pension Schemes

- SA200 – Short tax return

- Where the taxpayer's circumstances fall into one of the self-assessment individual exclusions for online filing.

(4) *Needs commercial software* – The following types of tax return and supplementary pages to the SA100 are not supported by the HMRC free software so require commercial software for submission:

- SA800 – Partnership tax return

- SA900 – Trust and estate return

- SA102M – Ministers of religion

- SA102MP – Members of Westminster Parliament

- SA102MLA – Members of Northern Ireland Assembly

- SA102MSP – Members of Scottish Parliament

- SA102WAM – Members of the National Assembly for Wales

- SA103L – Lloyds underwriters
- SA107 – Trust income
- SA109 – Residence, remittance basis etc.

Due dates for payment of tax

(TMA 1970, ss 59A, 59B)

Due date	What is payable:
31 January in the tax year	1st payment on account
31 July following tax year end	2nd payment on account
31 January following tax year end	Balancing payment and any CGT due

Notes

(1) *No payments on account* – These are not required where:

- More than 80% of the previous year's tax liability was covered by tax deducted at source and dividend tax credits; or
- the previous year's liability (net of tax deducted at source) was less than £1,000 *(SI 1996/1654, SI 2008/838)*.
- the payment is due on 31 July 2020 for 2020/21, these payments are automatically deferred until 31 January 2021 because of the COVID19 crisis (see www.gov.uk/pay-self-assessment-tax-bill).

(2) *Late notice* – If a return (or a notice to file) was not issued until after 31 October following the end of the tax year, and the taxpayer notified HMRC of chargeability by 5 October following the tax year, the due date for the final payment (including any CGT) is three months from the issue of the return/notice *(TMA 1970, s 59B(3), (4))*.

(3) *Penalties* – For penalties and interest that may apply to late payments see **Chapter 17**.

ASSESSMENTS, CLAIMS AND ELECTIONS

Normal time limits

(TMA 1970, ss 34, 43; FA 2008, s 118, Sch 39)

Tax year	Claim by
2021/22	5 April 2026
2020/21	5 April 2025
2019/20	5 April 2024
2018/19	5 April 2023
2017/18	5 April 2022
2016/17	5 April 2021

Notes

(1) *Timing of claim* – Except where otherwise specified, a relief claim for income tax and capital gains purposes must be made within four years after the end of the tax year. A self-assessment must be made within four years of the tax year it relates to (*TMA 1970, ss 8, 8A*).

(2) *Form of claim* – Claims or elections should generally be made on the tax return, in the online personal account, or on a form specifically provided for the claim, such as form P87, or by an amendment to the tax return.

(3) *Claims by phone* – HMRC will accept claims for relief on employment expenses if:

- a P87 form has not been sent to the taxpayer to complete;

- the claim is for less than £1,000, or £2,500 for professional subscriptions; and

- the taxpayer made a similar claim for an earlier tax year which was accepted by HMRC.

Expenses and benefits

COMPANY CAR BENEFIT CHARGES

(*ITEPA 2003, ss 139–142*)

Appropriate percentages from 6 April 2020 to 5 April 2022

For cars registered on and after 6 April 2020

CO_2 emissions g/km	Hybrid range with zero emissions miles	2020/21		2021/22	
		Petrol & electric %	Diesel %	Petrol & electric %	Diesel %
0	N/A	0	N/A	1	N/A
1–50	130 or more	0	4	1	5
1–50	70–129	3	7	4	8
1–50	40–69	6	10	7	11
1–50	30–39	10	14	11	15
1–50	Less than 30	12	16	13	17
51–54	N/A	13	17	14	18
54–59	N/A	14	18	15	19
60–64	N/A	15	19	16	20
65–69	N/A	16	20	17	21
70–74	N/A	17	21	18	22
75–79	N/A	18	22	19	23
80–84	N/A	19	23	20	24
85–89	N/A	20	24	21	25
90–94	N/A	21	25	22	26
95–99	N/A	22	26	23	27
100–104	N/A	23	27	24	28
105–109	N/A	24	28	25	29
110–114	N/A	25	29	26	30
115–119	N/A	26	30	27	31
120–124	N/A	27	31	28	32

CO$_2$ emissions g/km	Hybrid range with zero emissions miles	2020/21		2021/22	
		Petrol & electric %	Diesel %	Petrol & electric %	Diesel %
125–129	N/A	28	32	29	33
130–134	N/A	29	33	30	34
135–139	N/A	30	34	31	35
140–144	N/A	31	35	32	36
145–149	N/A	32	36	33	37
150–154	N/A	33	37	34	37
155–159	N/A	34	37	35	37
160–164	N/A	35	37	36	37
165–169	N/A	36	37	37	37
170 and over	N/A	37	37	37	37

Appropriate percentages from 6 April 2020 to 5 April 2022

For cars registered before 6 April 2020

CO$_2$ emissions g/km	Hybrid range with zero emissions miles	2020/21		2021/22	
		Petrol & electric %	Diesel %	Petrol & electric %	Diesel %
0	N/A	0	N/A	1	N/A
1–50	130 or more	2	6	2	6
1–50	70–129	5	9	5	9
1–50	40–69	8	12	8	12
1–50	30–39	12	16	12	16
1–50	Less than 30	14	18	14	18
51–54	N/A	15	19	15	19
54–59	N/A	16	20	16	20
60–64	N/A	17	21	17	21
65–69	N/A	18	22	18	22
70–74	N/A	19	23	19	23
75–79	N/A	20	24	20	24
80–84	N/A	21	25	21	25
85–89	N/A	22	26	22	26
90–94	N/A	23	27	23	27
95–99	N/A	24	28	24	28

continued

CO_2 emissions g/km	Hybrid range with zero emissions miles	2020/21		2021/22	
		Petrol & electric %	Diesel %	Petrol & electric %	Diesel %
100–104	N/A	25	29	25	29
105–109	N/A	26	30	26	30
110–114	N/A	27	31	27	31
115–119	N/A	28	32	28	32
120–124	N/A	29	33	29	33
125–129	N/A	30	34	30	34
130–134	N/A	31	35	31	35
135–139	N/A	32	36	32	36
140–144	N/A	33	37	33	37
145–149	N/A	34	37	34	37
150–154	N/A	35	37	35	37
155–159	N/A	36	37	36	37
160 and above	N/A	37	37	37	37

Appropriate percentages from 6 April 2017 to 5 April 2020

CO_2 emissions (g/km) (see Note 1 below)	2019/2020		2018/2019		2017/2018	
	Petrol & electric %	Diesel %	Petrol & electric %	Diesel %	Petrol & electric %	Diesel %
0–50	16	20	13	17	9	12
51–75	19	23	16	20	13	16
76–94	22	26	19	23	17	20
95–99	23	27	20	24	18	21
100–104	24	28	21	25	19	22
105–109	25	29	22	26	20	23
110–114	26	30	23	27	21	24
115–119	27	31	24	28	22	25
120–124	28	32	25	29	23	26
125–129	29	33	26	30	24	27
130–134	30	34	27	31	25	28
135–139	31	35	28	32	26	29
140–144	32	36	29	33	27	30
145–149	33	37	30	34	28	31
150–154	34	37	31	35	29	32

CO$_2$ emissions (g/km) (see Note 1 below)	2019/2020		2018/2019		2017/2018	
	Petrol & electric %	Diesel %	Petrol & electric %	Diesel %	Petrol & electric %	Diesel %
155–159	35	37	32	36	30	33
160–164	36	37	33	37	31	34
165–169	37	37	34	37	32	35
170–174	37	37	35	37	33	36
175–179	37	37	36	37	34	37
180 -184	37	37	37	37	35	37
185–189	37	37	37	37	36	37
190 and above	37	37	37	37	37	37

Appropriate percentages from 6 April 2014 to 5 April 2017

CO$_2$ emissions (g/km) (see Note 1 below)	2016/17		2015/16		2014/15	
	Petrol & electric %	Diesel %	Petrol & electric %	Diesel %	Petrol & electric %	Diesel %
0	7	10	5	8	0	0
1–50	7	10	5	8	5	8
51–75	11	14	9	12	5	8
76–94	15	18	13	16	11	14
95–99	16	19	14	17	12	15
100–104	17	20	15	18	13	16
105–109	18	21	16	19	14	17
110–114	19	22	17	20	15	18
115–119	20	23	18	21	16	19
120–124	21	24	19	22	17	20
125–129	22	25	20	23	18	21
130–134	23	26	21	24	19	22
135–139	24	27	22	25	20	23
140–144	25	28	23	26	21	24
145–149	26	29	24	27	22	25
150–154	27	30	25	28	23	26
155–159	28	31	26	29	24	27
160–164	29	32	27	30	25	28

continued

CO_2 emissions (g/km)	2016/17		2015/16		2014/15	
(see Note 1 below)	Petrol & electric %	Diesel %	Petrol & electric %	Diesel %	Petrol & electric %	Diesel %
165–169	30	33	28	31	26	29
170–174	31	34	29	32	27	30
175–179	32	35	30	33	28	31
180–184	33	36	31	34	29	32
185–189	34	37	32	35	30	33
190–194	35	37	33	36	31	34
195–199	36	37	34	37	32	35
200–204	37	37	35	37	33	35
205–209	37	37	36	37	34	35
210–214	37	37	37	37	35	35
215–219	37	37	37	37	35	35
220 and above	37	37	37	37	35	35

Notes

(1)   *Zero CO_2 emissions* – Vehicles which cannot produce CO_2 emissions under any circumstances when driven (*ITEPA 2003, s 140(3A)*).

(2)   *Rounding* – The income tax charge is based on a percentage of the car's list price graduated according to the level of CO_2 emissions measured in grams per kilometre (g/km) and rounded down to the nearest 5g/km. Rounding does not apply to cars with emissions below 75g/km in 2014/15.

(3)   *Measure of emissions* – For cars first registered on or after 6 April 2020 the measure of CO_2 emissions uses the Worldwide Harmonised Light Vehicle Test Procedure (WLTP) rather than New European Driving Cycle (NEDC). As the WLTP results in higher values the appropriate percentages are reduced by 2% for each band. This means there are different percentage values for cars registered before and on/after 6 April 2020.

(4)   *Appropriate percentages* – These will only increase for cars registered on and after 6 April 2020; by 1% in 2021/22 and by 1% in 2022/23. From 2022/23 all cars registered from 1 October 1999 will be taxed according to the same table of appropriate percentages.

(5)   *Car not available* – The car benefit is proportionately reduced if the company car is not available for part of the year, where the benefit ceases part way through a tax year (and is not reinstated in that year), or where the benefit of the company car is shared (*ITEPA 2003, ss 143, 148*).

(6)   *Payment for use* – From 6 April 2017 where an employee makes a payment for private use of the car or fuel to reduce the chargeable benefit, that payment must be made by 6 July after the end of the tax year in which the benefit was provided (*ITEPA 2003, s 144(1)*).

(7) *Diesel cars* – The diesel supplements in the tables above apply to diesel cars first registered on or after 1 September 2017 that don't meet Euro 6d emission standards. New diesel models do meet that standard. The diesel supplement also applies to all diesel cars first registered on or after 1 January 1998 and before 1 September 2017 (*FA 2018, s 9*).

(8) *OpRA vehicles* – Where a car or van is provided under an optional remuneration arrangement (salary sacrifice) the amount foregone includes all costs connected with the vehicle which are regarded as part of the benefit in kind (*FA 2019, s 7*).

(9) *Further Information* – See *Payroll Management* (Bloomsbury Professional).

Cars registered with no CO_2 emission figures

(*ITEPA 2003, ss 140–142;* see also EIM24950, EIM24975)

Registered at any time	2020/21– 2021/22 %	2019/20 %	2018/19 %	2017/18 %	2016/17 %
1,400 cc or less	24	23	20	18	16
Over 1,400 cc to 2,000 cc (note 2)	35	34	31	29	27
Over 2,000 cc (note 2)	37	37	37	37	37

Notes

(1) *Diesel cars* – A 3% supplement (4% from 6 April 2018) applies to diesel cars up to a maximum of 37%, see note 7: **diesel cars** above.

(2) *2015/16 and earlier* – If the vehicle was registered before 1998 the appropriate percentage was 22 for engines 1400cc to 2000 cc, and 32 for engines over 2000 cc.

Fuel benefit charges

(*ITEPA 2003, ss 149–153; SI 2018/1176*)

Car fuel benefit multiplier

Tax year	£	Tax year	£
2021/22	24,600	2018/19	23,400
2020/21	24,500	2017/18	22,600
2019/20	24,100	2016/17	22,200

Notes

(1) *Nil fuel benefit* – This applies in the following circumstances:

• if the employee is required to make good the full cost of all fuel provided for private use, and actually does so by 6 July following the tax year for 2017/18 and later years;

19

- if fuel is made available only for business travel (*ITEPA 2003, s 151*); or
- where the employer provides free charging for electric vehicles, as electricity is not classified as a 'road fuel' for car benefit purposes.

(2)   *Reductions* – The fuel benefit is proportionately reduced if the company car is only available for part of the year, where the benefit ceases part way through a tax year (and is not reinstated in that year), or where the benefit of the company car is shared (*ITEPA 2003, ss 152–153*).

(3)   *Cash equivalent* – The benefit charge for fuel provided for private motoring is calculated by applying the appropriate percentage to the relevant multiplier in the table above. The 'appropriate percentage' is broadly that used to calculate the car benefit (*ITEPA 2003, s 150*).

(4)   *Online tools* – The HMRC company car and car fuel calculator can be used to compute the benefit charge for tax years from 2015/16 to 2021/22 see: www.gov.uk/calculate-tax-on-company-cars.

Fuel benefit charges from 6 April 2017 to 5 April 2022

(*ITEPA 2003, s 150*)

Petrol and hybrid engines

CO_2 emissions (g/km)	Hybrid electric only range (miles)	2021/22 £ (note 4)	2020/21 £ (note 4)	2019/20 £	2018/19 £	2017/18 £
0–50	All	246	0	3,856	3,042	2,034
0–50	>130	246	0	3,856	3,042	2,034
0–50	70–129	984	735	3,856	3,042	2,034
0–50	40–69	1,722	1,470	3,856	3,042	2,034
0–50	30–39	2,706	2,450	3,856	3,042	2,034
0–50	<30	3,198	2,940	3,856	3,042	2,034
51–54		3,444	3,185	4,579	3,744	2,938
55–59		3,690	3,430	4,579	3,744	2,938
60–64		3,936	3,675	4,579	3,744	2,938
65–69		4,182	3,920	4,579	3,744	2,938
70–74		4,428	4,165	4,579	3,744	2,938
75–79		4,674	4,410	5,302	4,446	3,842
80–84		4,920	4,655	5,302	4,446	3,842
85–89		5,166	4,900	5,302	4,446	3,842
90–94		5,412	5,145	5,302	4,446	3,842
95–99		5,658	5,390	5,543	4,680	4,068

CO$_2$ emissions (g/km)	Hybrid electric only range (miles)	2021/22 £ (note 4)	2020/21 £ (note 4)	2019/20 £	2018/19 £	2017/18 £
100–104		5,904	5,635	5,784	4,914	4,294
105–109		6,150	5,880	6,025	5,148	4,520
110–114		6,396	6,125	6,266	5,382	4,746
115–119		6,642	6,370	6,507	5,616	4,972
120–124		6,888	6,615	6,748	5,850	5,198
125–129		7,134	6,860	6,989	6,084	5,424
130–134		7,380	7,105	7,230	6,318	5,650
135–139		7,626	7,350	7,471	6,552	5,876
140–144		7,872	7,595	7,712	6,786	6,102
145–149		8,118	7,840	7,953	7,020	6,328
150–154		8,364	8,085	8,194	7,254	6,554
155–159		8,610	8,330	8,435	7,488	6,780
160–164		8,856	8,575	8,676	7,722	7,006
165–169		9,102	8,820	8,917	7,956	7,232
170–174		9,102	9,065	8,917	8,190	7,458
175–179		9,102	9,065	8,917	8,424	7,684
180–184		9,102	9,065	8,917	8,658	7,910
185–189		9,102	9,065	8,917	8,658	8,136
190–194		9,102	9,065	8,917	8,658	8,362
195–199		9,102	9,065	8,917	8,658	8,362
Over 200		9,102	9,065	8,917	8,658	8,362

Diesel and hybrid engines

CO$_2$ emissions (g/km)	Hybrid electric only range (miles)	2021/22 £ (note 4)	2020/21 £ (note 4)	2019/20 £	2018/19 £	2017/18 £
0–50	all		0	4,820	3,978	2,712
0–50	>130	1,230	980	4,820	3,978	2,712
0–50	70–129	1,968	1,715	4,820	3,978	2,712
0–50	40–69	2,706	2,450	4,820	3,978	2,712
0–50	30–39	3,690	3,430	4,820	3,978	2,712
0–50	<30	4,182	3,920	4,820	3,978	2,712
51–54		4,428	4,165	5,543	4,680	3,616
55–59		4,674	4,410	5,543	4,680	3,616
60–64		4,920	4,655	5,543	4,680	3,616
65–69		5,166	4,900	5,543	4,680	3,616

continued

CO$_2$ emissions (g/km)	Hybrid electric only range (miles)	2021/22 £ (note 4)	2020/21 £ (note 4)	2019/20 £	2018/19 £	2017/18 £
70–74		5,412	5,145	5,543	4,680	3,616
75–79		5,658	5,390	6,266	5,382	4,520
80–84		5,904	5,635	6,266	5,382	4,520
85–89		6,150	5,880	6,266	5,382	4,520
90–94		6,396	6,125	6,266	5,382	4,520
95–99		6,642	6,370	6,507	5,616	4,746
100–104		6,888	6,615	6,748	5,850	4,972
105–109		7,134	6,860	6,989	6,084	5,198
110–114		7,380	7,105	7,230	6,318	5,424
115–119		7,626	7,350	7,471	6,552	5,650
120–124		7,872	7,595	7,712	6,786	5,876
125–129		8,118	7,840	7,953	7,020	6,102
130–134		8,364	8,085	8,194	7,254	6,328
135–139		8,610	8,330	8,435	7,488	6,554
140–144		8,856	8,575	8,676	7,722	6,780
145–149		9,102	8,820	8,917	7,956	7,006
150–154		9,102	9,065	8,917	8,190	7,232
155–159		9,102	9,065	8,917	8,424	7,458
160–164		9,102	9,065	8,917	8,658	7,684
165–169		9,102	9,065	8,917	8,658	7,910
170–174		9,102	9,065	8,917	8,658	8,136
175–179		9,102	9,065	8,917	8,658	8,362
180–184		9,102	9,065	8,917	8,658	8,362
185–189		9,102	9,065	8,917	8,658	8,362

Notes

(1) *Electric vehicles* – No fuel benefit arises where employees are provided with free electricity for their company-owned vehicles (*ITEPA 2003, s 149(4)*).

(2) *Employer provided power* – Before 6 April 2018 where employees were provided with free electricity at work to charge their own vehicles, or through a charge card, or where the employer pays for a charging point at the employee's home, those employees should be taxed on the cost of the electricity or service provided (EIM23900).

(3) *Charging at work* – From 6 April 2018 there is no chargeable benefit where an employee is permitted to charge a privately owned vehicle at or near their place of work (*ITEPA 2003, s 237A*).

(4) *Calculation* – For cars registered on and after 6 April 2020.

Mileage allowances

Advisory fuel rates for company cars

(www.gov.uk/government/publications/advisory-fuel-rates)

Engine size	Rate per Mile		
	Petrol	**Diesel**	**LPG**
From 1 March 2021		Electric cars: 4p/mile	
Up to 1,400 cc	10p		7p
1,401–2,000 cc	12p		8p
Over 2,000 cc	18p		12p
Up to 1,600 cc		9p	
1,601–2,000 cc		11p	
Over 2,000 cc		12p	
From 1 December 2020		Electric cars: 4p/mile	
Up to 1,400 cc	10p		7p
1,401–2,000 cc	11p		8p
Over 2,000 cc	17p		12p
Up to 1,600 cc		8p	
1,601–2,000 cc		10p	
Over 2,000 cc		12p	
From 1 September 2020		Electric cars: 4p/mile	
Up to 1,400 cc	10p		7p
1,401–2,000 cc	12p		8p
Over 2,000 cc	17p		12p
Up to 1,600 cc		8p	
1,601–2,000 cc		10p	
Over 2,000 cc		12p	
From 1 June 2020		Electric cars: 4p/mile	
Up to 1,400 cc	10p		6p
1,401–2,000 cc	12p		8p
Over 2,000 cc	17p		11p
Up to 1,600 cc		8p	
1,601–2,000 cc		9p	
Over 2,000 cc		12p	
From 1 March 2020		Electric cars: 4p/mile	
Up to 1,400 cc	12p		8p
1,401–2,000 cc	14p		10p
Over 2,000 cc	20p		14p
Up to 1,600 cc		9p	
1,601–2,000 cc		11p	
Over 2,000 cc		13p	

continued

Engine size	Rate per Mile		
	Petrol	**Diesel**	**LPG**
From 1 December 2019		Electric cars: 4p/mile	
Up to 1,400 cc	12p		8p
1,401–2,000 cc	14p		9p
Over 2,000 cc	21p		14p
Up to 1,600 cc		9p	
1,601–2,000 cc		11p	
Over 2,000 cc		14p	
From 1 September 2019		Electric cars: 4p/mile	
Up to 1,400 cc	12p		8p
1,401–2,000 cc	14p		10p
Over 2,000 cc	21p		14p
Up to 1,600 cc		10p	
1,601–2,000 cc		11p	
Over 2,000 cc		14p	
From 1 June 2019		Electric cars: 4p/mile	
Up to 1,400 cc	12p		8p
1,401–2,000 cc	15p		9p
Over 2,000 cc	22p		14p
Up to 1,600 cc		10p	
1,601–2,000 cc		12p	
Over 2,000 cc		14p	
From 1 March 2019		Electric cars: 4p/mile	
Up to 1,400 cc	11p		7p
1,401–2,000 cc	14p		8p
Over 2,000 cc	21p		13p
Up to 1,600 cc		10p	
1,601–2,000 cc		11p	
Over 2,000 cc		13p	
From 1 December 2018		Electric cars: 4p/mile	
Up to 1,400 cc	12p		8p
1,401–2,000 cc	15p		10p
Over 2,000 cc	22p		15p
Up to 1,600 cc		10p	
1,601–2,000 cc		12p	
Over 2,000 cc		14p	
From 1 September 2018		Electric cars: 4p/mile	
Up to 1,400 cc	12p		7p
1,401–2,000 cc	15p		9p
Over 2,000 cc	22p		13p
Up to 1,600 cc		10p	
1,601–2,000 cc		12p	
Over 2,000 cc		13p	

Notes

(1)   *Quarterly updates* – The advisory fuel rates are reviewed quarterly and updated as necessary to be effective from 1 March, 1 June, 1 September and 1 December.

(2)   *Hybrids* – Petrol hybrid cars are treated as either petrol or diesel cars for this purpose.

(3)   *VAT* – HMRC accept these figures for VAT purposes, ie a business can reclaim the VAT element on the amount attributable to fuel or mileage allowances paid to employees or subcontractors.

(4)   *Earlier periods* – Advisory fuel rates for periods from 1 June 2014: tinyurl.com/AFrts14-19.

Approved mileage allowance payments (AMAPs) rates for private vehicles

(ITEPA 2003, ss 229–232, 235, 236)

	Rate per business mile			
	From 2011/12		2002/03 to 2010/11	
	First 10,000 miles	Over 10,000 miles	First 10,000 miles	Over 10,000 miles
Cars	45p	25p	40p	25p
For each passenger making the same business journey	5p	5p	5p	5p
Motorcycles	24p	24p	24p	24p
Bicycles	20p	20p	20p	20p

Notes

(1)   *Additional claims* – Where the employer pays less than the authorised rate, the employee may claim tax relief (mileage allowance relief) on the difference.

(2)   *Passengers* – The additional rate which applies when carrying passengers was extended to volunteers with effect from 6 April 2011.

Company vans

(ITEPA 2003, ss 154–164; SI 2018/1176)

Tax Year	Cash equivalent of private use		
	Ordinary van £	Fuel £	Zero emissions £
2021/22	3,500	669	Nil (note 1)
2020/21	3,490	666	2,792
2019/20	3,430	655	2,058
2018/19	3,350	633	1,340
2017/18	3,230	610	646
2016/17	3,170	598	634

Notes

(1)   *Zero emissions* – The cash equivalent for private use of zero emission vans is calculated as a percentage of the benefit of an ordinary van: 60% for 2019/20 and 80% for 2020/21 (*ITEPA 2003, s 155(1C)*). From 6 April 2021, the cash equivalent of the van benefit charge for zero emission vans is nil where the van cannot emit CO_2 under any circumstances when being driven (*Finance Bill 2021, cl 23*).

(2)   *No benefit* – No charge arises if the restricted private use condition is satisfied (*ITEPA 2003, s 155(4)*).

(3)   *Definition* – Commercial vehicles with 'crew cabs' that are capable of carrying 3 or 4 people in addition to the driver may be considered to be cars with effect from 2018/19 (*see Payne, Garbett, Coca-Cola v HMRC* [2020] EWCA Civ 889, *ITEPA 2003, s 115*).

Buses

(*ITEPA 2003, ss 242, 243*)

(1)   *Works buses* – No income tax charge arises on the provision for employees of a works transport service, if the following conditions are satisfied:

   (a)   the service is available generally to employees of the employer (or each employer) concerned;

   (b)   the main use of the service is for qualifying journeys by those employees; and

   (c)   the service:

      (i)   is used only by the employees for whom it is provided or their children, or

      (ii)   is substantially used only by those employees or children.

(2)   *Local buses* – No charge to tax arises in respect of financial or other support provided for local bus services, if the following conditions are satisfied:

   (a)   the service is available to employees generally;

   (b)   it is used for qualifying journeys by employees of one or more employers; and

   (c)   either:

      (i)   it is a local bus service, discounts for regional or zonal tickets are not permitted; or

      (ii)   the bus must be provided to other passengers on terms that are as favourable as the terms on which the bus is provided to employees.

(3)   *Further information* – See EIM21850.

Bicycles

(ITEPA 2003, s 244)

(1) *Loan of bicycle* – No income tax charge arises on the provision for employees of cycles and/or cyclists' safety equipment, if the following conditions are satisfied:

    (a) the cycles are available to all employees generally; and

    (b) the cycles are used mainly for qualifying journeys, but other use of the cycle use does not disqualify the exemption.

(2) *Covid concession* – Employees who received a cycle or cyclist's safety equipment on or before 20 December 2020 will not have to meet the qualifying journeys condition between 16 March 2020 and 5 April 2022 (*Finance Bill 2021, cl 25*).

(3) *Transfer of ownership* – No charge to tax arises if the cycle is transferred to an employee after a period of use in return for the market value of the cycle at the time of transfer, see **Valuation of used cycles**.

(4) *Further information* – See HMRC's Employment Income Manual at EIM21665-21668.

Valuation of used cycles

Age of cycle	Original price of the cycle	
(years)	less than £500	£500+
1	18%	25%
1.5	16%	21%
2	13%	17%
3	8%	12%
4	3%	7%
5	Negligible	2%
6 or over	Negligible	Negligible

TRAVEL AND SUBSISTENCE

(SI 2015/1948)

Meal allowance while travelling

Duration of travel in the day	Rate per day (maximum) £	Additional claim if travel ongoing at 8pm £
5 hours or more	5	10
10 hours or more	10	10
15 hours or more and travel is ongoing at 8pm	25	–

Notes

(1) *What it applies to* – For payments made from 6 April 2016 to reimburse an employee for meals taken while in the course of qualifying travel (*ITEPA 2003, s 289A*).

(2) *Tax free* – These are the maximum amounts which when paid to employees, are exempt from income tax and NIC, but an employer may pay less if they want to.

(3) *Excess* – If the employer pays more than these amounts only the excess over the published rate is subject to tax and NIC.

(4) *Further information* – See HMRC's Employment Income Manual at EIM30240.

Personal incidental expenses

(*ITEPA 2003, ss 240, 241*)

From	Permitted amount per night	
	In UK £	Overseas £
6 April 1995	5	10

Notes

(1) *What it applies to* – Employees' minor personal expenditure, incurred whilst on business-related activities away from home. If the permitted amount is exceeded, the whole sum provided is taxable, unless it is refunded to the employer within a reasonable time.

(2) *Further information* – See HMRC's Employment Income Manual at EIM02730.

Lorry drivers' overnight subsistence allowance

(*ITEPA 2003, ss 289A, 289B*)

Period:	Permitted expense claim per night	
	No sleeper cab £	Sleeper cab £
From 2013 (note 1)	34.90	26.20
Year 2012	33.85	25.39

Notes

(1) *Approval needed* – From 6 April 2017 the employer must apply for approval from HMRC to pay or reimburse employees at the above rates to apply to overnight allowances for lorry drivers when working in the UK.

(2) *Evidence* – From 6 April 2017 HMRC require employers to carry out random checks to ensure that drivers are incurring an expense for food or accommodation, so the drivers need to retain at least some receipts.

(3) *Bespoke agreements* – Payments in excess of the above rates can be paid tax free if the employer has agreed a bespoke rate with HMRC.

(4) *Further information* – See HMRC's Employment Income Manual: EIM30255, EIM30260, EIM66205.

MOBILE PHONES

(ITEPA 2003, s 319)

(1) *One phone policy* – From 6 April 2006 no chargeable benefit arises where the employer provides one mobile phone per employee. There is no tax exemption for mobile phones provided for family members.

(2) *Top-up vouchers* – There is no tax charge on the provision of top-up payments for use of a mobile phone which is owned by the employer and provided to the employee.

(3) *What is a mobile phone?* – Includes a SIM card provided independently of a phone. Does not include devices that are solely PDAs, tablets or laptop computers (EIM21779).

CHILDCARE

Employer provided childcare vouchers

(ITEPA 2003, ss 270A, 318A; SI 2013/513)

Year	Weekly tax-free limit:		
Taxpayer's marginal rate	Basic rate £	Higher rate £	Additional rate £
2013/14 and later years	55	28	25
2012/13	55	28	22

Notes

(1) *Pre-April 2011* – Employees who joined the employer-provided childcare voucher scheme before 6 April 2011, and who are still employed by that employer, can continue to receive a tax-free benefit of £55 per week, whatever their marginal rate of tax.

(2) *Leave employer's scheme* – Within three months of opening a tax-free childcare account (see below) the parents must notify their employer that they are no longer eligible for employer-supported childcare.

(3) *Stay in employer's scheme* – Members of an employer-provided childcare voucher scheme can stay in that scheme or opt to open a tax-free childcare account (see **Chapter 5**).

(4) *Closure of voucher scheme* – No new employees can join the employer-provided childcare voucher scheme from 4 October 2018 (*SI 2018/462*).

HEALTH RELATED BENEFITS

(ITEPA 2003, Pt 4)

Benefit	Limit of tax & NI exemption
Recommend medical treatment (see note 1)	£500 per employee per year *(ITEPA 2003, s 320C)*
Eye test and spectacles or lenses	Required solely for VDU use *(ITEPA 2003, s 320A)*
Health screening or medical check-up	One screening per tax year *(ITEPA 2003, s 320B)*
Overseas medical treatment	Only when working abroad *(ITEPA 2003, s 325)*

Notes

(1) *Recommend treatment* – From 1 January 2015 the health-related intervention must be recommended by occupational health services and must be provided to help the employee return to work *(SI 2014/3226)*.

(2) *Further information* – See HMRC's Employment Income Manual at EIM21765-21766.

HOME WORKING ALLOWANCE

(ITEPA 2003, ss 316A, 336)

Period	Per week £	Per month £
From 6 April 2020	6	26
6 April 2003–5 April 2020	4	18

Notes

(1) *Paid by employer* – The above amounts may be paid free of tax and NIC to employees who regularly work from home under an agreed homeworking arrangement with their employer. HMRC will accept there is a homeworking arrangement where the employee is required to work at home because their employer's office has closed, or the employee has been advised to self-isolate.

(2) *Employee's costs* – Where the employer does not pay the homeworking allowance to the employee but the individual is required to work at home, HMRC will accept the employee's claim for a tax deduction at the same amount as the homeworking allowance, without proof of the additional costs incurred. This deduction may be claimed for the whole of 2020/21 irrespective of the amount of time the employee works at home. The cost of business telephone calls can be claimed in addition to this deduction, *(EIM32815, ITEPA 2003, s 336)*.

(3) *Equipment* – Where employees have purchased equipment to allow them to work at home and that purchase would have been exempt under *ITEPA 2003, s 316* if the employer had incurred the cost directly, the employer may reimburse those costs from 11 June 2020 to 5 April 2021 with no tax or NI charges. In addition, HMRC will not collect tax or NI on similar costs reimbursed from 16 March 2020 to 10 June 2020 *(SI 2020/524, https://tinyurl.com/rr9x8jap)*.

(4)　*Further information* – See HMRC's Employment Income Manual at EIM01472, EIM32760 and EIM32815.

RELOCATION EXPENSES

(ITEPA 2003, ss 271–289)

(1)　*Exemption* – Up to £8,000 of reimbursed expenses for qualifying removal costs incurred on a change of the employee's residence.

(2)　*Conditions* – The change of residence must be connected with starting a new employment or change of place of work or duties with an existing employer. The old residence must not be within reasonable commuting distance of the new work location.

(3)　*Further information* – See HMRC's Employment Income Manual EIM03100-EIM03139.

TERMINATION PAYMENTS

(ITEPA 2003, Pt 6, Ch 3)

Tax year	Maximum tax free amount
From 1998/99 onwards	£30,000

Notes

(1)　*Commencement* – All of the conditions described below apply where the employment ended, and the relevant termination benefits or payments were received, on or after 6 April 2018. Please refer to an earlier edition of *Bloomsbury's Tax Rates and Tables* for the conditions which applied to termination payments made before that date.

(2)　*Relevant termination award* – This must be split between amount treated as employment income (PENP) and any residue which may be covered by the tax free amount.

(3)　*Tax free amount* – No tax or National Insurance (employers' or employees') is payable to the extent that the residue of the 'relevant termination award' above the 'post-employment notice pay' (PENP) is sheltered by the available tax free amount. Payments taxed as earnings can't be sheltered by the tax free amount and are liable to NIC *(ITEPA 2003, s 402C)*.

(4)　*Post-employment notice pay* – PENP = $((BP \times D) \div P) - T$ where:

　　BP = employee's basic pay for last pay period before trigger date

　　D = number of days in post-employment period

　　P = number of calendar days in last pay period

　　T = payment or benefit received in connection with termination of employment which is taxable earnings

(5)　*Exemptions* – Statutory redundancy pay and approved contractual payments, to the extent that they are exempt under *ITEPA 2003, s 309*, don't form part of the 'relevant termination award' but count towards the tax free amount.

(6)   *Class 1A NIC* – Applies to taxable termination payments in excess of the tax free amount of £30,000, for payments made on and after 6 April 2020, see **Chapter 14**.

(7)   *Further information* – HMRC's Employment Income Manual EIM138744+.

SCHOLARSHIPS

(ITTOIA 2005, s 776(1); SP 4/86)

Period	Specified amount
From 1 September 2007	£15,480
From 1 September 2005–31 August 2007	£15,000
From 6 April 1992–31 August 2005	£7,000

Notes

(1)   *Exemption* – No liability to income tax arises in respect of scholarship income, but only for the holder of the scholarship.

(2)   *Benefit charge* – A scholarship will give rise to a chargeable benefit where it is provided to a member of the family or household of a director or employee, by reason of the employment of that director or employee *(ITEPA 2003, ss 211–215)*.

EMPLOYMENT RELATED LOANS

Actual official rates of interest

(ITEPA 2003, s 181; SI 2017/305)

Period	Rate %
From 6 April 2021	2.00
6 April 2020–5 April 2021	2.25
6 April 2017–5 April 2020	2.50
6 April 2015–5 April 2017	3.00
6 April 2014–5 April 2015	3.25

Average official rates of interest

(ITEPA 2003, s 182)

Year	Average official rate %
2020/21	2.25
2019/20	2.50
2018/19	2.50
2017/18	2.50
2016/17	3.00
2015/16	3.00

Notes

(1)   *Maximum value* – No liability to tax or NIC arises where the combined value of all loans made by the employer to the employee in the year do not exceed £10,000 (£5,000 before 6 April 2014).

(2)   *Interest charged* – No tax or NIC liability arises where the interest charged to the employee is equal to or higher than the official rate of interest at the time the loan was taken out.

(3)   *Average rate* – The average official rates of interest are used if the loan was outstanding throughout the year and the normal averaging method of calculation is being used. The employer can use the alternative precise method to calculate the benefit.

(4)   *Close company* – Where the loan is made by a close company to the directors or shareholders of that company, a corporation tax charge may also be due, see **Chapter 7**.

FLAT RATE ALLOWANCES

(ITEPA 2003, s 367; EIM32712)

Occupation			Deduction from 2013/14 onwards £	Deduction for 2008/09 to 2012/13 £
Agriculture		All workers	100	100
Airlines		Uniformed flight deck crew see EIM50050	1,022	850
		Cabin crew see EIM50070	720	–
Aluminium	A	Continual casting operators, process operators, de-dimplers, driers, drill punchers, dross unloaders, firemen (see Note 3), furnace operators and their helpers, leaders, mouldmen, pourers, remelt department labourers, roll flatteners	140	140
	B	Cable hands, case makers, labourers, mates, truck drivers and measurers, storekeepers	80	80
	C	Apprentices	60	60
	D	All other workers see EIM50125	120	120
Armed forces	A	Royal Navy ratings	80	80
	B	Other ranks in Army, RAF and Royal Marines	100	100

continued

Occupation			Deduction from 2013/14 onwards £	Deduction for 2008/09 to 2012/13 £
Banks and Building societies		Uniformed doormen and messengers	60	60
Brass and copper		Braziers, coppersmiths, finishers, fitters, moulders, turners and all other workers.	120	120
Building	A	Joiners and carpenters	140	140
	B	Cement works and roofing felt and asphalt labourers	80	80
	C	Labourers and navvies	60	60
	D	All other workers	120	120
Building materials	A	Stone-masons	120	120
	B	Tilemakers and labourers	60	60
	C	All other workers	80	80
Clothing	A	Lacemakers, hosiery bleachers, dyers, scourers and knitters, knitwear bleachers and dyers	60	60
	B	All other workers	60	60
Constructional engineering (see Note 4)	A	Blacksmiths and their strikers, burners, caulkers, chippers, drillers, erectors, fitters, holders up, markers off, platers, riggers, riveters, rivet heaters, scaffolders, sheeters, template workers, turners, welders	140	140
	B	Banksmen labourers, shop-helpers, slewers, straighteners	80	80
	C	Apprentices and storekeepers	60	60
	D	All other workers	100	100
Electrical and electricity supply	A	Those workers incurring laundry costs only	60	60
	B	All other workers	120	120
Trades ancillary to Engineering	A	Pattern makers	140	140
	B	Labourers, supervisory and unskilled workers	80	80
	C	Apprentices and storekeepers	60	60
	D	Motor mechanics in garage repair shop	120	120
	E	All other workers	120	120

Occupation			Deduction from 2013/14 onwards £	Deduction for 2008/09 to 2012/13 £
Fire service		Uniformed firefighters and fire officers	80	80
Food		All workers	60	60
Forestry		All workers	100	100
Glass		All workers	80	80
Healthcare	A	Ambulance staff on active service (ie excluding staff who take telephone calls or provide clerical support)	185	140
	B	Nurses and midwives, chiropodists, dental nurses, occupational speech physios and therapists, phlebotomists, radiographers. For shoes, stocking and socks where style/ colour is obligatory, see EIM67200	125 18	100 18
	C	Plaster room orderlies, hospital porters, ward clerks, sterile supply workers, hospital domestics, hospital catering staff	125	100
	D	Laboratory staff, pharmacists, pharmacy assistants	80	60
	E	Uniformed ancillary staff – maintenance workers, grounds staff, drivers, parking attendants and security guards, receptionists and other uniformed staff	80	60
Heating	A	Pipe fitters and plumbers	120	120
	B	Coverers, laggers, domestic glaziers, heating engineers and all their mates	120	120
	C	All gas workers and all other workers	100	100
Iron Mining	A	Fillers, miners and underground workers	120	120
	B	All other workers	100	100

continued

35

Occupation			Deduction from 2013/14 onwards £	Deduction for 2008/09 to 2012/13 £
Iron and steel	A	Day labourers, general labourers, stockmen, time-keepers, warehouse staff and weighmen	80	80
	B	Apprentices	60	60
	C	All other workers	140	140
Leather	A	Curriers (wet workers), fellmongering workers, tanning operatives (wet)	80	80
	B	All other workers	60	60
Particular engineering (see Note 5)	A	Pattern makers	140	140
	B	Chainmakers; cleaners, galvanisers, tinners and wire drawers in the wire drawing industry; tool-makers in the lock making industry	120	120
	C	Apprentices and storekeepers	60	60
	D	All other workers	80	80
Police force	A	Police officers (ranks up to and including Chief Inspector)	140	140
	B	Community support officers, see EIM68130	140	140
	C	Other uniformed police employees	60	60
Precious metals		All workers	100	100
Printing	A	Letterpress Section – Electrical engineers (rotary presses), electrotypers, ink and roller makers, machine minders (rotary), maintenance engineers (rotary) and stereotypers	140	140
	B	Bench hands (periodical and bookbinding), compositors and readers (letterpress section) telecommunications and electronic section wireroom operators, warehousemen (paper box making section)	60	60
	C	All other workers	100	100

Occupation			Deduction from 2013/14 onwards £	Deduction for 2008/09 to 2012/13 £
Prisons		Uniformed prison officers	80	80
Public service: docks and inland waterways	A	Dockers, dredger drivers, hopper steerers	80	80
	B	All other workers	60	60
Public service: public transport	A	Garage hands (including cleaners and mechanics)	80	80
	B	Conductor and drivers	60	60
Quarrying		All workers	100	100
Railways	A	See the appropriate category for craftsmen, eg engineers, vehicle builders etc.		
	B	All other workers	100	100
Seamen	A	Carpenters on passenger liners	165	165
	B	Carpenters on cargo vessels, tankers, coasters and ferries	140	140
Shipyards	A	Blacksmiths and their strikers, boilermakers, burners, carpenters, caulkers, drillers, furnacemen (platers), holders up, fitters, platers, plumbers, riveters, sheet iron workers, shipwrights, tubers, welders	140	140
	B	Labourers	80	80
	C	Apprentices and storekeepers	60	60
	D	All other workers	100	100
Textiles and textile printing	A	Carders, carding engineers, overlookers and technicians in spinning mills	120	120
	B	All other workers	80	80
Vehicles	A	Builders, railway wagon etc. repairers and railway wagon lifters	140	140
	B	Railway vehicle painters and letterers, railway wagon etc. builders' and repairers' assistants	80	80
	C	All other workers	60	60

continued

Occupation			Deduction from 2013/14 onwards £	Deduction for 2008/09 to 2012/13 £
Wood and furniture	A	Carpenters, cabinet makers, joiners, wood carvers and woodcutting machinists	140	140
	B	Artificial limb makers (other than in wood), organ builders and packaging case makers	120	120
	C	Coopers not providing own tools, labourers, polishers and upholsterers	60	60
	D	All other workers	100	100

Notes

(1) *Flat rate allowance* – For most classes of industry a tax deduction is given for certain amounts 'representing the average annual expenses incurred by employees of the class to which the employee belongs in respect of the repair and maintenance of work equipment'.

(2) *'Workers' and 'all other workers'* – These are references to manual workers or to workers who have to pay for the upkeep of tools and special clothing.

(3) *'Firemen'* – Means persons engaged to light and maintain furnaces.

(4) *'Constructional engineering'* – Means engineering undertaken on a construction site, including buildings, shipyards, bridges, roads and other similar operations.

(5) *'Particular engineering'* – Means engineering undertaken on a commercial basis in a factory or workshop for the purposes of producing components such as wire, springs, nails and locks.

(6) *Healthcare staff* – The rates shown for 2013/14 onwards generally only apply from 6 April 2014.

(7) *Other occupations* – If the occupation is not listed in the table, a standard amount of £60 can be claimed for the laundry costs of uniforms or protective clothing (tinyurl. com/flatra).

3

Payroll matters

REAL TIME INFORMATION (RTI)

RTI procedures

(SI 2003/2682, regs 67B–67H)

PAYE procedure	Under RTI
Application of PAYE to employees' pay.	The amounts of PAYE deductions and payments must be reported online, generally on or before the contractual payment date (note 3).
Payment of PAYE must be made by:	Nil payments must be reported monthly on EPS, unless the scheme is registered as an annual scheme (see below).
• 19th of the month if paying by cheque; or	Where employees are paid quarterly, a nil EPS must be submitted for months in which no payment is made.
• 22nd of the month, for electronic payments.	HMRC match the employer's liability for PAYE to the payments made by the employer each month or quarter. Any apparent underpayments will be chased promptly.
End of year	Last FPS for the tax year marked as 'final' to be submitted by the last payment date in the year, or EPS can be used as the final submission by 19 April following the year end.
	Forms P60 to given to those employed on 5 April, by 31 May following the tax year end.
Starters	New worker's details are sent to HMRC in the FPS that includes the first payment to that person.
Leavers	Date the worker left employment should be included on the FPS when making the final payment to that employee, or include the leaving date on next FPS with zero amounts for pay. Leavers are given a P45 or leaver statement, but the P45 is not sent to HMRC.
Annual PAYE scheme: all employees are paid once per year in the same tax month	The PAYE scheme must be registered as 'annual' with HMRC, in which case one FPS should be submitted for the month of payment. Nil EPS are not required for the months when no payments are made.
Expenses and benefits reporting	Forms P11D, and P11D(b) must be submitted to HMRC and given to employees by 6 July after the tax year end.

continued

PAYE procedure	Under RTI
Construction Industry Scheme (CIS)	CIS reports are submitted monthly outside RTI. Companies (not unincorporated businesses) can set off CIS tax against their own PAYE liabilities by reporting CIS deductions on the EPS each month.
Statutory payments (see **Chapter 16**)	Payments of statutory pay are recorded on the FPS. Recovery of statutory parental pay must be claimed on the EPS each month and once a recovery has been made in a tax year the YTD figure must continue to be reported for that year. There is a separate system for reclaiming SSP.

Notes

(1)   *Commencement* – All employers must report under RTI from 6 April 2014. However, employers who can't use a computer due to a disability or a religious objection can ask HMRC for permission to submit paper forms.

(2)   *Universal Credit* – RTI is required in order to implement Universal Credit (see **Chapter 15**) and to improve fraud detection for Tax Credits.

(3)   *Payment date* – If this falls at a weekend or bank holiday and payment to the employees is brought forward to the first banking day before or after the weekend/bank holiday the contractual payment date must still be used to report for RTI not the actual date when the employee was paid; see RTI reports below.

(4)   *Further information* – See tinyurl.com/RTrunpay, tinyurl.com/RTIestaff, and tinyurl.com/RTIwtdwed.

RTI Reports

(SI 2003/2682, regs 67B–67H)

Reports	Function and submission period
Full Payment Submission (FPS)	Must be submitted on or before the 'actual payment' date, when the employees are contractually due to be paid, see notes for exceptions.
Employer Payment Summary (EPS)	To report nil payments to employees, claim set-off of statutory payments or CIS deductions against PAYE due. To correct EPS figures send a new EPS using the appropriate EPS for the year affected.
Earlier Year Update (EYU)	Ideally submit before 19 May following tax year end, to correct any of the year-to-date totals submitted in the final FPS for the previous tax year, but can be submitted at any time post tax year end. The FPS can now report revised YTD figures after the year end so the EYU is not necessary in most cases.
NI Number Verification Request (NVR)	To verify or obtain a National Insurance number for new employees. Can only be submitted after an EAS or the first FPS has been submitted.

Notes

(1)   *Cash payments to casuals* – Where the employee is paid in cash for work done on the day, at a time when it would be impractical to make an RTI report, the FPS can be submitted on the earliest of the next regular RTI report date, or seven days after the payment date.

(2)   *Notional payments* – Where there is no transfer of money from the employer to the employee, such as an award of shares, the RTI report can be made at the earliest of the time the employer operates PAYE on the notional payment or 14 days after the end of the tax month.

(3)   *Late reporting code* – When the FPS is late the employer should include the appropriate code in the late reporting reason field on the FPS.

(4)   *Late reporting* – Situations for which an FPS can be submitted after the date of payment see: tinyurl.com/RTIfpsaPay, and note the codes for late reporting reasons: tinyurl.com/RTIltrp.

(5)   *Earlier Year Update (EYU)* – Will not be a valid submission from April 2021.

Other PAYE returns

(SI 2003/2682, regs 85, 90)

Forms	Due Date
P11D, P11D(b) (note 2)	6 July following the end of the tax year
P46 (Car) (note 2)	When a car is first provided report by:
	• 2 May for q/e 5 April;
	• 2 August for q/e 5 July;
	• 3 November for q/e 5 October; and
	• 2 February for q/e 5 January.

Notes

(1)   *Payrolling* – To payroll benefits the cash equivalent of the employee's benefit is added to the payroll and taxed using the employee's tax code.

(2)   *Fewer forms* – Where the provision of benefits in kind has been payrolled using the HMRC online service the forms P11D and P46 (car) are not required, but the P11D(b) is needed.

(3)   *Further information* – To payroll benefits the employer should apply in advance of the start of the tax year (tinyurl.com/aprbnts).

PAYE thresholds

(SI 2003/2682, reg 9)

	2021/22 £	2020/21 £	2019/20 £	2018/19 £	2017/18 £	2016/17 £
LEL weekly	120	120	118	116	113	112
Weekly	242	240	240	228	221	212
Monthly	1048	1042	1042	988	958	917
Annual	12,570	12,500	12,500	11,850	11,500	11,000

Notes

(1)   *Tax thresholds* – The above thresholds are the level of earnings at which income tax becomes payable, but NICs will be due at lower thresholds (see **Chapter 14**).

(2)   *PAYE requirement* – The employer must operate a PAYE scheme and report under RTI once an employee earns over the lower earnings limit (LEL).

PAYE codes

(SI 2003/2682, reg 7)

PAYE code	Application
Suffix	
L	For those eligible for the personal allowance. Also used for 'emergency' tax codes (note 3).
M	For those who have received the marriage allowance.
N	For those who have surrendered the marriage allowance.
T	Used where HMRC are reviewing other items in tax code (eg the income-related reduction in the personal allowance). Also used if allowances have been used up or reduced to nil (0T).
BR	Deduct tax at 20% from all pay.
D0	Deduct tax at 40% on all pay.
D1	Deduct tax at 45% from all pay.
SD0	Deduct tax at 21% on all pay (note 4).
SD1	Deduct tax at 41% from all pay (note 4).
SD2	Deduct tax at 46% from all pay (note 4).
NT	No tax should be deducted from the pay or pension.
OT	Used as default PAYE tax code to deduct tax at the basic, higher and additional rates where new employees have no form P45 or starter information, and for pension income of a person still in receipt of employment income.
Prefix:	
K	Used where total coding 'deductions' (eg other income) exceed allowances.
S	Scottish taxpayer
C	Welsh taxpayer

Notes

(1)   *Use of codes* – PAYE codes are used by employers or pension providers to calculate the amount of tax, if any, to be deducted from an individual's pay or pension.

(2)   *Maximum deduction* – The maximum which can be deducted using any PAYE code is 50% of gross taxable pay this pay period.

(3)   *Emergency code* – The emergency tax codes for 2020/21 are:

●   1257L W1(week 1);

●   1257L M1(month 1).

(4)   *Scottish tax codes* – Apply from 2018/19 although SDO applied in 2017/18 to take tax at 40%. SD2 is Scotland only (see **Chapter 18**).

(5)   *Welsh tax codes* – Apply from 2019/20 (see **Chapter 18**).

(6)   *Further information* – see www.gov.uk/employee-tax-codes.

PAYE and Class 1 NIC – accounting periods

(SI 2003/2682, regs 69, 70)

| Tax Period | Tax Month | Tax quarter | Payment must clear HMRC's bank account: | |
			When paid electronically	Paid by other means
6 Apr–5 May	1	–	22 May	19 May
6 May–5 Jun	2	–	22 June	19 June
6 Jun–5 Jul	3	1	22 July	19 July
6 Jul–5 Aug	4	–	22 August	19 August
6 Aug–5 Sep	5	–	22 September	19 September
6 Sept–5 Oct	6	2	22 October	19 October
6 Oct–5 Nov	7	–	22 November	19 November
6 Nov–5 Dec	8	–	22 December	19 December
6 Dec–5 Jan	9	3	22 January	19 January
6 Jan–5 Feb	10	–	22 February	19 February
6 Feb–5 Mar	11	–	22 March	19 March
6 Mar–5 Apr	12	4	22 April	19 April

Notes

(1)   *Electronic payment* – HMRC recommend that all employers pay electronically, but employers with 250 or more employees must pay PAYE liabilities electronically.

(2)   *Non-banking day* – Where due day falls on a weekend or a bank holiday, the payment must reach HMRC on the previous working day.

(3)   *Non-electronic payments* – When paying by post employers must enclose a pre-printed payslip for the correct period. HMRC treat payments as being received on third day after the cheque is received.

(4)   *Quarterly payment* – Where the employer has reasonable grounds to believe their 'average monthly amount' will be less than £1,500 he can ask HMRC for permission to pay quarterly, in which case the payment for all months in the quarter is due after the end of the quarter as shown above. Call the HMRC payment enquiry line: 0300 200 3401 to discuss quarterly or annual payments.

(5)   *Further information* – For available payment methods and timings see www.gov.uk/pay-paye-tax.

PAYE PENALTIES

RTI returns

(FA 2009, Sch 55)

Number of employees in PAYE scheme	Amount of monthly late filing penalty £
1 to 9	100
10 to 49	200
50 to 249	300
250 or more	400

Notes

(1)   *Not automatic* – Penalties for late or non-filing of the FPS due within the tax year are only issued to employers after a manual risk assessment by HMRC officers. When the RTI data collection mechanism is sufficiently robust these penalties will be issued automatically (*FA 2009, s 106, Sch 55, paras 6B–6D*).

(2)   *One default* – Each PAYE scheme is permitted one default for late filing per tax year when no penalty charged (*FA 2009, Sch 55, para 6C*).

(3)   *Grace period* – For periods ending after 6 March 2015 no penalty is applied if the FPS is submitted within three days of the payment date. Employers who persistently file late, but within three days of the payment date may be considered for a penalty.

(4)   *New employer* – The first FPS submitted by a new employer within 30 days of paying its employees for first time will not attract a penalty.

(5)   *Frequency* – Only one penalty is issued per month even if FPS reports are submitted more frequently. Penalties are charged quarterly at the end of: July, October, January and April.

(6)   *Tax-geared penalties* – Where FPS is more than three months late, a penalty of 5% of the amount showing on the missing returns applies (*FA 2009, Sch 55 para 6D*).

(7) *Appeals* – Employers can appeal online against the penalty quoting the unique ID shown on the penalty notice, or submit an appeal in writing. The penalty must be paid within 30 days unless an appeal is lodged.

(8) *Specified charge* – An estimated PAYE charge based on the PAYE liability for the previous tax year. It is raised if the employer has not submitted an FPS or EPS for the tax month and the scheme is not registered as annual. The specified charge is payable until it is replaced by EPS or FPS (*SI 2003/2682, reg 75A*).

(9) *Inaccuracies* – The penalty regime for errors or inaccuracies in RTI returns is the same as applies to all other tax returns – see **Chapter 17: Structure of penalties** (*FA 2007, s 97, Sch 24, para 1*).

(10) *Further information* – For guidance on RTI penalties see: tinyurl.com/whydrprt.

Late payments of PAYE

(*FA 2009, s 107, Sch 56*)

Default penalties

Number of times payment is late in a tax year	Penalty %
1	No penalty (as long as the payment is less than 6 months late – see below)
2–4	1
5–7	2
8–10	3
11 or more	4

Notes

(1) *Small differences* – Where the difference in PAYE owed (according to HMRC) and the amount paid for the month is £100 or less no penalty will be charged, but interest will still accrue on underpayments.

(2) *Percentage applies to* – Each late payment due within the tax year, ie each month or quarter, and are charged automatically each quarter. For earlier periods the percentage applies to the total amount which is late in the tax year.

(3) *Further penalties* – In addition to the above, a 5% penalty is imposed:

• where monthly or quarterly payments remain unpaid after six months; and

• where payments remain outstanding after 12 months.

Such penalties apply even where only one payment in the tax year is late.

(4) *Small employers* – A small employer who makes quarterly payments can only have a maximum of four failures in a tax year, so the maximum initial default penalty rate is 1% (CH152550). However, further penalties may still arise for prolonged lateness (see note 3).

(5)   *Suspension or reduction* – HMRC may reduce a penalty due to 'special circumstances' at its discretion. Penalties are suspended if the employer has an agreement for deferred payment in place (ie a 'time to pay' arrangement) with HMRC, which is not broken.

(6)   *Appeals* – Employers can appeal using HMRC's online PAYE service, or using paper form. Tax agents can submit online appeals for clients. Penalty should be cancelled if there is a 'reasonable excuse' for the failure (*FA 2009, Sch 56, paras 9, 10, 13, 16*).

(7)   *Further information* – See: tinyurl.com/PAYEltpd.

Interest on PAYE paid late

(SI 2003/2682, regs 82, 83)

(1)   *In year charges* – Interest is charged on any PAYE payments including specified charges, not paid by the due date within the tax year (see **Chapter 17** for rates).

(2)   *Additional debt* – Interest on late paid PAYE is charged in addition to and separate from any penalties for late payment of PAYE. Interest is also charged on PAYE penalties which are not paid within 30 days of the penalty notice.

RECOVERY OF TAX DEBTS THROUGH PAYE

(ITEPA 2003, s 684(2), (3A); SI 2011/1585)

Debt from:	Maximum recovery in PAYE code
Operation of PAYE	£3,000
Underpaid Class 2 NICs	£3,000
Self-assessment balancing payment	£3,000
Other taxes, overpaid tax credits and penalties where PAYE earnings are:	(see note 4)
less than £30,000	£3,000
£30,000 to £40,000	£5,000
£40,001 to £50,000	£7,000
£50,001 to £60,000	£9,000
£60,001 to £70,000	£11,000
£70,001 to £80,000	£13,000
£80,001 to £90,000	£15,000
Over £90,000	£17,000

Notes

(1)   *Amend code* – HMRC may alter an employee's PAYE code, to recover all or part of a relevant debt up to the above limits (*SI 2003/2682, reg 14A(1)*), (*SI 2011/1584, reg 2(2)*).

(2)   *Process* – HMRC should write to the taxpayer explaining the intention to code out. The taxpayer has the right to object to coding out, and may arrange to pay the debt by another method.

(3)   *Limits* – The total deductions made through the PAYE code cannot exceed 50% of the employee's relevant pay.

(4)   *Graduated limits* – Limits above £3,000 apply from 2015/16 *(SI 2014/2483)*.

AUTO-ENROLMENT FOR A WORKPLACE PENSION

(FA 2016, Pt 6)

Year	Annual qualifying earnings			Minimum contributions	
	Lower earnings £	Earnings trigger £	Upper earnings £	Employer %	Employee %
2021/22	6,240	10,000	50,270	3	5
2020/21	6,240	10,000	50,000	3	5
2019/20	6,136	10,000	50,000	3	5
2018/19	6,032	10,000	46,350	2	3
2017/18	5,876	10,000	45,000	1	1
2016/17	5,824	10,000	43,000	1	1

Notes

(1)   *Who to auto-enrol* – All employees aged between 22 and state pension age who earn over the earnings trigger threshold must be automatically enrolled into the workplace pension. They can then choose to opt out/cease membership after enrolment.

(2)   *Contributions calculated on* – For most pension schemes the contributions are only paid in respect of earnings in the band between the lower and upper earnings thresholds. Some schemes use a pensionable earnings basis where the contributions are based on the employee's earnings from £1 upwards and not by reference to earnings within the bands. Public sector schemes have much more complex scheme rules on pensionable pay.

(3)   *Regular review* – Every three years those employees who have opted out of the workplace pension must be re-enrolled into the workplace pension scheme with a fresh opportunity to opt out.

(4)   *Further information* – The Pensions Regulator www.thepensionsregulator.gov.uk/en.

APPRENTICESHIP LEVY

(FA 2016, Pt 6)

From	Annual charge on payroll	Annual allowance
6 April 2017	0.5%	£15,000

Notes

(1)   *Payable by* – All employers in the UK who have 'pay subject to employers' Class 1 NIC'. This includes employers who pay other employment levies such as in the construction, engineering and film industries. Also applies to pay of 'deemed employees' subject to the off-payroll rules in the public sector.

(2)   *Pay bill* – This is the total pay of all employees who have earnings liable to NI, including where the NI is due at 0%, such as for apprentices aged under 25. The levy is paid on the entire pay bill where earnings are subject to Class 1 NIC, but not on the value of benefits subject to Class 1A NIC.

(3)   *Allowance* – The levy is only payable to the extent that it is not covered by the annual allowance. Effectively employers with a pay bill of no more than £3 million will not pay the levy. Only one annual allowance can be claimed per group of companies or connected employers, but it can be apportioned amongst the group's PAYE schemes, apportionment being reported on the April EPS and is fixed for the tax year.

(4)   *Period of payment* – The levy is payable monthly with PAYE deductions by 22nd of each month, and reported in each month's EPS.

(5)   *Apprenticeship funding* – From May 2017 employers in England who pay the apprenticeship levy can access the amount they have paid as levy to fund the cost of training apprentices. Different arrangements apply in Scotland, Northern Ireland and Wales.

(6)   *Further information* – See tinyurl.com/jfu78m2.

STUDENT LOANS

(SI 2009/470, reg 29; SI 2011/784, reg 6)

Tax Year	Pay deducted above threshold	Undergraduate Plan 1 loan threshold			Undergraduate Plan 2 loan threshold		
		Annual £	Monthly £	Weekly £	Annual £	Monthly £	Weekly £
2021/22	9%	19,895	1,657.91	382.59	27,295	2,274.58	524.90
2020/21	9%	19,390	1,615.83	372.88	26,575	2,214.58	511.05
2019/20	9%	18,935	1,577.92	364.14	25,725	2,143.75	494.71
2018/19	9%	18,330	1,527.50	352.50	25,000	2,083.33	480.77
2017/18	9%	17,775	1,481.25	341.82	21,000	1,750.00	403.84
2016/17	9%	17,495	1,457.91	336.44	21,000	1,750.00	403.84
2015/16	9%	17,335	1,444.58	333.36	N/A	N/A	N/A

Tax Year	Pay deducted above threshold	Postgraduate loan thresholds		
		Annual £	Monthly £	Weekly £
2021/22	6%	21,000	1,750	403.84
2020/21	6%	21,000	1,750	403.84
2019/20	6%	21,000	1,750	403.84

Notes

(1)   *Payroll deduction* – Employers are responsible for deducting student loan repayments from employees' pay at the percentage shown, and passing the payment to HMRC, who will in turn account for the funds to the Student Loan Company.

(2)   *Plan 1* – Where students began their course prior to 1 September 2012 or are from Scotland or Northern Ireland they repay the loan under Plan 1.

(3)   *Plan 2* – Students from England and Wales who began their course on or after 1 September 2012 repay student loans under Plan 2 from 6 April 2016.

(4)   *Postgraduate loan (PGL)* – Repayments due from 6 April 2019 can be collected concurrently with repayments for any Plan 1 or Plan 2 undergraduate loan which is still outstanding for English and Welsh former students.

(5)   *Reporting* – Student loan deductions must be reported on each FPS, and from 6 April 2019 the data is immediately passed to the Student Loans Company.

(6)   *Further information* – See guidance for employers on the deduction of student loans: tinyurl.com/gsr4sl.

CONSTRUCTION INDUSTRY SCHEME (CIS)

CIS deductions and returns

(FA 2004, ss 62, 70; SI 2005/2045, regs 4, 7, 8)

Sub-contractors:	Rate of deduction
Registered to receive payments gross	0%
Registered with HMRC	20%
Not registered with HMRC	30%

Notes

(1)   *Returns* – Contractors must file a monthly CIS return online of the deductions taken from payments made to subcontractors, by 19th of the month following the last tax month.

(2)   *Payments* – The CIS deductions must reach HMRC by 22nd of the following month if made electronically, or by 19th of that month if paying by post.

(3)   *Quarterly payments* – A contractor who believes their 'average monthly amount' will be less than £1,500 can choose to pay tax on a quarterly basis (ie for quarters ending 5 July, 5 October, 5 January and 5 April). The CIS return must be filed monthly.

(4)   *'Nil' returns* – Contractors who have not paid any subcontractors in the previous tax month are not required to submit a nil return (*SI 2015/429*).

(5)   *Penalties* – For late CIS returns or late payment see **Chapter 17**.

(6)   *Further information* – See: www.gov.uk/what-you-must-do-as-a-cis-contractor.

CORONAVIRUS JOB RETENTION SCHEME (CJRS)

(*Coronavirus Act 2020, ss 71, 76*; Treasury Directions: tinyurl.com/CVA2020dir)

Furlough periods within:	1–31 Aug 2020	1–30 Sept 2020	1–31 Oct 2020	1 Nov to 30 April 2021 (note 10)	1 May to 30 June 2021	1–31 July 2021	1 Aug– 30 Sept 2021
Employee wages covered by grant (note 1)	80% ref salary	70% ref salary	60% ref salary	80% ref salary	80% ref salary	70% ref salary	60% ref salary
Maximum wages per month	£2,500	£2,187.50	£1,875	£2,500	£2,500	£2,187.50	£1,875
Employer NIC covered by grant? (note 3)	No	No	No	No	No	No	No
Employer pension contributions covered by grant? (note 4)	No	No	No	No	No	No	No
Employer must pay amount of furlough wages per month:	–	10% of usual up to £312.50	20% of usual up to £625	–		10% of usual up to £312.50	20% of usual up to £625
Employee should receive at least per month for furloughed periods (note 2):	80% of usual up to £2,500	80% of usual up to £2,500	80% of usual up to £2,500	80% of usual up to £2,500	80% of usual up to £2,500	80% of usual up to £2,500	80% of usual up to £2,500

Notes

(1)   *Reference salary* – This is determined by when the employee's pay was first reported on an FPS under RTI by the employer as follows:

- First on FPS by 19 March 2020 – reference pay is the last pay period before this date.

- First on FPS between 20 March 2020 and 30 October 2020 – reference pay is the last pay period before 30 October 2020.

- First on FPS between 31 October 2020 and 2 March 2021 – reference pay is the last pay period before 2 March 2021.

The reference pay doesn't change even if the contractual pay has increased or decreased.

(2) *Employee receives* – Under the furlough scheme the employee should receive at least 80% of their ref salary, but the employer may choose to pay a higher amount. A reduction in the employee's wages to 80% of the usual level while on furlough must be agreed with the employee. The employer will be expected to pay 80% of the ref salary for all periods the employee is furloughed up until 30 September 2021 when the scheme will end.

(3) *Employer's NIC* – For furlough periods to 31 July 2020 the CJRS grant covered the employer's class 1 NIC on the furloughed pay. For furlough periods from 1 August 2020 onwards the employer's class 1 NIC is not covered by the CJRS grant.

(4) *Pension contributions* – For furlough periods to 31 July 2020 the CJRS grant covers the employer's minimum contribution to the workplace pension (3%), where employee is enrolled in such a scheme. For furlough periods from 1 August 2020 the CJRS does not cover any of the employer's pension contributions.

(5) *Conditions for furlough* – For periods before 1 July 2020 the employee must agree to be furloughed for an initial period of least three weeks and must have been on the payroll by 19 March 2020 with some pay for 2019/20 reported to HMRC through RTI by that date. While on furlough the employee can do no work for the employer or for any connected business, but they can undertake training (see note 8).

(6) *Sick pay* – The CJRS grant does not cover Statutory Sick Pay paid to the employee, but where SSP is paid in respect of coronavirus absence it may be reclaimed by smaller employers (see **Chapter 16**).

(7) *Apprenticeship Levy* – The CJRS grant does not cover the Apprenticeship Levy.

(8) *Flexible furlough* – From 1 July 2020 the furlough periods can be flexible down to a few days or hours per week, with the employee working for the rest of his or her normal hours. The employee must agree to written terms for flexible furlough.

(9) *CJRS version 2* – From 1 July to 31 October 2020 to be included in a CJRS claim, the employee must have been furloughed for at least three weeks before July and included in an earlier CJRS claim by the same employer. The CJRS claims for periods up until 30 June 2020 must be submitted by 31 July 2020. A furlough period cannot straddle a month end. The number of employees in a claim cannot exceed the maximum number claimed for in CJRS claims for periods before July 2020.

(10) *CJRS version 3* – From 1 November 2020 there is no requirement for an employee to have been included in an earlier CJRS claim. The employee's pay must have been reported under RTI between 20 March and 30 October 2020.

(11) *Directors* – If the company has agreed to the directors being furloughed, the employer can claim for the relevant percentage of the director's salary but NOT for any dividend payments. The director can undertake statutory duties while furloughed but must not provide any services to or on behalf of the company, or a connected person, that generate any income for the company.

(12) *NMW rates* – While furloughed the employees are not working so NMW or NLW rates do not apply. Usual wages can be reduced to below NMW rates. If employees undertake training while furloughed they must be paid at least NMW or NLW for that training time as appropriate for age of employee.

(13) *Data for a claim* – For each employee the employer needs to provide: name; NINO; and dates of furlough period. For furlough periods from 1 July 2020 the employer must report the actual hours worked and the usual hours for each furloughed employee. The employer also has to provide: PAYE scheme number; UTR number or company registration number; business name; address, bank account details; and number of employees covered by the claim.

(14) *Taxable* – CJRS grants are taxable income of the business in the period for which the grant is designed to refund the employer for furlough wages, but the grants are outside the scope of VAT.

(15) *Further information* – See Government guidance: tinyurl.com/CJRSckcl, tinyurl.com/CJRSwkcl and tinyurl.com/CJRS0511.

4

Shares and share options

ADMINISTRATION

Tax-advantaged share schemes

Notes

(1) *Registration* – Employers must register a share scheme with HMRC, whether it is tax advantaged or not, when there is a reportable event for the scheme by 6 July following the end of the tax year in which the scheme commenced.

(2) *Self-certification* – New tax advantaged schemes must be registered and self-certified by 6 July following the end of the tax year in which the scheme is implemented.

(3) *Online filing* – Employers must use the online ERS system to file the annual return for each share scheme by 6 July after the end of the tax year where there is a reportable event in the scheme in that tax year (ERS Bulletin: July 2015).

(4) *Penalties* – An automatic penalty of £100 applies for late submission of an annual share scheme return. Additional penalties of £300 apply on 7 October, and 7 January, following the end of the tax year if the annual return is still not filed by those dates. Coronavirus will be considered a reasonable excuse for missing the July 2020 filing deadline.

(5) *Making good amounts of tax paid* – Where tax is due on the award of shares or options the employee must reimburse the employer any tax and NIC paid by the employer in respect of the shares/options. This must be done by 6 July following the end of the tax year in which that event occurred (*ITEPA 2003, s 222*).

(6) *Further information* – Guidance for employees: www.gov.uk/tax-employee-share-schemes. Guidance for advisers: tinyurl.com/emrltdscits.

ENTERPRISE MANAGEMENT INCENTIVES (EMI)

(*ITEPA 2003, Pt 7, Ch 9, Sch 5*)

Action	Tax & NIC Implications
Grant of option	No income tax or NICs arise
Exercise of option	No income tax or NIC charges, if exercised within 10 years of grant and no disqualifying events have occurred. Employee must pay at least market value of shares as at the date of grant (*ITEPA 2003, ss 529–530*).

continued

Action	Tax & NIC Implications
Disposal of shares	Gain subject to CGT. Shares disposed of from 6 April 2013 can qualify for entrepreneurs' relief where the option grant date falls at least 1 year before disposal date; the requirement to hold 5% of ordinary share capital is ignored (*FA 2013, Sch 24*).

Notes

(1) *Purpose* – To help small, higher risk companies recruit and retain employees. EMI options must be granted for qualifying purposes (*ITEPA 2003, Sch 5, para 4*).

(2) *Number of employees* – The company must have fewer than 250 'full-time equivalent employees' at the option grant date (sum of all employees of a parent company and qualifying subsidiaries). Employees on furlough are counted as part of these numbers as if they were working their normal hours (*ITEPA 2003, Sch 5, para 12A*).

(3) *Available to* – Companies or groups with assets of no more than £30 million at the option grant. The company's activities must not be in an excluded sector including: banking, farming, property development, and legal services (*ITEPA 2003, Sch 5, para 12*).

(4) *Maximum options* – The total value of shares under EMI options granted by the company must not exceed £3 million (*ITEPA 2003, Sch 5, para 7*).

(5) *Employee entitlement* – An employee must work at least 25 hours a week or 75% of their working time for the employer to be entitled to participate in the EMI scheme. However, if these thresholds are not met during the coronavirus pandemic HMRC will accept the employee qualifies if they would have otherwise qualified. An employee may be granted qualifying options over shares with a total value not exceeding £250,000 (*SI 2012/1360*).

(6) *Notice required* – Options granted must be notified to HMRC using the ERS service within 92 days of the option grant (*ITEPA 2003, Sch 5, para 44*). Send reasonable excuse for late notification including unique scheme number, name of the company and scheme name to: shareschemes@hmrc.gov.uk.

(7) *Annual return* – Employers operating an EMI scheme must submit an annual return using the ERS online service by 6 July in the immediately following tax year (*ITEPA 2003, Sch 5, para 52*).

(8) *Call for evidence* – A call for evidence was published in March 2021, seeking views on how the EMI scheme is operating and whether it should be expanded.

(9) *Further information* – See HMRC's Employee Tax Advantaged Share Scheme User Manual para ETASSUM50000, and Employment Related Securities Bulletin 36.

SHARE INCENTIVE PLAN (SIP)

(ITEPA 2003, Pt 7, Ch 6, Sch 2; ITTOIA 2005, ss 392–396, 405–408, 770; SI 2001/1004, reg 22(8), Sch 3, Pt 9, para 7)

Type of share and annual limit per employee	When shares acquired	Shares taken from plan during the first 3 years	Shares taken from plan during years 3 to 5	Shares taken from plan after 5 years
Free shares up to £3,600 and Matching shares (maximum 2:1 to partnership shares)	No income tax or NICs to pay on the value of the shares *(ITEPA 2003, s 490)*	Income tax payable on the market value of the shares when taken out of the plan *(ITEPA 2003, s 505(2))*	Income tax payable on the lower of the market value of the shares: • when awarded, or • when taken out of plan *(ITEPA 2003, s 505(3))*	No income tax or NICs to pay
Partnership shares up to £1,800	No income tax or NICs to pay on the money used to buy the shares *(ITEPA 2003, s 492)*	Income tax payable on the market value of the shares when taken out of the plan *(ITEPA 2003, s 506(2))*	Income tax payable on the lower of: • the pay used to buy the shares, or • the market value of the shares when taken out of the plan *(ITEPA 2003, s 506(3))*	No income tax or NICs
Dividend shares	No income tax or NICs on dividends used to buy dividend shares *(ITEPA 2003, ss 490(1(b), 493, 496; ITTOIA 2005, s 770(2))*	Dividends used to buy shares are taxed as a dividend in the year the shares are taken out of the plan *(ITTOIA 2005, ss 394(2), 407(2))*	No income tax or NICs	No income tax or NICs

Notes

(1) *All employees* – Participation in the SIP cannot be restricted to particular groups or individuals. However, the employer can exclude employees who haven't worked for the company for a minimum period of time, which may be no longer than 18 months *(ITEPA 2003, Sch 2, paras 7, 8, 16)*.

(2) *NI exemption* – There is generally no National Insurance liability when an employee acquires shares from a SIP. However, a Class 1 NIC liability (and an income tax charge) may arise if the employee leaves the company, or takes shares out of the plan, within five years of joining it (see National Insurance Manual, NIM06806-06807).

(3) *Further information* – See HMRC's Employee Tax Advantaged Share Scheme User Manual para ETASSUM20000+.

COMPANY SHARE OPTION PLAN (CSOP)

(ITEPA 2003, Pt 7, Ch 8, Sch 4)

Action:	Tax & NIC Implications
Grant of option	No income tax or NICs arise, unless option was granted at a discount (*ITEPA 2003, s 526*).
Exercise of option	No income tax or NIC charges if the option is exercised between 3 and 10 years of the date of grant, or under 'good leaver' provisions within 3 years of the grant, (*ITEPA 2003, s 524*).
Disposal of shares	Gains are subject to CGT.

Notes

(1) *Tax advantaged* – The company can only grant share options if the CSOP has been registered and self-certified with HMRC (*ITEPA 2003, Sch 4, Pt 7*).

(2) *Maximum per employee* – Approved options with a market value of no more than £30,000, calculated at the date of grant (*ITEPA 2003, Sch 4, Pt 2*).

(3) *Eligible employees* – The individuals who receive the CSOP options must be either a full time director or a 'qualifying employee' of the scheme organiser (or constituent company in a group scheme), and must not have a material interest (more than 30% of ordinary share capital) in the company in which the options are granted. Full time directors and employees on furlough remain qualifying as if they were working their normal hours (*ITEPA 2003, Sch 4, Pt 3*; Employment Related Securities Bulletin 35).

(4) *Further information* – See HMRC's Tax Advantaged Share Scheme User Manual para ETASSUM40000+.

SAVE AS YOU EARN (SAYE)

(ITEPA 2003, Pt 7, Ch 7, Sch 3)

Action	Tax & NIC Implications
Grant of option	No income tax or NICs arise, unless option was granted at a discount. If options are accidentally granted at a discount to the market value of the shares on the agreed valuation date in excess of the permitted 20%, the option is treated as not having been granted, and will attract no tax advantages.
Exercise of option	No income tax or NIC charges if the option is exercised 3 years or more after the date of grant or if within 3 years of grant, in certain defined circumstances such as injury, disability or redundancy (*ITEPA 2003, s 519*).
Interest and bonuses	No income tax liability arises on interest and any bonus payable under a certified SAYE savings arrangement (*ITTOIA 2005, ss 702–703*). No NIC liability arises when proceeds of savings are used to buy shares.
Disposal of shares	Gains are subject to CGT. If shares are transferred into an ISA or pension fund on acquisition no CGT is payable.

Notes

(1) *Purpose* – SAYE, also known as Sharesave, allows employees to save, by having amounts deducted from their pay after income tax and NIC. This money is used to provide share options to current employees and directors of the scheme organiser or constituent company in a group scheme, to purchase the company's shares in the future, at a price determined at the time of invitation (*ITEPA 2003, Sch 3, Pt 3*).

(2) *Self-certification* – SAYE option schemes must be self-certified by the scheme organiser and registered with HMRC (*ITEPA 2003, Sch 3, Pt 8*).

(3) *Linked savings arrangements* – Individuals may contract to make monthly contributions over a three or five-year period, and may choose to leave the contributions in their accounts for an additional two years (ETASSUM34170–34180).

(4) *Contribution breaks* – Individuals can suspend contributions to the SAYE for up to 12 months without leaving the scheme or their options lapsing. This payment holiday may be extended for employees on furlough or unpaid leave, due to coronavirus (ETASSUM34140).

(5) *Contribution limits* – Maximum contribution permitted is £500 per month. The minimum contribution cannot exceed £10 per month (*ITEPA 2003, Sch 3, Pt 5*).

(6) *Bonus and interest rates* – The bonus rate is set at the time the savings contract is entered into, and is unaffected by any subsequent change to the rate.

(7) *Further information* – See HMRC's Employee Tax Advantaged Share Scheme User Manual para ETASSUM30000, and Employment Related Securities Bulletin 36.

EMPLOYEE SHAREHOLDER SHARES

(ITEPA 2003, ss 226A–226D, 326B; ITTOIA 2005, s 385A; TCGA 1992, ss 236B–236G; CTA 2009, s 1038B)

Action:	Tax & NIC implications
Award of shares before 1 December 2016	Up to £2,000 of shares awarded to each employee are free of income tax and NIC. Employees are deemed to have the value of the shares acquired (*ITEPA 2003, ss 226A–226D*).
Sale of shares back to issuing company	No income tax charge arises where the shares are sold back to the company if the individual is not an employee (or office-holder) of the employer company or of an associated company at the time of disposal (*ITTOIA 2005, s 385A*).
Disposal of shares	Capital gains realised on the disposal of up to £50,000 of shares (valued on acquisition) are exempt from CGT when the employee disposes of them (see notes 7–9) (*TCGA 1992, ss 236B–236G*).

Notes

(1) *Cancelled* – This scheme was effectively cancelled for shares issued from December 2016. If the employee received independent advice on their shareholder agreement prior to 1.30pm on 23 November 2016, the agreement could be signed by 2 December 2016 with the tax reliefs for the shares intact.

(2) *Period of scheme* – The tax and NI exemptions apply to shares awarded to employees who signed an employee shareholder status contract under the *Growth and Infrastructure Act 2013, s 31* on or after 1 September 2013 and before 1 December 2016, or 2 December 2016 as detailed in note 1.

(3) *Taxable* – Income tax and NICs are due on any value of shares awarded that exceeds £2,000.

(4) *Employment rights* – By taking up employee shareholder status, in order to receive the shares, the employee had to opt out of a package of employment rights. The employee was not treated as disposing of an asset by relinquishing the employment rights.

(5) *No connection* – The employee shareholder must not have a 'material interest' in the company (or its parent company) when the shares are issued or allotted, or within one year prior to that date, and must not be connected with an individual with such an interest (*ITEPA 2003, s 226D; TCGA 1992, s 236D*).

(6) *Corporation tax* – The deemed payment of up to £2,000 for the shares for income tax purposes is disregarded for the corporation tax deduction under *CTA 2009, Pt 12*, but where shares worth more than £2,000 are awarded, the excess over £2,000 qualifies for a corporation tax deduction.

(7) *Restricted gains on disposal* – Where the shares were acquired in connection with an employee shareholder agreement entered into on or after 16 March 2016 and before 1 December 2016, the gains made on the disposal of those shares are exempt from CGT up to a maximum of £100,000 for the person making the disposal. This is a lifetime limit.

(8) *Unrestricted gains* – Gains made on disposal of employee shareholder shares acquired from 1 September 2013 and 15 March 2016 do not count towards that £100,000 limit (*FA 2016, s 88*).

(9) *No transfer* – Shares acquired under this scheme enjoy CGT exemption on disposal if and only if they are held by the employee who received them under the shareholder agreement, subject to these limits. Where the shares are transferred to a spouse or civil partner the exemption will not apply on disposal by that spouse/partner.

(10) *Further information* – See tinyurl.com/Emshtx.

Pensions and investments

PENSION CONTRIBUTIONS

(FA 2004, Pt 4, Schs 28–36)

Individual has	Annual maximum relievable contributions
Relevant UK earnings	100% of earnings capped by annual allowance
Little or no UK earnings	£3,600 gross contribution

Notes

(1) *Individual's contributions* – Income tax relief is generally given at the basic rate by the registered pension scheme claiming 25% of the net contribution from HMRC. This also applies to contributions made by individuals who pay no tax, or who are taxed at rates lower than 20%.

(2) *Higher rate relief* – Tax relief is given at the individual's marginal rate of tax (where higher than 20%) by claiming through the tax return or the PAYE code, on relievable contributions made by the individual within the above annual limits. Additional contributions may be made by the individual, but no further tax relief is available *(FA 2004, s 190)*.

(3) *Employer contributions* – The individual's employer may make pension contributions on behalf of the individual up to the limit of the annual allowance (see below). These contributions do not attract income tax relief but in general will be a qualifying deduction for tax purposes for the employer.

(4) *Excluded contributions* – Contributions made after the individual has reached age 75 don't attract income tax relief *(FA 2004, s 188(3))*.

Annual allowances

(FA 2004, ss 218, 228)

Tax year:	2021/22 £	2020/21 £	2019/20 £	2018/19 £	2017/18 £	2016/17 £
Annual Allowance	40,000	40,000	40,000	40,000	40,000	40,000
Restricted AA (note 7)	4,000	4,000	10,000	10,000	10,000	10,000
MPAA	4,000	4,000	4,000	4,000	4,000	10,000

Notes

(1)   *Annual allowance charge* – This is levied at the individual's marginal income tax rate charged on earned income. Scottish taxpayers pay the charge at their highest Scottish income tax rate. The charge does not apply in the tax year the individual dies, retires due to severe ill-health, or is a deferred member whose benefits cannot increase (*FA 2004, ss 229(3), 230*).

(2)   *Scheme pays* – Where the annual allowance charge exceeds £2,000, the member can ask his pension scheme to pay the liability, with the scheme benefits being actuarially reduced accordingly (*FA 2004, ss 237A, 237B*).

(3)   *PIP alignment* – All pension input periods (PIPs) are aligned with the tax year from 2016/17. All earlier PIPs were deemed to end on 8 July 2015 and recommenced on 9 July 2015 to allow for this adjustment (*FA 2004, ss 238ZA, 238ZB*).

(4)   *Double allowance* – For 2015/16 only it was possible to enjoy two annual allowances of £40,000 each; for a PIP ending on 8 July 2015, and for a PIP ending on 5 April 2016. The maximum unused allowance which can be carried forward to 2016/17 is £40,000 (*FA 2004, s 228C*).

(5)   *Carry forward* – Unused annual allowance from the three tax years preceding the current tax year may be added to the current year's allowance, using the earliest years' allowance first. This does not apply for the MPAA. The taxpayer must have been a member of a registered pension scheme for the years from which the allowance is carried forward (*FA 2004, s 228A*).

(6)   *MPAA* – Money purchase annual allowance applies to restrict contributions to the same or other money purchase/defined contribution schemes, where a taxpayer has flexibly accessed their defined contribution scheme or SASS. The MPAA doesn't apply when only the tax-free cash is taken (*FA 2004, 227B*). The MPAA is £20,000 if the flexible access occurred before 9 July 2015 (*FA 2004, s 228C*).

(7)   *Restricted allowance* – Since 2020/21 the annual allowance is tapered down by £1 for every £2 of the taxpayer's adjusted income (including pension contributions) over £240,000, but the taxpayer's net income (excluding contributions) must also exceed £200,000. For earlier years those thresholds were £150,000 and £110,000 respectively (*F(No 2)A 2015, Sch 4, Pt 4*).

PENSION WITHDRAWALS

Lifetime allowance

(*FA 2004, s 215*)

Tax year	2021/22 £	2020/21 £	2019/20 £	2018/19 £	2017/18 £	2016/17 £
Allowance	1.0731m	1.0731m	1.055m	1.03m	1m	1m

Notes

(1)   *Pension age* – This is the minimum age from which a person can draw their pension. It is normally 55, but members of certain professions and occupations can draw

pension benefits earlier (see protected retirement ages). Pension age is due to be raised in future years.

(2) *Lifetime allowance charge* – This tax charge is calculated as a percentage of the excess pension pot above the lifetime allowance, measured at the time benefits are first taken. If the benefits are taken as a pension the charge is 25%: where the benefits are taken as a lump sum the charge is 55%. These rates also apply to Scottish taxpayers.

(3) *Individual protection 2016* – Individuals who expect to have pension savings over £1 million at 5 April 2016 can apply online to protect their lifetime allowance up to £1.25 million, but this needs to happen before pension benefits are taken (*FA 2016, Sch 4*).

(4) *Fixed protection 2016* – Individuals who have not applied for the previous versions of fixed protection can apply to protect their lifetime allowance at £1.25m, where an online election is made from July 2016. To meet the conditions of fixed protection there must be no further contributions into their pension fund from 6 April 2016 onwards (*FA 2016, Sch 4*).

(5) *Further information* – See: HMRC's Pension Tax Manual para PTM094100+.

Tax charges on withdrawals

(FA 2004, Pt 4, Ch 5)

Charge	Tax rates
Lifetime allowance charge (*FA 2004, s 215*)	See note 2 under **Lifetime allowance:** 55% on lump sum, 25% on pension
Annual allowance charge (*FA 2004, s 227*)	See note 1 under **Annual allowance:** highest marginal rate
Unauthorised payments charge (*FA 2004, s 208*)	40%
Unauthorised payments surcharge (*FA 2004, s 209*)	15%
Short service refund lump sum charge (*FA 2004, s 205; SI 2010/536*)	20% on first £20,000, 50% on amounts over £20,000. These rates also apply to Scottish taxpayers
Serious ill-health lump sum charge (*FA 2004, Sch 29 para 4*)	Charged at the recipient's marginal rate where the individual is over 75
Special lump sum death benefits charge when paid to non-qualifying person (*FA 2004, s 206*)	45%
Authorised surplus payments charge (*FA 2004, s 207*)	35%
Scheme sanction charge (*FA 2004, s 240*)	15%–40%
De-registration charge (*FA 2004, s 242*)	40%

Notes

(1)   *Pension freedoms* – From 6 April 2015 members of defined contribution pension schemes who are aged 55 or over can draw all of their pension savings without restriction, without having to purchase an annuity at that point. However, withdrawals in excess of the 25% tax-free amount are taxed at the individual's marginal tax rate for the year of withdrawal. For 2014/15 the pension access rules were relaxed as described in notes 2 to 4 below (*FA 2014, ss 41–42, Sch 5*).

(2)   *Flexible drawdown* – Where the individual has guaranteed pension income of £12,000 (£20,000 before 27 March 2014) all their pension funds can be taken in cash; 25% tax free and the rest is taxed at their marginal income tax rate for earned income.

(3)   *Capped drawdown* – Where the individual does not qualify for flexible drawdown, the maximum drawdown cash that can be taken is 150% (120% before 27 March 2014) of the equivalent single life annuity.

(4)   *Trivial commutation* – Where an individual over age 60 has total pension rights under all registered pension schemes of less than £30,000 (£18,000 before 27 March 2014) the total can be taken in cash: 25% tax free, the rest taxed at the taxpayer's marginal rate for earned income.

(5)   *Small lump sums* – Up to three pension pots with a value of less than £10,000 (£2,000 prior to 27 March 2014) can be taken as a lump sum.

(6)   *Tax free pensions advice* – From 6 April 2017 an employer may pay for relevant pensions advice for an employee, former employee, or prospective employee, who is within five years of retirement age. The benefit of receiving this advice is exempt from tax and NIC where the cost doesn't exceed £500 per person per year (*ITEPA 2003, s 308C*). A similar exemption applied from 14 December 2004 for employees only, where the advice cost no more than £150 per person (*SI 2002/205*).

PROTECTED RETIREMENT AGES

(*FA 2004, Sch 36, paras 21, 23; SI 2005/3451, reg 3, Sch 2*)

The following professions and occupations have lower retirement ages than the standard of age 55.

Athletes	Members of the Reserve Forces
Badminton players	Motor racing drivers and motor cycle riders
Boxers	Rugby players
Cricketers	Skiers (downhill)
Cyclists	Snooker or billiards players
Dancers	Speedway riders
Divers (saturation, deep sea and free swimming)	Squash players
Footballers	Table tennis players
Golfers	Tennis players (including real tennis)
Ice hockey players	Trapeze artists
Jockeys – flat racing and national hunt	Wrestlers

Notes

(1) *Normal retirement age* – Retirement benefits can generally only be taken from a registered pension scheme from the minimum pension age of 55. Lower pension ages for certain qualifying occupations were generally abolished from 6 April 2006.

(2) *Protected age* – The above occupations and professions have protected pre-existing rights to take benefits under a personal pension scheme or retirement annuity contract before the age of 50. This is the individual's protected pension age (see HMRC's Pensions Tax Manual, PTM062220).

INDIVIDUAL SAVING ACCOUNTS (ISA)

(ITTOIA 2005, Pt 6, Ch 3; SI 1998/1870, reg 4)

ISAs	2021/22 £	2020/21 £	2019/20 £	2018/19 £	2017/18 £	2015/16 & 2016/17 £
Overall limit	20,000	20,000	20,000	20,000	20,000	15,240
Cash limit	20,000	20,000	20,000	20,000	20,000	15,240
Junior ISA	9,000	9,000	4,368	4,260	4,128	4,080
Lifetime ISA (note 5)	4,000	4,000	4,000	4,000	4,000	N/A
Help to save	50 per month	50 per month	50 per month	N/A	N/A	N/A

Notes

(1) *Combination of savings* – From 1 July 2014, investors can invest any combination of cash or shares in an ISA up to the limits shown (*SI 2014/1450*).

(2) *Junior ISA (JISA)* – Available to UK residents who are under 18 and who don't have a Child Trust Fund (CTF) account. The investment limit can be divided between cash and stocks and shares. When the holder reaches age 18, their JISA becomes an adult ISA (*ITTOIA 2005, s 695A*).

(3) *Young people* – Whether or not a person aged 16 to 18 holds a Junior ISA, they may invest in an adult cash ISA up to the cash limit, but not in a stocks and shares ISA.

(4) *Help to buy ISA* – From 1 December 2015 to 30 November 2019 individuals could open a help to buy ISA to save for their first home. The saver may deposit up to £1,000 initially and then up to £200 per month. The Government contributes 25% bonus, up to £3,000 per ISA payable only when the funds are used to buy the home (*Help to Buy ISA factsheet*).

(5) *Lifetime ISA* – Available to UK resident individuals aged between 18 and 40, from 6 April 2017. All deposits count towards the overall savings limit of £20,000. Government adds a 25% bonus of up to £1,000 per year, which is surrendered together with a 5% penalty if funds are withdrawn for a non-qualifying purpose. The funds may be withdrawn from age 60 onwards, when the saver is terminally ill, or used to help purchase the saver's first home worth up to £450,000, once the account

has been open for at least 12 months. From 6 March 2020 to 5 April 2021 the penalty for withdrawing funds for a non-qualifying purpose is removed, but the Government bonus is lost (*Lifetime ISA fact sheet*).

(6)   *Inherited ISA allowance* – For deaths on or after 2 December 2014 the surviving spouse/civil partner has an additional ISA allowance for the year of death equivalent to the value of the deceased person's savings at the date of death (*SI 2015/869*).

(7)   *Help to save* – From 1 September 2018 individuals receiving tax credits or universal credit can open a help to save account with NS&I. The Government will contribute 50% bonus on the second and fourth anniversaries of opening the account (*SI 2018/87*).

(8)   *Further information* – For ISAs see www.gov.uk/individual-savings-accounts. For help to save see www.gov.uk/get-help-savings-low-income.

INVESTMENTS BY PARENTS

(*ITTOIA 2005, s 629*)

Assets given by each parent to:	Annual income derived per child	Treated as income of
Their child	Up to £100	Child
Their child	Over £100	Parent
Their child's cash ISA	Up to £100	Child, but tax free
Their child's cash ISA	Over £100	Capital treated as part of parent's ISA limit
Their child's JISA or child trust fund account	Unlimited	Child, but tax free

Notes

(1)   *Applies* – Where the child is aged under 18, and is neither married nor in a civil partnership.

(2)   Cash gifts which are not invested by, or on behalf of, the child are not counted in the above limits.

(3)   *Further information* – ISA guidance notes: tinyurl.com/ISAmGn.

Tax-free childcare accounts

(*SI 2015/488; SI 2015/522; Childcare Payments Act 2014*)

	Maximum contribution per child:		
	Parent contributes £	Government matches £	Total per year £
Child aged 11 or under	8,000	2,000	10,000
Disabled child under 17	16,000	4,000	20,000

Notes

(1)   *Savings account* – Parents can apply for an online savings account, into which the government will contribute funds as indicated above. The funds from the tax-free childcare account can only be spent with registered childcare providers who are signed up to the scheme.

(2)   *Earnings limits* – To qualify for the matching funds both partners must be employed or self-employed earning at least the National Minimum Wage for 16 hours per week, with neither having an adjusted net income of over £100,000. The self-employed are not required to earn the minimum amount in the first 12 months of their business. Claimants of tax credits or universal credit do not qualify for the tax-free childcare account.

(3)   *Further information* – See www.gov.uk/tax-free-childcare.

ENTERPRISE INVESTMENT SCHEME (EIS)

(ITA 2007, Pt 5; TCGA 1992, s 150A, Sch 5B)

Shares issued in:	Maximum investment per tax year £	Rate of income tax relief	Amount permissible to carry back £
From 2018/19 (note 1)	2,000,000	30%	All
2012/13 to 2017/18	1,000,000	30%	All
2011/12	500,000	30%	All
2008/09 to 2010/11	500,000	20%	50,000 for 2008/09 See Note 2
2006/07 to 2007/08	400,000	20%	50,000

Notes

(1)   *Knowledge intensive* – Any investment over £1 million per tax year must be invested in knowledge intensive companies *(FA 2018, Sch 4)*.

(2)   *New shareholders only* – For shares issued on or after 18 November 2015, EIS relief can only apply if the shareholder did not previously own any shares in the company other than subscriber shares, or shares issued under the EIS, SEIS or VCT schemes *(ITA 2007, s 164A)*.

(3)   *Carry back* – EIS relief is available for the tax year in which the shares are issued, but the investor may carry back some or all of the tax relief to the immediately preceding year, subject to the overriding tax relief limit for that earlier year *(ITA 2007, s 158(4))*.

(4)   *Disposal relief* – A gain made on the disposal of EIS shares after holding them for at least three years is exempt from CGT to the extent that full income tax relief has been claimed, and not withdrawn, on the investment *(TCGA 1992, s 150A)*.

(5)   *Deferral relief* – Where the disposal proceeds from any capital gain are reinvested in a subscription for EIS shares in the four-year period that starts one year before the date of the gain, all or part of the original gain can be deferred. The deferred gain is brought back into charge on the disposal of the EIS shares or on a breach of the investment conditions (*TCGA 1992, Sch 5B*).

(6)   *Further information* – See HMRC's Venture Capital Schemes Manual at VCM10000.

SEED ENTERPRISE INVESTMENT SCHEME (SEIS)

(*TCGA 1992, ss 150E–150G; ITA 2007, Pt 5A*)

Shares issued in:	Maximum investment £	Rate of income tax relief %	Rate of CGT reinvestment relief %
2013/14 onwards	100,000	50	50
2012/13	100,000	50	100

Notes

(1)   *Small companies* – SEIS can be used by companies with gross assets of no more than £200,000, and up to 25 full-time equivalent employees. There is no minimum investment for the investor.

(2)   *Scope* – A company can accept up to £150,000 as SEIS investments in any three-year period, but it can go on to raise money under EIS or VCT at a later stage. SEIS cannot be used after permission to use EIS has been granted.

(3)   *Income tax relief* – The relief may be claimed in respect of investments in SEIS shares issued on or after 6 April 2012. The relief is given as a reduction in the individual's tax liability for the tax year in which the investment was made.

(4)   *Carry back* – A claim can be made to treat the investment as having been made in the immediately preceding tax year (but not before 2012/13). This election is also effective for CGT reinvestment relief (see HMRC's Venture Capital Manual at VCM45010).

(5)   *Reinvestment relief* – This exempts from CGT 100% or 50% of a gain where the disposal proceeds are reinvested in new SEIS shares, within the same tax year in which the disposal occurs (*TCGA 1992, Sch 5BB*). Income tax relief must be given for the SEIS investment and not withdrawn.

(6)   *Disposal relief* – A gain on the disposal of SEIS shares after the relevant three-year period is exempt from CGT to the extent that income tax relief has been given, and not withdrawn, for the investment in the shares.

(7)   *Further information* – See HMRC's Venture Capital Schemes Manual at VCM30000.

SOCIAL INVESTMENT TAX RELIEF (SITR)

(ITA 2007, Pt 5B; TCGA 1992, ss 255A–255B, Sch 8B)

Shares issued in:	Maximum investment per tax year £	Rate of income tax relief	Amount permissible to carry back £
2015/16 to 2022/23	1,000,000	30%	All
2014/15	1,000,000	30%	none

Notes

(1) *Social enterprises* – SITR is a venture capital scheme for investments in social enterprises (eg charities, community interest companies), which have fewer than 250 employees and a maximum of £15 million gross assets.

(2) *Applies to* – Subscriptions for new shares and debt instruments issued by social enterprises between 6 April 2014 and 5 April 2023.

(3) *Income tax relief* – Tax relief is given as a tax reduction following a claim, which must be made no later than the fifth anniversary of 31 January following the tax year of investment. The tax relief may be reduced or withdrawn in certain circumstances, broadly on a disposal of the SITR investment or a breach of the investment conditions, within three years.

(4) *Disposal relief* – A gain on the disposal of SITR investment realised at least three years after it was acquired is exempt from CGT to the extent that income tax relief has been given on the investment, and has not been withdrawn.

(5) *Hold-over relief* – Where a gain is reinvested in SITR shares or debt instruments in a four-year period that begins one year before the gain arose, all or part of the original gain can be held-over. That gain is brought back into charge to CGT on the disposal of the SITR investment or a breach of the investment conditions.

(6) *Further information* – Outline guidance is found at: tinyurl.com/SIRTapply.

VENTURE CAPITAL TRUSTS (VCT)

(ITA 2007, Pt 6)

Shares issued from	Maximum annual investment £	Rate of relief
6 April 2006	200,000	30%
6 April 2004	200,000	40%
6 April 2000	100,000	20%

Notes

(1)   *Income tax relief* – This is given for the tax year in which the shares are issued by the VCT. The relief available is the lower of 30% of the investment value, and the amount which reduces the individual's income tax liability to nil.

(2)   *Dividend exemption* – Individual investors are exempt from income tax on dividends in respect of ordinary VCT shares acquired with the above maximum amounts, provided that the shares were acquired for genuine commercial reasons and not for a tax avoidance purpose (*ITTOIA 2005, Pt 6, Ch 5*).

(3)   *CGT exemption* – Disposals of VCT shares by individual investors are exempt from CGT (and losses are not allowable) where the shares were acquired within the above permitted maximum amounts, and if certain other conditions are satisfied (*TCGA 1992, ss 151A, 151B*).

(4)   *From 6 April 2014* – Tax relief is withdrawn if the VCT shares are disposed of within five years of acquisition and income tax relief is restricted where investments are conditionally linked to a VCT share buy-back or have been made within six months of a disposal of shares in the same VCT (*FA 2014, Sch 10*).

(5)   *Further information* – See HMRC's Venture Capital Schemes Manual at VCM50000.

COMMUNITY INVESTMENT TAX RELIEF (CITR)

(*ITA 2007, Pt 7; CTA 2010, Pt 7*)

Investor:	Rate of relief of invested amount	Given over:	Maximum relief:
Individual	25%	5 years	Unlimited
Company	25%	5 years	€200,000

Notes

(1)   *For investments in* – Accredited Community Development Finance Institutions (CDFIs), for a period of at least five years.

(2)   *Given as* – Reduction in the investor's tax liability, limited to the amount of tax liability for each year.

(3)   *Carry forward* – For investments made from April 2013, the tax relief can be carried forward to the next year or accounting period if it is not fully relieved in the relevant tax year (*ITA 2007, s 335A; CTA 2010, s 220A*).

(4)   *Claimed for* – Tax year or accounting period in which the investment falls and the four subsequent tax years or accounting periods (*ITA 2007, s 335(3); CTA 2010, s 220(4)*).

(5)   *Further information* – See tinyurl.com/kxxtpmf.

EMPLOYEE OWNERSHIP TRUST

(TCGA 1992, ss 236H–236P; ITEPA 2003, Pt 4, Ch 10A; IHTA 1984, ss 13, 28, 75, 86; CTA 2009, s 1292)

Relief from	Type of relief	Starts from	Maximum relief:
Capital gains tax	No gain, no loss on shares transferred	6 April 2014	unlimited
Inheritance tax	Exempt disposal on transfer to EOT	6 April 2014	unlimited
Income tax	Tax exempt bonuses paid to employees of the company controlled by the EOT	1 October 2014	£3,600 per year per employee
Corporation tax	Deduction given for tax exempt bonuses paid	1 October 2014	£3,600 per year per employee

Notes

(1) *Controlling interest* – The tax reliefs described above apply when shares in a trading company are transferred to an employee-ownership trust (EOT), and within that tax year the EOT has acquired a controlling interest in that company.

(2) *Individuals* – The reliefs are only available for transfers of shares made by individuals, trustees or personal representatives of deceased individuals, not by companies.

(3) *After the disposal* – The transferor must not hold 5% or more of shares in the company, or less than two-fifths of the employees and office holders in the company must hold 5% or more in the company.

(4) *Further information* – HMRC's Capital gains manual CG67800.

6

Business profits

MAKING TAX DIGITAL (MTD)

Timetable

(F(No 2)A 2017, ss 60–62, Sch 14)

Commencing	Businesses which are:	Must file:
VAT periods starting on and after 1 April 2019	VAT registered with annual VATable turnover of £85,000 or more and are not deferred	VAT return using MTD-compatible software
VAT periods starting on and after 1 October 2019	VAT registered and annual VATable turnover over £85,000 who are deferred (note 2)	VAT return using MTD-compatible software
VAT periods starting on and after 1 April 2022	VAT registered with turnover under VAT registration threshold	VAT return using MTD-compatible software
Accounting periods for income tax starting on or after 6 April 2023	Unincorporated traders or landlords who have annual turnover over £10,000	Quarterly reporting of income and expenses plus annual adjustments in end of period statement
Accounting periods starting no earlier than 1 April 2026	Companies and all bodies paying corporation tax	Quarterly reports of income and expenditure plus annual adjustments to bring totals in line with GAAP

Notes

(1) *MTD for VAT* – Most VAT registered businesses (see note 5) were required to enter the MTD regime for VAT periods commencing on and after 1 April 2019. Businesses in the deferred categories had a later start date (see note 2).

(2) *Deferred categories* – Businesses who are required to make payments of VAT on account, as they pay VAT of more than £2m per year, plus those in the following

categories could not commence VAT filing under MTD until their first VAT period which began on or after 1 October 2019:

- VAT groups
- VAT divisions
- traders based overseas
- trusts
- unincorporated not-for-profit organisations
- certain public sector bodies and local authorities
- annual account scheme users

(3) *Digital records* – Businesses must keep the records required to make the returns under MTD, in a digital format. This can be within MTD-functional accounting software or in spreadsheets (*SI 2018/261, reg 6*; *VAT Notice 700/22, section 4*).

(4) *Digital links* – Where more than one software package or spreadsheet is used, those packages should be digitally linked so the data can be transferred without a person having to retype it. Digital links are compulsory for VAT periods starting on and or after 1 April 2021, unless the business has applied for an extension to the soft-landing period (VAT Notice 700/22, 4.2.1.1).

(5) *VAT reporting* – The VAT return figures must be submitted to HMRC directly from the MTD-compatible software by way of an API (application programming interface) to HMRC. No further information is required to be, or can be, submitted under MTD at this time.

(6) *Voluntary VAT registered* – Businesses which are VAT registered on a voluntary basis will be required to enter the MTD regime from VAT return periods starting on and after 1 April 2022; until then they are not required to file using MTD software (VAT Notice 700/22, section 2).

(7) *Exemptions* – Businesses exempt from online filing for VAT pre-MTD are also automatically exempt from filing VAT returns using MTD compatible software. Other businesses must apply to HMRC for exemption from MTD on the grounds of: insolvency; religion; or that it is not reasonably practical to keep digital records by reason of: age; disability; remoteness of location; or other reason (VAT Notice 700/22 section 3).

(8) *MTD ITSA* – Businesses and landlords with total gross annual turnover of £10,000 or more will be required to enter the MTD for income tax regime from the first accounting period that starts on or after 6 April 2023. A taxpayer with several businesses may have several start dates for MTD.

(9) *MTD for corporation tax* – No firm start date has been proposed other than it will not be earlier than April 2026.

(10) *Further information* – See VAT notice 700/22 and Bloomsbury Professional: MTD Tracker, available as part of all Bloomsbury Professional tax packages.

CASH BASIS

Trading business

(ITTOIA 2005, s 25A, Pt 2, Ch 3A, ss 33A, 51A, 56A, Ch 17A, Pt 3, Ch 3)

Tax Year	Entry turnover £	Exit turnover £
2021/22	150,000	300,000
2020/21	150,000	300,000
2019/20	150,000	300,000
2018/19	150,000	300,000
2017/18	150,000	300,000
2016/17	83,000	166,000

Notes

(1) *Elect in* – Unincorporated trading businesses can elect to calculate profits/losses for tax purposes on the basis of the cash received and expenses paid out, known as the cash basis. This cash basis replaces the cash basis used by barristers, with some transitional arrangements *(ITTOIA 2005, s 25A)*.

(2) *Permitted turnover* – For the first period of using the cash basis the business' turnover must be no more than the entry level. Where the business is operated by a universal credit claimant, it can start to use the cash basis if its turnover is less than the exit level *(ITTOIA 2005, s 31B)*.

(3) *Excluded businesses* – The following businesses cannot use the cash basis *(ITTOIA 2005, s 31C)*:

- companies;
- LLPs;
- farmers using the herd basis;
- persons using profit averaging for farmers and artists;
- persons carrying on a mineral extraction trade;
- persons who have claimed business premises renovation allowance or R&D allowance; and
- Lloyd's underwriters.

(4) *Exit* – The business must cease to use the cash basis when its annual turnover exceeds the exit turnover. Alternatively, the business may leave the cash basis when its commercial circumstances change such that the cash basis is no longer appropriate.

(5) *Loan interest* – The deduction for loan interest paid is limited to £500 per year, although a full deduction for hire purchase costs and credit card interest for business purchases is permitted *(ITTOIA 2005, s 57B)*.

(6) *Losses* – Trade losses can only be carried forward to the following tax year. No sideways or carry back of loss relief is permitted *(ITA 2007, s 74E)*.

(7) *Accounting year* – The business can make up its accounts to any date in the year and use the cash basis.

(8) *Further information* – Outline guidance is found at: www.gov.uk/simpler-income-tax-cash-basis. Technical guidance found in HMRC's Business Income Manual at BIM70000.

(9) *Three line accounts* – Where the trader has turnover below the VAT registration threshold he may submit just three totals (turnover, expenses and profit) on the self-employment short SA return (see: tinyurl.com/zvz43uj).

Property businesses

(ITTOIA 2005, ss 271A–271E, 272ZA, 276A, 307A–307F, 329A, 334A)

Tax Year	Entry turnover £	Exit turnover £
2021/22	150,000	150,000
2020/21	150,000	150,000
2019/20	150,000	150,000
2018/19	150,000	150,000
2017/18	150,000	150,000

Notes

(1) *Opt out* – From 6 April 2017 the cash basis for unincorporated property businesses is the default accounting treatment, but the landlord may opt out by making an election on his tax return (*ITTOIA 2005, s 271A(10)*).

(2) *Excluded* – The following are not permitted to use the cash basis for property businesses (*ITTOIA 2005, s 271A(2), (7)*):

- companies;
- LLPs;
- partnerships with one or more partners who are not individuals;
- trustees;
- where the property is jointly owned by spouses or civil partners, and one of those individuals uses the GAAP basis of accounting for their share of the joint property income;
- where the receipts for the year, calculated on the cash basis, exceed £150,000.

(3) *Finance costs* – These costs may be deducted as incurred, subject to a restriction where the capital value of the loans outstanding at the end of the period exceeds the value of the let property when it was first let by the taxpayer plus any improvements made by that landlord since that date (*ITTOIA 2005, ss 307C, 307D*).

(4) *Residential property* – The restriction outlined in note 3 applies before, and in addition to, the restriction on the deduction of finance costs described under Residential Property Lettings below.

FIXED RATE DEDUCTIONS

(ITTOIA 2005, Ch 5A)

Optional use – From 6 April 2013 any unincorporated trading business or profession, can use the following fixed rate deductions, also known as simplified expenses, to replace the calculation of actual costs incurred. These rates can be used whether or not the business also opts to use the cash basis *(ITTOIA 2005, s 94B)*.

Not companies – Any firm which includes a company as a partner is prohibited from using these fixed rate deductions *(ITTOIA 2005, s 94C)*.

Motor expenses

(ITTOIA 2005, ss 94D–94G)

Vehicle	Business use	Rate per mile
Car or goods vehicle	First 10,000 miles per year (833 per month)	45p
Car or goods vehicle	In excess of 10,000 miles per year (833 per month)	25p
Motor cycle	All such journeys	24p

Notes

(1)   *Other deductions* – These rates do not cover the finance element of a finance lease or hire purchase, which may be claimed in addition to the mileage rate, subject to private use adjustment. In addition, journey-specific costs such as parking, toll and congestion charges may be claimed.

(2)   *Excluded vehicles* – Goods vehicles or motorcycles acquired under the cash basis where a full deduction has been made for the cost, and vehicles for which capital allowances have previously been claimed, cannot use these mileage rates *(ITTOIA 2005, s 94E)*.

(3)   *More than one car* – Where a business uses more than one car, including vehicles used by employees, it must aggregate all business mileage across all the vehicles that qualify for a fixed rate deduction to calculate the overall deduction *(ITTOIA 2005, s 94F)*.

(4)   *Further information* – See HMRC's Business Income Manual at BIM75005.

Use of home for business purposes

(ITTOIA 2005, s 94H)

Home used for working hours per month	Claim per month £
25 to 50 or more	10
51 to 100 or more	18
101 or more	26

Notes

(1) *Which costs* – Businesses that use the home for business purposes can opt to use the above fixed deduction in place of the business proportion of home expenses including; power, telephone, internet or broadband. These rates don't cover council tax (domestic rates in Northern Ireland), insurance and mortgage interest, so a business proportion of those costs can be claimed in addition.

(2) *Separate months* – The fixed rate expense claimed can be different for each month, depending on the use of the property in that month. There is no pro-rata reduction where the home is only used for part of the month.

(3) *Partners* – From 6 April 2016 partners in partnerships can claim the use of home deduction (*FA 2016, s 24*).

(4) *Further information* – See HMRC's Business Income Manual at BIM75010.

Business premises used partly as a home

(*ITTOIA 2005, s 941*)

Number of relevant occupants	Applicable amount per month £
1	350
2	500
3 or more	650

Notes

(1) *Where it applies* – For business premises, such as a hotel or bed and breakfast, which are used partly for private purposes as a home. The applicable amount is deducted from the actual expenses such that the cost net of private use is deducted in the accounts.

(2) *Relevant occupant* – This is any individual who at any time during the month (or part of the month) occupies the premises as a home, otherwise in the course of the trade. From 6 April 2016 the individual may be a partner in the business (*FA 2016, s 24*).

(3) *Further information* – See HMRC's Business Income Manual at BIM75015.

AVERAGING PROFITS FOR FARMERS AND ARTISTS

(*ITTOIA 2005, Pt 2, Ch 16*)

One year's profits are:	Less than 70% of other year	Less than 75% of other year	70% to 75% of other year
	May apply full averaging	Full averaging from 2016/17 onwards	Marginal relief (note 5)

Notes

(1)   *Farmers* – Individuals and partnerships (not companies) engaged in farming, market gardening, the intensive rearing in the UK of livestock or fish on a commercial basis for human food production.

(2)   *Artists* – Individuals and partnerships (not companies) who personally create literary, dramatic, musical or artistic works or designs.

(3)   *Which profits to include* – Profits arising in consecutive tax years. A trading loss is treated as a nil profit for these averaging purposes.

(4)   *Averaging period* – From 2016/17 farmers (as defined above) can average their profits and losses over two years (as per earlier years) or over a period of five years (*FA 2016, s 25*).

(5)   *Marginal relief* – This form of averaging relief is abolished from 2016/17. If the profits for one year exceed 70% of the profits for the other, but are less than 75% of those profits, marginal relief was calculated as follows (*ITTOIA 2005, s 223(4)*):

Step 1 – Calculate the adjustment, using the following formula:

$$(D \times 3) - (P \times 0.75)$$

where: D is the difference between the relevant profits for the two years; and

P is the higher relevant profits of the two years

Step 2 – Add the adjustment to the relevant profits of the tax year of which those profits are lower.

Step 3 – Deduct the adjustment from the relevant profits of the tax year of which those profits are higher.

(6)   *How to claim* – In the self-assessment return for the later year, within 12 months of 31 January following the later of the two tax years to be averaged. This time limit may be extended if profits are adjusted for some other reason (*ITTOIA 2005, s 222(6)*; see BIM73155).

(7)   *Further information* – See HMRC's Business Income Manual at BIM73000–73190, and HMRC Helpsheets HS224 and HS234.

CAR HIRE COSTS

(ITTOIA 2005, s 48; CTA 2009, ss 56, 1251(2))

CO_2 emissions in g/km				Car hire or lease commencing in tax year:
2009/10 to 2012/13	**2013/14 to 2017/18**	**2018/19 to 2020/21**	**From 2021/22**	
Up to 130	Up to 130	Up to 110	Up to 50	Full leasing costs deductible
Over 160	Over 130	Over 110	Over 50	Tax deductible leasing costs reduced by 15%

Notes

(1) *Hire or lease period* – Begins on the first day on which the car is required to be made available for use under the hire/lease agreement.

(2) *No restriction* – The above restriction does not apply to:

   • cars first registered before 1 March 2001;

   • hire periods beginning before 1 April 2009

   • electrically propelled cars; and

   • qualifying hire cars.

(3) *Further information* – HMRC's Business Income Manual BIM47714.

RESIDENTIAL PROPERTY LETTINGS

Restriction of finance costs

(ITTOIA 2005, ss 272A–272B, 274A–274B)

Tax year	Proportion of finance costs deductible
2017/18	75%
2018/19	50%
2019/20	25%
2020/21 and later	nil

Notes

(1) *Restrictions* – Deductions for finance costs, including interest payments, relating to the letting of residential properties is restricted to the proportions shown above *(ITTOIA 2005, s 272A)*.

(2) *Applies to* – Individual landlords, partnerships of individuals and trustees. Corporate landlords are not affected, even where the company carries on a property letting business in partnership with individuals *(ITTOIA 2005, s 272A(5))*.

(3) *Tax credit* – The landlord can claim a tax credit to set against their income tax liability for the year equal to 20% of the lower of:

   • finance costs which have been restricted for the tax year;

   • profits of the property business for the tax year; or

   • total income that exceeds the taxpayer's personal allowances for the tax year *(ITTOIA 2005, s 274AA)*.

(4) *Further information* – See tinyurl.com/lndlrds1718tx.

Qualifying periods for FHL

(ITTOIA 2005, s 325; CTA 2009, s 267)

Condition:	Applies in accounting period or tax year:
Available for commercial letting	At least 210 days
Actually let on commercial basis	At least 105 days (see Note 2).
Pattern of occupation	No more than 155 days of longer-term occupation.

Notes

(1) *Qualify as FHL* – Furnished accommodation which is let during the tax year (or accounting period, for companies) qualifies as furnished holiday lettings (FHL) for that year or accounting period if all of the conditions set out above are satisfied.

(2) *Longer-term occupation* – A continuous period of more than 31 days during which the accommodation is let to the same person, other than under circumstances that are not normal.

(3) *First or last periods* – When letting starts or finishes count the first or last 12 months as the relevant period (*ITTOIA 2005, s 324; CTA 2009, s 266*).

(4) *Averaging election* – Where several properties are let as FHL the owner can elect for the number of days of actual lettings to be averaged over two or more properties, such that all the properties reach the minimum threshold of 105 days let for the relevant period (see *ITTOIA 2005, s 326; CTA 2009, s 268*).

(5) *'Period of grace' election* – Where a property has qualified as FHL on the actual days let or due to the averaging election in the previous relevant period, the owner can elect to treat the property as continuing to qualify for up to two later years or accounting periods. This applies even though the property does not satisfy the letting condition in those periods. The election must be made in the first tax year or accounting period in which the letting condition is not met (see *ITTOIA 2005, s 326A; CTA 2009, s 268A*).

(6) *Further information* – See HMRC's Property Income Manual at PIM4100, and HMRC's Helpsheet HS253 'Furnished holiday lettings'.

TIME LIMITS FOR CLAIMS AND ELECTIONS

(TMA 1970, s 43(1))

(1) Claims must be made on the tax return or by an amendment to the return. Except where another period is expressly prescribed, a claim for relief in respect of income tax must be within four years after the end of the tax year. For claims relating to companies, see **Chapter 7**.

(2)   Specific exceptions in respect of business profits and losses include the following:

Provision	Time limit
Averaging of profits of farmers or creative artists (*ITTIOA 2005, ss 222(5), 222A(6)*)	First anniversary of 31 January after the end of the last tax year to which the claim relates
Stock transferred to a connected party on cessation of trade to be valued at higher of cost or sale price (*ITTOIA 2005, s 178(4)*)	First anniversary of 31 January following the tax year of cessation
Herd basis (*ITTOIA 2005, s 124(2); CTA 2009, s 122(2)*)	First anniversary of 31 January following the tax year in which the first relevant period of account ends
Change of accounting date (*ITTOIA 2005, s 217(2)*)	Filing date for the relevant tax return
Post-cessation relief (*ITTOIA 2005, s 257(4); ITA 2007, s 96(4)*)	First anniversary of 31 January following the tax year
Furnished holiday lettings: averaging of letting periods (*ITTOIA 2005, s 326(6)*)	First anniversary of 31 January following the tax year
Furnished holiday lettings: grace period election (*ITTOIA 2005, s 326A(2)*)	First anniversary of 31 January following the tax year
Current and preceding year set-off of trading losses (*ITA 2007, s 64(5)*)	First anniversary of 31 January following the loss-making year
Three year carry back of trading losses in opening years of trade (*ITA 2007, s 72(3)*)	First anniversary of 31 January following the tax year in which the loss is made
Relief for trade etc losses against capital gains of the year in which the loss was made or the previous year (*TCGA 1992, s 261B(8)*)	First anniversary of 31 January following the tax year in which the loss was made

LEASE PREMIUMS

Short leases

(*ITTOIA 2005, s 277; CTA 2009, s 217*)

$$P \times \frac{(50-Y)}{50}$$

Where:

P is the premium, and

Y is the number of complete periods of 12 months (other than the first) comprised in the effective duration of the lease.

Notes

(1)   *What is a short lease* – Broadly a lease with 50 years or less to run.

(2)   *Property income* – The amount calculated using the above formula is treated as a property business receipt for the tax year or accounting period in which the lease is granted.

(3)   *Capital deduction* – The amount of the premium for the grant of a short lease which is brought into account as a property business receipt is deducted from the consideration taken into account for capital gains purposes, in accordance with *TCGA 1992, Sch 8, paras 5, 7*.

(4)   *Which percentage* – The percentages of short lease premium charged as a property business receipt and taken into account for capital gains purposes are summarised in the table below (see PIM1205):

Length of lease in years	Percentage of premium taxable as receipt of property business	Percentage of premium chargeable as a capital gain
More than 50	0	100
50	2	98
49	4	96
48	6	94
47	8	92
46	10	90
45	12	88
44	14	86
43	16	84
42	18	82
41	20	80
40	22	78
39	24	76
38	26	74
37	28	72
36	30	70
35	32	68
34	34	66
33	36	64
32	38	62
31	40	60
30	42	58
29	44	56
28	46	54
27	48	52
26	50	50
25	52	48
24	54	46

Length of lease in years	Percentage of premium taxable as receipt of property business	Percentage of premium chargeable as a capital gain
23	56	44
22	58	42
21	60	40
20	62	38
19	64	36
18	66	34
17	68	32
16	70	30
15	72	28
14	74	26
13	76	24
12	78	22
11	80	20
10	82	18
9	84	16
8	86	14
7	88	12
6	90	10
5	92	8
4	94	6
3	96	4
2	98	2
1 or less	100	0

Long Leases

- Where the payment relates to a lease of more than 50 years, a premium is treated as being within the lease premium regime if it falls within *ITTOIA 2005 s 303;* or *CTA 2009, s 243.*

- For leases granted on and after 1 April 2013 for companies, and on and after 6 April 2013 for unincorporated businesses, the lease premium relief is limited (*FA 2013, Sch 28*).

Leases which are wasting assets

(TCGA 1992, Sch 8, para 1)

A short lease is a wasting asset. The allowable expenditure attributable to a short lease therefore reduces over its term. The rate at which the expenditure is written off is fixed in accordance with the table in *TCGA 1992, Sch 8, para 1* (see **Chapter 8: Capital Gains Tax**).

Relief for premiums paid

(ITTOIA 2005, s 61; CTA 2009, s 63)

(a)   Tenant occupies the whole of the land

$$\frac{A}{TRP}$$

Where:

A is the unreduced amount of the taxed receipt; and

TRP is the number of days in the receipt period of the taxed receipt.

(b)   Tenant occupies part of the land

$$\frac{F \times A}{TRP}$$

Where:

F is the fraction of the land occupied (calculated on a just and reasonable basis); and

A and TRP have the same meaning as in (a) above.

Notes

(1)   *Land used in a trade* – The income element of a short lease premium is allowable as a deduction from the tenant's business profits for income tax or corporation tax purposes. The above formulae are used to calculate the allowable proportion of the 'taxed receipt' (broadly the amount of the lease taxed on the landlord as a rental business receipt) available as a deduction for the tenant. Relief is also available if the land is sub-let.

(2)   *Occupation* – The formula in (a) should be used if the tenant occupies the whole of the land for trading purposes. The formula in (b) applies if only part of the land is so used.

SELF-EMPLOYMENT INCOME SUPPORT SCHEME (SEISS)

(Coronavirus Act 2020, First HMRC Direction: tinyurl.com/SEISSDIR)

Grant number	Percentage of average monthly profits	Maximum per month £	Maximum grant £	Deadline for applications
1	80%	2,500	7,500	13 July 2020
2	70%	2,190	6,570	19 October 2020
3	80%	2,500	7,500	29 January 2021
4	80%	2,500	7,500	1 June 2021
5	80%	2,500	7,500	TBA

Notes

(1) *Established traders* – Only self-employed individuals and partners who have submitted a tax return for 2018/19 reporting trading income can qualify, and they must receive at least half of their average annual income as self-employed trading profits. Individuals who started trading after 5 April 2019 are not eligible for the first three grants.

(2) *Average profits* – For the first three grants the average taxable profits are calculated by HMRC from the self-employed income reported in the individual's tax returns for 2016/17 to 2018/19. If the trader started trading within that period the profits are averaged over the actual trading period. Either the profits for 2018/19 must not exceed £50,000 or the average annual profits for 2016/17 to 2018/19 don't exceed £50,000.

(3) *Partner's eligibility* – This is calculated from the partner's reported profit share not from the profits of the entire partnership.

(4) *Trading conditions* – For grants 1 and 2 the business must have been adversely affected by the coronavirus during a specified period that varies for each grant. For grant 3 the sales must have decreased due to coronavirus.

(5) *Continuing business* – The trader must have been in business in 2019/20 and would have traded in 2020/21 if it hadn't been for the coronavirus. The business must not have ceased permanently at the date of the claim. If the trade has temporarily ceased there must be an intention to resume trading.

(6) *Use of losses* – Losses brought forward from before 2016/17 are ignored. Losses are not carried back from 2019/20.Trading losses in 2016/17 to 2018/19 are netted against trading profits to calculate the average net annual profit, which is measured against the £50,000 threshold and used to determine the amount of the grant.

(7) *Farmer's averaging* – This adjustment of taxable profits for farmers or creative artists is not taken into account when calculating annual average profits for SEISS.

(8) *Landlords* – Property letting is not a trade, so landlords don't qualify for the SEISS grant in respect of property income or furnished holiday lettings

(9) *Taxable* – The first three SEISS grants must be declared as income on 2020/21 tax returns, and are subject to tax and NIC for that year, no apportionment of the grant should be made to 2019/20 tax year. The fourth and fifth SEISS grants must be declared as taxable income for 2021/22.

(10) *Further information* – See guidance: tinyurl.com/SEISSclaim, tinyurl.com/SEISSpfts, and tinyurl.com/SEISSEx.

7

Taxation of companies

RATES OF CORPORATION TAX

(CTA 2010, Pt 2, Chs 2, 3, Pt 3)

	Financial year commencing 1 April:				
	2022	**2021**	**2020**	**2019**	**2018**
Main rate	19%	19%	19%	19%	19%
	2017	**2016**	**2015**	**2014**	**2013**
Main rate	19%	20%	20%	21%	23%
Small Profits Rate	–	–	–	20%	20%
Small Profits Rate can be claimed by qualifying companies with profits not exceeding	–	–	–	£300,000	£300,000
Marginal Relief Lower Limit	–	–	–	£300,000	£300,000
Marginal Relief Upper Limit	–	–	–	£1,500,000	£1,500,000
Standard fraction	–	–	–	1/400	3/400

Notes

(1) *From 1 April 2015* – All profits are charged at a single rate of corporation tax, with an exception for profits made by companies within a ring fence trade (see note 5), *(FA 2014, Sch 1)*. See Note 9 for the position from 1 April 2023.

(2) *Prior to 1 April 2015* – The Small Profits Rate applied and the lower and upper limits were reduced proportionately for accounting periods of less than 12 months. The limits are also divided by the number of associated companies carrying on a trade or business for all or part of the accounting period *(CTA 2010, s 25)*. The Small Profits Rate did not apply to 'Close Investment Holding Companies' *(CTA 2010, s 18(b))*.

(3) *Patent Box* – For accounting periods beginning on and after 1 April 2013, any company can elect for a reduced rate of corporation tax to be applied to all profits attributable to qualifying intellectual property (see **Patent Box**).

(4) *Unit trusts and OEICs* – These companies are subject to corporation tax set at the basic income tax rate charged for the tax year beginning on 6 April in that financial year *(CTA 2010, ss 614, 618)*. For financial years 2008 to 2018, the applicable tax rate was 20%.

(5) *Oil and gas* – For companies with ring fence profits from oil-related activities, the Main Rate still applies at 30%, the Small Profits Rate is 19%, and the ring fence fraction is 11/400, all for financial years 2008 to 2018 *(CTA 2010, Pt 8, Ch 3A)*.

Companies in the oil and gas industries also pay the supplementary charge of corporation tax and petroleum revenue tax (PRT), see HMRC's Oil Taxation Manual.

(6) *Restitution interest* – From 21 October 2015 restitution interest paid to companies when a dispute concerning HMRC's mistake in law is resolved, is taxed at 45% rather than at the normal CT rates. Where HMRC pays restitution interest it withholds tax at 45% from the payment (*F(No 2)A 2015, s 38*).

(7) *Non-resident landlords* – From 6 April 2020 non-resident corporate landlords must pay corporation tax on their UK property income instead of income tax (*FA 2019, Sch 5*).

(8) *Special rate* – The Northern Ireland Assembly is to be given the power to set a special rate of corporation tax (expected to be 12.5%), for companies trading in Northern Ireland. However, the devolution of this power will not commence until the Northern Ireland Executive demonstrates its finances are on a sustainable footing (*Corporation Tax (Northern Ireland) Act 2015*).

(9) *Proposed two rates* – From 1 April 2023, the main corporation tax rate will increase to 25% where a company has profits exceeding £250,000. Companies with profits of £50,000 or less will pay corporation tax at the small profits rate of 19%. Marginal relief will apply to companies with profits between £50,000 and £250,000.

Effective marginal rates for small profits

(*CTA 2010, s 19*)

Financial Year (Commencing 1 April)	Marginal Small Profits Rate %
2014	21.25
2013	23.75
2012	25.00
2011	27.50
2010	29.75

Marginal relief

(*CTA 2010, s 19*)

The corporation tax charged on the company's taxable total profits of the accounting period is reduced by an amount equal to:

$$F \times (U - A) \times \frac{N}{A}$$

Where:

F is the standard fraction,

U is the upper limit,

A is the amount of the augmented profits, and

N is the amount of the taxable total profits.

Notes

(1)   *The standard fraction* – See table of Rates of Corporation Tax (*CTA 2010, s 19(3)*).

(2)   *Augmented Profits* – This is defined as the company's taxable total profits plus any franked investment income received by the company, excluding any franked investment income received by the company from a company which is a 51% subsidiary of the receiving company or a company of which the receiving company is a 51% subsidiary, or from a trading company or relevant holding company that is a quasi-subsidiary of the receiving company.

(3)   *Quasi-subsidiary* – This is a company owned by a consortium of which the recipient company is a member, which is not a 75% subsidiary of any company, where no arrangements exist for it to become a 75% subsidiary of any company (*CTA 2010, ss 32, 33*).

RESEARCH AND DEVELOPMENT (R&D)

(CTA 2009, ss1039–1142; FA 2012, Sch 3)

Expenditure incurred on and after:	SME companies	Large companies		
	Enhanced deduction	Enhanced deduction	Vaccines research	RDEC
1 April 2020	230%	N/A	N/A	13%
1 Jan 2018	230%	N/A	N/A	12%
1 April 2017	230%	N/A	N/A	11%
1 April 2016	230%	N/A	140%	11%
1 April 2015	230%	130%	140%	11%
1 April 2014	225%	130%	140%	10%

Notes

(1)   *Company conditions* – To claim R&D tax relief the company must incur qualifying expenditure on qualifying R&D projects which relate to its own trade, or to qualifying R&D projects it works on as a subcontractor for another organisation. The company must also be a going concern as shown in its latest accounts, and from 1 August 2015 it must not be an ineligible company (*CTA 2009, Pt 13*).

(2)   *Time limits* – The relief must be claimed in the corporation tax return within two years of the end of the accounting period in which the qualifying R&D expenditure was incurred (*CTA 2009, ss 1044, 1074*).

(3)   *Qualifying R&D* – Each R&D project must be carried on in a field of science or technology and be undertaken with an aim of extending knowledge in a field of science or technology, and must fall within the former DTI guidelines (see CIRD 813000).

(4) *Qualifying expenditure* – Restricted to the areas of staffing costs, external workers (conditions relaxed from April 2020), software, materials consumed or transformed, utilities (not rent) and payments to clinical volunteers. No minimum spend on qualifying costs is required. From 1 April 2015 materials which are included in a saleable product do not qualify (*CTA 2009, ss 1127–1140*).

(5) *Definition of SME* – For this purpose an SME is a company with fewer than 500 employees and turnover not exceeding €100 million or balance sheet value not exceeding €86 million. SMEs can claim a payable tax credit – see table below (*CTA 2009, ss 1119, 1120*).

(6) *R&D expenditure credit (RDEC)* – From 1 April 2016 this is the only means of claiming R&D relief for large companies (*CTA 2009, Pt 3, Ch 6A*).

(7) *Vaccines research* – Abolished from 1 April 2017. It applied to R&D projects connected with research on TB, malaria or AIDS, (see CIRD 75000; *CTA 2009, Pt 13, Ch 7; FA 2016, s 43*).

(8) *Consultation* – The structure of R&D tax reliefs is under review until June 2021 with the possibility of changing the scope or having variable rates for different sectors, to target the relief more effectively (Consultation: https://tinyurl.com/rdtxrv).

(9) *Further information* – See: tinyurl.com/R-DTXRLF and HMRC's Corporate Intangibles Research and Development Manual at CIRD80000.

Payable tax credit

(*CTA 2009, ss 1054–1060*)

Expenditure incurred in financial year starting 1 April	Percentage of loss given as tax credit
2021 (note 3)	14.50%
2020	14.50%
2019	14.50%
2018	14.50%
2017	14.50%
2016	14.50%
2015	14.50%

Notes

(1) *Conditions* – Payable tax credits are only available to SME companies which have not started to trade, or have made a loss after the deduction of R&D enhanced expenditure (*CTA 2009, s 1054*).

(2) *Amount* – The tax credit is given in exchange for the loss, calculated as the percentage of the surrendered loss shown in the table above (*CTA 2009, s 1058*).

(3)   *Cap* – From 1 April 2021 the tax credit paid will be limited to £20,000 plus three times the company's total PAYE and NIC contributions for the year the claim relates to, but some exceptions apply.

PATENT BOX

(CTA 2010, Pt 8A)

Financial Year starting 1 April	Effective patent box rate when companies pay:	
	Main CT rate %	Small profits rate %
2021	10.00	10.00
2020	10.00	10.00
2019	10.00	10.00
2018	10.00	10.00
2017	10.00	10.00
2016	11.00	11.00

Notes

(1)   *Election* – Companies may elect for a reduced rate of corporation tax rate for profits attributable to qualifying patents and similar intellectual property (IP). The legislation provides a formula to calculate the deduction *(CTA 2010, s 357A)*.

(2)   *Time limit* – This election only applies to accounting periods beginning on or after 1 April 2013. It must be made (or revoked) within two years of the end of the accounting period *(CTA 2010, ss 357G, 357GA)*.

(3)   *Qualifying patents* – The company must own, or exclusively licence, patents issued by the UK Intellectual Property Office, European Patent Office or any of these countries: Austria, Bulgaria, Czech Republic, Denmark, Estonia, Finland, Germany, Hungary, Poland, Portugal, Romania, Slovakia, and Sweden. Plant breeders' rights also qualify *(CTA 2010, s 357BB)*.

(4)   *Only IP income* – Profits from creating or developing the patented product, or a product containing the patented item, qualify for the relief. Profits from holding patents as investments do not qualify *(CTA 2010, ss 357BC–357BE)*.

(5)   *Streaming* – Costs and revenues are streamed on a patent-by-patent or product-by-product basis for new entrants from 1 July 2016, and for all eligible companies from 1 July 2021 *(FA 2016, s 64)*.

(6)   *Cost sharing* – From 1 April 2017 the streaming rules are amended where R&D is undertaken collaboratively by two or more companies under a cost sharing arrangement *(CTA 2010, s 357GC)*.

(7)   *Further Information* – Outline guidance: tinyurl.com/CTptntbx, for detailed guidance see HMRC's Corporate Intangibles Research & Development Manual (para CIRD200000).

FILM TAX RELIEF

(CTA 2009, Pt 15; SI 2015/1741)

Method of tax relief	From 1 April 2015 (note 2)	To 31 March 2015
Additional deduction		
● Limited budget films:	100% of core expenditure	100% of core expenditure
● Other films:	80% of core expenditure	80% of core expenditure
Payable tax credit		
● Limited budget films:		25% of loss surrendered
● Other films:		20% of loss surrendered
● All films:	25% of loss surrendered, up to 'unused 25% band'; plus 20% of any remaining loss.	

Notes

(1) *Eligible* – Film tax relief (FTR) can by claimed by film production companies in respect of British films intended for commercial release. At least 10% (25% before application of *FA 2014, s 32*) of the core expenditure on the film must be UK expenditure (*CTA 2009, s 1198*).

(2) *Revised rates* – These rates apply to films of which principal photography is not completed before 1 April 2015 (*FA 2015, s 29*).

(3) *Additional deduction* – This is calculated on the basis of UK qualifying core expenditure. Budget films are those with core expenditure up to £20 million (*CTA 2009, ss 1184(2), 1199–1200*).

(4) *Payable tax credits* – If FTR is available, the company may claim a film tax credit for an accounting period in which it has a 'surrenderable loss' (*CTA 2009, ss 1201–1203*).

(5) *Further information* – Outline guidance: tinyurl.com/criTxrlf. Detailed guidance in HMRC's Film Production Company Manual.

CREATIVE INDUSTRIES TAX RELIEFS

(CTA 2009, Pts 15A, 15B)

Method of tax relief	Relief rate
Additional deduction	100% of qualifying core expenditure (see Note 2)
Payable tax credit	25% of loss surrendered

Notes

(1) *Available to* – Companies in the creative sectors including; TV and video game production, theatre productions, orchestras and museums. All cultural reliefs follow the structure of film tax relief, and some require a 'British' cultural test to be passed to qualify (*SI 2015/86*).

(2)   *Qualifying core expenditure* – For most of the creative sector reliefs at least 25% of the core expenditure must be on goods or services used or provided from within the EEA countries, but see note (3). The additional deductions, and the payable tax credit, are calculated on the basis of UK core expenditure, up to a maximum of 80% of the total qualifying expenditure by the eligible company (*CTA 2009, ss 1216CG, 1217CG*).

(3)   *High-end TV* – From 1 April 2013, relief for production of TV programmes of 30 minutes or more intended for broadcast to the general public, which may be: drama, documentary and animation, but not: advertising, current affairs, entertainment shows, competitions, live performances or training programmes. From 1 April 2015 at least 10% of the core expenditure must be in the UK (*CTA 2009, Pt 15A, Ch 3*).

(4)   *Video games development* – From 1 April 2014, relief for the production of video games intended for supply to the general public which are not produced for advertising, promotional or gambling purposes (*CTA 2009, Pt 15B*).

(5)   *Theatre productions* – From 1 September 2014, relief for costs of dramatic or ballet productions performed live to the general public, but not for productions including wild animals, or which are made to promote goods or services. The tax credit available is 25% for touring productions and at 20% for other productions (*CTA 2009, Pt 15C*).

(6)   *Children's TV* – From 1 April 2015, relief for producing programmes intended for children aged under 15 (*CTA 2009, Pt 15A*).

(7)   *Orchestral concerts* – From 1 April 2016, relief for the cost of live orchestral concerts performed before a paying audience. There must be at least 12 musicians and most of the instruments must not be electronically or directly amplified (*CTA 2009, Pt 15D*).

(8)   *Museums and galleries* – From 1 April 2017, relief for the costs of new exhibitions including those which are toured. Maximum amount which can be paid to the company per exhibition is £100,000 for a touring exhibition, or £80,000 for a non-touring exhibition (*CTA 2009, Pt 15E*).

(9)   *Further information* – Outline guidance at: tinyurl.com/criTxrlf. Detailed guidance in following HMRC manuals: Museums and Galleries Exhibition Tax Relief Manual, Orchestra Tax Relief, Television Production Company Manual, Theatre Tax Relief Manual, Video Games Development Company Manual.

LOANS TO PARTICIPATORS

(CTA 2010, Pt 10, Ch 3)

Loan advanced:	**Before 6 April 2016**	**From 6 April 2016**
Rate of charge	25% of loan value	32.5% of loan value

Notes

(1)   *When the charge applies* – If a close company makes a loan or advances money to any of the following who are participators or associates of a participator in the company:

   •   an individual (or company acting in a representative capacity for the individual);

- a trustee in a settlement where trustees or actual or potential beneficiaries are participators;

- a member of an LLP or other partnership (*CTA 2010, s 455*).

(2) *Charge treated as* – Corporation tax chargeable for the accounting period in which the loan or advance is made. It is not payable in respect of the portion of loan repaid, released or written off before the CT becomes payable. Can choose which outstanding loan a repayment is set against.

(3) *When charge is repaid* – Where the loan or advance is subsequently repaid, released or written off, the tax charge can be reclaimed (*CTA 2010, s 458*).

(4) *Replacing the loan* – From 20 March 2013 additional conditions must be met for a repayment of a loan to be counted as a repayment for the purposes of *CTA 2010, s 455*, see notes (5) to (8) below.

(5) *30-day rule* – Where a loan of £5,000 or more is repaid to the company, but within 30 days amounts totalling £5,000 or more are borrowed by the same borrower or one of his associates, the first loan is treated as not having been repaid and is treated as continuing for the purposes of calculating the corporation tax charge (*CTA 2010, s 464C(1)*).

(6) *Arrangements in place* – Where the loan is £15,000 or more, the 30-day rule is ignored if, at the time of the repayment of the first loan arrangements are in place for it to be replaced by the company with an amount of at least £5,000. If the later loan is made, it is treated as a continuation of the first loan (*CTA 2010, s 464C(3)*).

(7) *Taxed income* – Where the repayments made in (5) or (6) above give rise to an income tax charge on the participator or associate who took out the loan (eg the repayment was made as a declared dividend or bonus), that repayment is not caught by the rules in *CTA 2010, s 464C (CTA 2010, s 464C(5)*).

(8) *Conferring a benefit* – A charge at the rate in the table above applies to the value of the benefit is due when arrangements which confer a benefit on a participator (eg by transferring value from the company to the participator in an indirect fashion) such that is it not caught by *CTA 2010, s 455*. The charge can be reclaimed if the benefit is returned to the company (*CTA 2010, ss 464A, 464B*).

(9) *Benefit in kind* – See **Chapter 2** for the benefit in kind tax charge that arises on the individual who receives an employment related loan.

(10) *Further information* – See HMRC Corporation Tax Manual para CTM61500+.

COMPANY TAX RETURNS AND PAYMENTS

Filing dates

(*FA 1998, Sch 18, para 14*)

The filing date for a company tax return is the later of the following periods:

(a) 12 months from the end of the return period;

(b) If the company's relevant period of account is less than 18 months; 12 months from the end of that period;

(c)   If the company's relevant period of account is longer than 18 months; 30 months from the beginning of that period; or

(d)   three months from the date of a notice by HMRC to deliver the return.

Notes

(1)   *Relevant period of account* – In relation to a return for an accounting period this is defined as the period of account of the company in which the last day of that accounting period falls.

(2)   *Online filing* – Corporation tax returns (with a very few exceptions) must be filed online using iXBRL. This requires the majority of the figures in the company accounts and tax return to be 'tagged'. For further information see: http://tinyurl.com/l9v375a.

Due dates for CT payments

(TMA 1970, ss 59D, 59E, 59G, 59H; SI 1998/3175; ITA 2007, Pt 15, Ch 15; CTA 2010, s 455(3); SI 2017/1072)

Liability	Due Date
Mainstream corporation tax	9 months and 1 day following the end of the accounting period
Mainstream corporation tax payable by large companies (notes 1& 2)	1st – 6 months and 13 days from the start of the accounting period (or date of final instalment, if earlier); 2nd – 3 months after 1st instalment; 3rd – 3 months after 2nd instalment; 4th – 3 months and 14 days from the end of the accounting period.
Mainstream corporation tax payable by very large companies (note 4)	1st – 2 months and 13 days from the start of the accounting period (or date of final instalment, if earlier); 2nd – 3 months after 1st instalment; 3rd – 3 months after 2nd instalment; 4th – 3 months after 3rd instalment.
Income tax on interest, annual payments etc.	14 days after end of return period (note 3)
Charge on loans to participators in close companies (*CTA 2010, s 455*)	9 months and 1 day after the end of the accounting period in which the loan or advance was made.

Notes

(1)   *Instalment payments* – Large companies are liable to pay corporation tax in quarterly instalments: see note (2). From 1 April 2015 a 'large' company is one with annual taxable profits exceeding £1.5 million, divided by 1 plus the number of related 51% group companies. For earlier periods the number of associated companies were counted.

(2) *Not large* – A company is not large if its profits are £10,000 or less (reduced proportionately for periods shorter than 12 months), or if its profits for the accounting period are up to £10 million and it was not a large company in the 12 months preceding that accounting period (*TMA 1970, s 59E; SI 1998/3175*).

(3) *Amount due* – The CT due for each instalment is calculated using the following formula (*SI 1998/3175, regs 5–8*):

$$3 \times \frac{CTI}{n}$$

where:

CTI = the amount of the company's total liability for that accounting period; and

n = the number of whole months in the accounting period, plus the 'appropriate decimal' (ie broadly the proportion of a whole 30-day month, rounded to 2 decimal places).

(4) *Very large companies* – For accounting periods starting on and after 1 April 2019, where the annual profits are over £20 million for the company or group, instalments of CT are payable at advanced intervals as shown in table above (*SI 2017/1072*).

(5) *Taxes withheld* – Tax deducted from interest, annual payments and royalties paid overseas must be reported on a form CT61 for the quarterly periods ending on 31 March, 30 June, 30 September and 31 December and at the end of an accounting period. For further information see HMRC's Corporation Tax manual at CTM35000.

(6) *Section 455 charge* – This tax is not payable in respect of any loan or advance repaid before the date on which the tax under *CTA 2010, s 455* would otherwise become due. See **Loans to Participators** above.

TIME LIMITS FOR CLAIMS AND ELECTIONS

A claim or election for corporation tax purposes must generally be made in writing within four years of the end of the accounting period to which it relates, ie in the absence of any provisions to the contrary (*FA 1998, Sch 18, para 55*; see also *SI 2009/403*). Other common time limits are given below.

Provision	Time limit
Appropriation of asset to trading stock: election to adjust trading profit by the amount of the gain or loss on the deemed disposal at market value (*TCGA 1992, s 161(3)*).	2 years from the end of the accounting period in which the asset is appropriated as trading stock.
Reallocation of chargeable gain or an allowable loss within a group (*TCGA 1992, s 171A(5)*).	2 years from the end of the transferring company's accounting period in which the gain or loss accrues.
Stock transferred to a connected person on the cessation of trade to be valued at higher of cost or selling price (*CTA 2009, s 167(4)*).	2 years from the end of the accounting period of cessation. Election must be made jointly by both parties.

continued

Provision	Time limit
Relief for trading losses against total profits of the same, or an earlier, accounting period (*CTA 2010, s 37(7)*).	2 years from the end of the loss making accounting period. (note 3)
Terminal loss relief on the cessation of trade (*CTA 2010, s 39*).	2 years from the end of the loss making accounting period.
Group relief (*FA 1998, Sch 18, para 74*).	Group relief claims must be made or withdrawn by the later of the following:
	(1) 12 months from the filing date for the claimant company's tax return for the accounting period of the claim;
	(2) 30 days after the completion of an enquiry into that return;
	(3) 30 days after the issue of a notice of amendment by HMRC following the completion of an enquiry; or
	(4) 30 days after the determination of any appeal against an HMRC amendment (in (3) above).
Capital allowances (*FA 1988, Sch 18, para 82*).	As for group relief (see above).
Surrender of company tax refund within group (*CTA 2010, s 963(3)*).	Before the refund is made to the surrendering company.
Intangible fixed assets: election to write down cost for tax purposes at a fixed rate (*CTA 2009, s 730*).	2 years from the end of the accounting period in which the company creates or acquires the asset.
Set-off of loss on disposal of shares in unquoted trading company against income of investment company (*CTA 2010, s 70(4)*).	2 years from the end of the accounting period in which the loss was incurred.
Company distributions – election that distribution should not be treated as exempt (*CTA 2009, s 931R*).	2 years from the end of the accounting period in which the distribution is received.
Relief for a non-trading deficit on loan relationships (including any non-trading exchange losses) (*CTA 2009, ss 458(2), 460(1)*).	• Claim to carry forward the deficit to later accounting periods – 2 years from the end of the accounting period following the deficit period.
	• Claim to set off deficit against profits of the deficit period or earlier periods – 2 years from end of period in which deficit arises.

Notes

(1) *Extended time limits* – In some cases, HMRC may allow a longer claim period at its discretion.

(2) *Group relief* – The above references to an enquiry do not include a restricted enquiry into an amendment of a return (ie where the restriction arises because the time limit for enquiring into that return has expired), where the amendment consists of a group relief claim or the withdrawal of such a claim (*FA 1998, Sch 18, para 74(4)*).

(3) *Temporary extension to carry back trading loss relief* – Claims to extended relief for trading losses incurred in relevant accounting periods ending between 1 April 2020 and 31 March 2022 must be made within two years of the end of the accounting period in which the loss was incurred.

INDEXATION ALLOWANCE

(TCGA 1992, Ch IV)

Retail Prices Index (RPI)

	Jan	Feb	Mar	Apr	May	Jun	Jul	Aug	Sep	Oct	Nov	Dec
1982			79.44	81.04	81.62	81.85	81.88	81.90	81.85	82.26	82.66	82.51
1983	82.61	82.97	83.12	84.28	84.64	84.84	85.30	85.68	86.06	86.36	86.67	86.89
1984	86.84	87.20	87.48	88.64	88.97	89.20	89.10	89.94	90.11	90.67	90.95	90.87
1985	91.20	91.94	92.80	94.78	95.21	95.41	95.23	95.49	95.44	95.59	95.92	96.05
1986	96.25	96.60	96.73	97.67	97.85	97.79	97.52	97.82	98.30	98.45	99.29	99.62
1987	100.0	100.4	100.6	101.8	101.9	101.9	101.8	102.1	102.4	102.9	103.4	103.3
1988	103.3	103.7	104.1	105.8	106.2	106.6	106.7	107.9	108.4	109.5	110.0	110.3
1989	111.0	111.8	112.3	114.3	115.0	115.4	115.5	115.8	116.6	117.5	118.5	118.8
1990	119.5	120.2	121.4	125.1	126.2	126.7	126.8	128.1	129.3	130.3	130.0	129.9
1991	130.2	130.9	131.4	133.1	133.5	134.1	133.8	134.1	134.6	135.1	135.6	135.7
1992	135.6	136.3	136.7	138.8	139.3	139.3	138.8	138.9	139.4	139.9	139.7	139.2
1993	137.9	138.8	139.3	140.6	141.1	141.0	140.7	141.3	141.9	141.8	141.6	141.9
1994	141.3	142.1	142.5	144.2	144.7	144.7	144.0	144.7	145.0	145.2	145.3	146.0
1995	146.0	146.9	147.5	149.0	149.6	149.8	149.1	149.9	150.6	149.8	149.8	150.7
1996	150.2	150.9	151.5	152.6	152.9	153.0	152.4	153.1	153.8	153.8	153.9	154.4
1997	154.4	155.0	155.4	156.3	156.9	157.5	157.5	158.5	159.3	159.5	159.6	160.0
1998	159.5	160.3	160.8	162.6	163.5	163.4	163.0	163.7	164.4	164.5	164.4	164.4
1999	163.4	163.7	164.1	165.2	165.6	165.6	165.1	165.5	166.2	166.5	166.7	167.3
2000	166.6	167.5	168.4	170.1	170.7	171.1	170.5	170.5	171.7	171.6	172.1	172.2
2001	171.1	172.0	172.2	173.1	174.2	174.4	173.3	174.0	174.6	174.3	173.6	173.4
2002	173.3	173.8	174.5	175.7	176.2	176.2	175.9	176.4	177.6	177.9	178.2	178.5
2003	178.4	179.3	179.9	181.2	181.5	181.3	181.3	181.6	182.5	182.6	182.7	183.5
2004	183.1	183.8	184.6	185.7	186.5	186.8	186.8	187.4	188.1	188.6	189.0	189.9

continued

	Jan	Feb	Mar	Apr	May	Jun	Jul	Aug	Sep	Oct	Nov	Dec
2005	188.9	189.6	190.5	191.6	192.0	192.2	192.2	192.6	193.1	193.3	193.6	194.1
2006	193.4	194.2	195.0	196.5	197.7	198.5	198.5	199.2	200.1	200.4	201.1	202.7
2007	201.6	203.1	204.4	205.4	206.2	207.3	206.1	207.3	208.0	208.9	209.7	210.9
2008	209.8	211.4	212.1	214.0	215.1	216.8	216.5	217.2	218.4	217.7	216.0	212.9
2009	210.1	211.4	211.3	211.5	212.8	213.4	213.4	214.4	215.3	216.0	216.6	218.0
2010	217.9	219.2	220.7	222.8	223.6	224.1	223.6	224.5	225.3	225.8	226.8	228.4
2011	229.0	231.3	232.5	234.4	235.2	235.2	234.7	236.1	237.9	238.0	238.5	239.4
2012	238.0	239.9	240.8	242.5	241.8	242.8	242.1	243.0	244.2	245.6	245.6	246.8
2013	245.8	247.6	248.7	249.5	250.0	249.7	249.7	251.0	251.9	251.9	252.1	253.4
2014	252.6	254.2	254.8	255.7	255.9	256.3	256.0	257.0	257.6	257.7	257.1	257.5
2015	255.4	256.7	257.1	258.0	258.5	258.9	258.6	259.8	259.6	259.5	259.8	260.6
2016	258.8	260.0	261.1	261.4	262.1	263.1	263.4	264.4	264.9	264.8	265.5	267.1
2017	265.5	268.4	269.3	270.6	271.7	272.3	272.9	274.7	275.1	275.3	275.8	278.1

Acknowledgement: Office for National Statistics website: www.ons.gov.uk

Indexation formula

The formula for calculating indexation factors is as follows (*TCGA 1992, s 54(1)*):

$$\frac{(RD - RI)}{RI}$$

Where:

RD is the RPI for the month of disposal; and

RI is the RPI for March 1982 (or the month in which the expenditure was incurred, if later).

The resulting figure is applied to each item of qualifying expenditure in the computation, by multiplying the expenditure by the relevant indexation factor as calculated.

Notes

(1)   *Which periods* – The allowance adjusts the base value of the asset for the effects of inflation as measured by the RPI for periods from 31 March 1982 (or date of acquisition if later), to the month of disposal but no later than 31 December 2017. Indexation allowance is frozen for disposals made after 2017.

(2)   *Who can use it* – Only companies within the charge to corporation tax (*TCGA 1992, s 52A*). It can reduce an unindexed gain to nil, but it cannot be applied to create or increase a loss (*TCGA 1992, s 53(1)*).

(3)   *Publication* – Tables showing the indexed rise in respect of disposals taking place in particular months can be found here: tinyurl.com/odelvrk.

Capital Gains Tax

RATES AND ANNUAL EXEMPTIONS

(TCGA 1992, ss 1H, 1K, 1L, Sch 1B)

Tax Year	Annual exempt amount		Tax rate paid by		
	Individuals, PRs and trusts for disabled	General trusts	Individuals within:		Trustees and PRs
			Basic rate band	Higher tax bands	
	£	£	%	%	%
2021/22 (note 1)	12,300	6,150	10	20	20
2020/21 (note 1)	12,300	6,150	10	20	20
2019/20 (note 1)	12,000	6,000	10	20	20
2018/19 (note 1)	11,700	5,850	10	20	20
2017/18 (note 1)	11,300	5,650	10	20	20
2016/17 (note 1)	11,100	5,550	10	20	20
2015/16	11,100	5,550	18	28	28

Notes

(1) *Upper rates* – From 6 April 2016 taxable gains made on the disposal of residential property and carried interest gains are taxed at 18% (within the taxpayer's basic rate income tax band) or 28% where the gain is made by trustees or lies within the higher or additional rate income tax bands *(TCGA 1992, s 1H, Sch 1B)*.

(2) *Scottish taxpayers* – From 6 April 2016 these taxpayers are treated as if they are **not** Scottish taxpayers for CGT purposes, so they use the tax bands which apply in the rest of the UK *(TCGA 1992, s 1J(6))*.

(3) *Personal representatives* – The annual exemption is available to personal representatives in the tax year of death and the following two years *(TCGA 1992, s 1K(7))*.

(4) *Trustees* – The annual exemption for trustees is divided by the number of qualifying settlements created by one settlor, subject to a lower limit of 10% of the annual exemption for individuals for that tax year *(TCGA 1992, Sch 1C)*.

(5) *Remittance basis users* – An individual who claims to use the remittance basis for a tax year is not entitled to the annual exempt amount for that year *(ITA 2007, s 809G)*. However the annual exempt amount remains available where the remittance basis

applies without a claim – eg where the individual's unremitted foreign income and gains are less than £2,000 for the year (*ITA 2007, s 809D*).

(6)   *Business Asset Disposal Relief/Entrepreneurs' Relief* – From 23 June 2010 the 10% rate of CGT applies in respect of gains brought within a claim for entrepreneurs' relief (*TCGA 1992, s 169N(3); see **Business Asset Disposal Relief**).

(7)   *Investors' relief* – From 6 April 2019 the 10% rate of CGT applies in respect of gains qualifying for investors' relief (*TCGA 1992, s 169VC(2)*; see **Investors' relief**).

CHATTEL EXEMPTION

(TCGA 1992, s 262)

	Exemption (max sale proceeds)	Marginal relief (max chargeable gain)
From 1989/90 onwards	£6,000	5/3 of the excess over £6,000

BUSINESS ASSET DISPOSAL RELIEF

(TCGA 1992 ss 169H–169S)

Date of disposal	Lifetime limit	Rate of CGT on eligible gains
From 11 March 2020	£1 million	10%
6 April 2011–10 March 2020	£10 million	10%
23 June 2010–5 April 2011	£5 million	10%

Notes

(1)   *Rename* – This relief was formerly known as Entrepreneurs' Relief (*FA 2020, Sch 3, pt 2*).

(2)   *Qualifying disposals* – Disposals made by an individual or by certain trustees qualify if the disposal consists of:

- all or part of a trade carried on alone or in partnership;

- assets used by a partnership or company which are disposed of in association with a disposal of an interest in the partnership or company (see note 11);

- assets of such a trade following cessation; or

- shares or securities in the individual's 'personal company' (notes 3–5), where the company is a trading company (or the holding company of a trading group) and the individual is an officer or employee of the company (or of a trading group member) (*TCGA 1992, ss 169H, 169I*); and

- the relevant conditions are met throughout a period of at least 24 months (12 months for disposals before 6 April 2019) ending with the date of disposal or cessation of trade (*TCGA 1992, s 169I*).

(3) *Personal company* – The taxpayer must hold at least 5% of the ordinary share capital measured on nominal value and control at least 5% of the voting rights of the company. For disposals made on and after 29 October 2018 the shareholder must also meet the equity holder condition (note 4) or the sale proceeds condition (note 5) (*TCGA 1992, s 169S(3)(c)*).

(4) *Equity holder* – Taxpayer must be beneficially entitled to at least 5% of the amounts available for distribution to the equity holders, and to at least 5% of the assets available for distribution to equity holders on the winding up of the company.

(5) *Sale proceeds* – Taxpayer must be entitled to at least 5% of the sale proceeds of the company in the event of the disposal of the entire ordinary share capital of the company.

(6) *Diluted shares rights* – Where the company raises more equity capital by issuing new shares on or after 6 April 2019, which results in the rights of an existing shareholder being reduced below the 5% thresholds set out in note 3, that shareholder can elect to claim entrepreneurs' relief on the accrued gain to that date (*TCGA 1992, ss 169SB–169SH*).

(7) *Trust assets* – Where used for business purposes the gains arising can be eligible for relief if a qualifying beneficiary of the trust has an interest in possession in the whole or a relevant part of the settled property, and all the above conditions for the relief are satisfied by the beneficiary (*TCGA 1992, s 169J*).

(8) *Deferred gains* – Gains made before 6 April 2008 which were deferred using QCBs, EIS or VCT and become chargeable on or after that date may qualify for this relief (*FA 2008, Sch 3, paras 7, 8*). Also gains deferred under EIS or SITR can qualify for this relief when the deferred gain falls back into charge on or after 3 December 2014 (*TCGA 1992, Pt 5, Ch 4*).

(9) *EMI shares* – Gains made on shares from 6 April 2013 which were acquired through exercising EMI options on or after 6 April 2012 can qualify for this relief, even if the taxpayer holds less than 5% of the ordinary share capital and voting rights of the company.

(10) *Goodwill* – The relief is restricted for gains arising on the transfer of goodwill to a close company on or after 3 December 2014 (*TCGA 1992, s 169LA*).

(11) *Associated disposals* – From 18 March 2015 for a gain to qualify for this relief as an associated disposal, it must be connected with a disposal of at least 5% of the ordinary share capital of the individual's personal company or at least a 5% interest in the partnership assets of the partnership of which he is a member. This rule is relaxed for a retiring partner and an additional condition is added for assets acquired on and after 13 June 2016 (*TCGA 1992, s 169K*).

(12) *Reduced lifetime limit* – If the taxpayer has already made disposals subject to ER claims of £1 million or more by 11 March 2020, no further disposals can qualify, but earlier claims will not be disturbed. Forestalling rules apply for contracts exchanged after 6 April 2019 and before 11 March 2020 (*FA 2020, Sch 3, pt 1*).

(13) *Further information* – Chapter 12 of *Capital Gains Tax 2021/22* (Bloomsbury Professional).

INVESTORS' RELIEF

(TCGA 1992, ss 169VA–169VR, Sch 7ZB)

Date of disposal	Lifetime limit	Rate of CGT on eligible gains
From 6 April 2019	£10 million	10%

Conditions

(1)   *Qualifying shares* – Only gains made on the disposal of qualifying shares are eligible for this relief. The shares must be:

- subscribed for on or after 17 March 2016 by the taxpayer who is disposing of them;

- issued by an unquoted trading company or unquoted holding company of a trading group;

- held by the investor for a continuous period of at least three years to date of disposal, which cannot be before 6 April 2019.

(2)   *Connection to company* – The investor can become an employee of the company six months or more after acquiring the shares, but he must not be offered that employment as a condition of subscribing for the shares. Alternatively, the investor may become an unpaid director of the company *(TCGA 1992, s 169VB)*.

(3)   *Receipt of value* – The relief cannot apply where the investor has received value from the company at any time in the period starting one year before the issue of the shares to three years after the share issue *(TCGA 1992, Sch 7ZB)*.

(4)   *Further information* – Chapter 17 of *Capital Gains Tax 2021/22* (Bloomsbury Professional).

ROLLOVER RELIEF FOR BUSINESS ASSETS

(TCGA 1992, Pt 5, Ch 1)

Qualifying assets *(TCGA 1992, s 155)*:

Class of asset	Description
1A	Land and buildings occupied (and used) only for the purposes of a trade
1B	Fixed plant or machinery (not forming part of a building)
2	Ships, aircraft and hovercraft
3	Satellites, space stations and spacecraft (including launch vehicles)
4	Goodwill
5	Milk & potato quotas (both abolished)
6	Ewe and suckler cow premium quotas
7	Fish quotas
7A	Payment entitlements under Single Payment for farmers
7B	Payment entitlement under Basic Payment Scheme for farmers (note 2)
8A	Lloyd's underwriters' syndicate capacity
8B	Lloyd's members' agent pooling arrangements

Notes

(1) *Corporate claims* – For the purposes of corporation tax, assets in categories 4 to 7A listed above, if owned by a company at any time on or after 1 April 2002, would fall within the intangible assets regime and are therefore excluded from business asset rollover relief (*TCGA 1992, s 156ZB*).

(2) *Farmers' subsidies* – From 20 December 2013 the disposal of entitlements to the Basic Payment Scheme under EU regulation 1307/2013 qualifies for rollover relief (*FA 2014, s 61*).

(3) *Companies and intangibles* – From 19 March 2014, companies are specifically prohibited from claiming rollover relief where the proceeds on disposal of a tangible asset are reinvested in an intangible fixed asset (*CTA 2009, s 870A*).

MAIN RESIDENCE RELIEF

(TCGA 1992, ss 222–226B)

Deemed occupation due to:	Maximum period permitted:
Delay in taking up occupation	24 months (*TCGA 1992, s 223ZA*)
Job-related accommodation	No limit, includes those who receive armed forces allowance (*TCGA 1992, s 222(8)*)
Final period of ownership	9 months for disposals on or after 6 April 2020, or 36 months where owner or spouse is disabled or has moved to residential care home, (*TCGA 1992, s 225E*).

Taxpayer must occupy the home as their main residence both before and after and have no other qualifying residence in that period for these deemed periods of occupation to apply:

Employer requires taxpayer to live elsewhere in order to perform employment duties	4 years (*TCGA 1992, s 223(3)(c)*)
Taxpayer or spouse was employed outside the UK and duties performed outside of UK	No limit (*TCGA 1992, s 223(3)(b)*)
Absence for any reason	3 years (*TCGA 1992, s 223(3)(a)*)

Notes

(1) *The relief* – Also known as principal private residence relief (PPR). Relief from CGT is given on the disposal of (or of an interest in) a dwelling which has been the individual's only or main residence, and on land enjoyed with that residence as its garden or grounds up to half a hectare, or more if the additional land is required for the reasonable enjoyment of the property.

(2) *Period of occupation* – The relief is time apportioned for periods of occupation, and for certain periods of deemed occupation. Relief for the final period of ownership is given, if the property was at some time the individual's only or main residence (*TCGA 1992, s 223(1)*).

(3)   *Election as main residence* – Where an individual occupies two or more properties as their home, they may elect within two years of the second or subsequent property being used as their home, which property is to be treated as the main residence (*TCGA 1992 s 222(5)*). A late election may be accepted in some circumstances (*TCGA 1992 s 222(5A)*). Where the property is located in a country in which the owner is not resident for tax purposes, the property may only be subject to that election if the owner spends at least 90 midnights in the property in the tax year (*TCGA 1992, s 222A*).

(4)   *Married couples and civil partners* – Such couples may have only one main residence at any time between them which qualifies for the relief. From 6 April 2020 where the home is transferred between spouses the recipient inherits the ownership history of the transferring spouse (*TCGA 1992, s 222(6)*).

(5)   *Lettings relief* – For disposals from 6 April 2020 this relief only applies to periods where the owner was in occupation concurrently with the tenant, for earlier disposals it could apply where the main residence had been wholly or partly let as residential accommodation at any time in the period of ownership. The maximum relief is the lower of:

- the gain attributable to the let period;

- £40,000 per owner;

- the gain exempt as main residence relief.

(6)   *Non-residents* – From 6 April 2015 owners who are not resident for tax purposes in the UK are subject to non-resident CGT (NRCGT) on gains on the disposal of UK residential property. Individual non-resident owners can claim main residence relief, but only if they are present in the property for at least 90 midnights during the tax year (*FA 2015, Sch 7*).

(7)   *Rate of CGT* – Any gain on a residential property interest which is not covered by a relief above, is charged to CGT at 28% (18% within basic rate band) for disposals made on and after 6 April 2016.

(8)   *Payment of CGT* – Where the contract to dispose of UK residential property is exchanged and completed on or after 6 April 2020 and CGT is due, it must be paid 'on account' within 30 days of the completion date and a UK Property Disposal Return must be filed online to report the tax due (*TCGA 1992, Sch 2*).

(9)   *Further information* – Chapter 11 of *Capital Gains Tax 2021/22* (Bloomsbury Professional), Report and Pay CGT on UK Property: tinyurl.com/RPCGTUKPr.

ASSETS OF NEGLIGIBLE VALUE

(TCGA 1992, s 24(2))

Claim by	Time limit	Claim to be made
Individuals and trustees	2 years from end of tax year in which asset value became negligible or was noticed to be so.	In tax return or by later amendment
Companies	2 years from end of accounting period in which asset value became negligible or was noticed to be so.	In tax return or by later amendment

Notes

(1)   *Conditions* – The asset must have **become** of negligible value during the period of ownership, and it must still be of negligible value and be owned by the taxpayer at the date of claim.

(2)   *Effect* – The claimant is treated as having sold and immediately reacquired the asset at the time of the claim or (subject to certain conditions) at any earlier time specified in the claim, for consideration equal to the value specified in the claim.

(3)   *Form CG34* – This form may be used to establish whether the asset has a negligible value, which can then be used in a later claim on the tax return. See **Chapter 17: HMRC clearances** for the procedure to use form CG34.

(4)   *Negligible value list* – HMRC publishes a list of shares or securities formerly quoted on the London Stock Exchange, which have been officially declared of negligible value for the purposes of a claim under *TCGA 1992, s 24(2)* by HMRC Shares and Assets Valuation (SAV), see: tinyurl.com/NegValshs.

(5)   *Further information* – See HMRC Help Sheet HS286, HMRC's Capital Gains Manual at CG13128, and Share Valuation Manual at SVM107150.

CULTURAL GIFT SCHEME

Gifts of pre-eminent objects

(FA 2012, s 49, Sch 14)

	Taxes to be reduced	**Tax credit as percentage of the gift**
Individuals	Income tax and/or CGT	30%
Companies	Corporation tax	20%

Notes

(1)   *Applies from* – Tax years or accounting periods starting on or after 1 April 2012 *(SI 2013/587)*.

(2)   *Relief given* – A reduction in specified taxes is available where the donor makes a 'qualifying gift' of 'pre-eminent property' to be held for the benefit of the public or the nation. The gift offer must be registered and accepted under the Cultural Gifts Scheme.

(3)   *Individuals* – An individual (not trustee or PR) can allocate the tax reduction to the tax year in which the offer is registered and/or any of the following four tax years. Unless otherwise instructed, the tax reduction is first applied against income tax liabilities, then against CGT liabilities.

(4)   *Companies* – The tax reduction is treated as arising when the company's corporation tax liability for the period in which the gift is made becomes due, or the registration date of the gift, if later.

(5)   *Capital gains* – A gain on the gift of an object under the scheme is exempt from CGT or corporation tax *(TCGA 1992, s 258(1A))*.

(6)   *Inheritance tax* – Gifts of property under the scheme are exempt from inheritance tax under *IHTA 1984, s 25(3).*

(7)   *Further information* – Administered by the Department for Culture Media and Sport and the Arts Council, see: tinyurl.com/Cltgiftschm.

Charities and CASCs

(TCGA 1992, ss 256, 257)

(1)   Gains accruing to charities which are both applicable and applied for charitable purposes are generally exempt for CGT purposes.

(2)   Relief from CGT generally applies to gifts to charities and certain other bodies. The relief was extended from 6 April 2002 to asset disposals to Community Amateur Sports Clubs (CASCs).

LEASES WHICH ARE WASTING ASSETS

(TCGA 1992, Sch 8, para 1)

Depreciation table

Years	%	Monthly increment (note 2)	Years	%	Monthly increment (note 2)
50 or more	100	–	24	79.622	0.123
49	99.657	0.029	23	78.055	0.131
48	99.289	0.031	22	76.399	0.138
47	98.902	0.032	21	74.635	0.147
46	98.490	0.034	20	72.770	0.155
45	98.059	0.036	19	70.791	0.165
44	97.595	0.039	18	68.697	0.175
43	97.107	0.041	17	66.470	0.186
42	96.593	0.043	16	64.116	0.196
41	96.041	0.046	15	61.617	0.208
40	95.457	0.049	14	58.971	0.221
39	94.842	0.051	13	56.167	0.234
38	94.189	0.054	12	53.191	0.248
37	93.497	0.058	11	50.038	0.263
36	92.761	0.061	10	46.695	0.279
35	91.981	0.065	9	43.154	0.295
34	91.156	0.069	8	39.399	0.313
33	90.280	0.073	7	35.414	0.332
32	89.354	0.077	6	31.195	0.352

Years	%	Monthly increment (note 2)	Years	%	Monthly increment (note 2)
31	88.371	0.082	5	26.722	0.373
30	87.330	0.087	4	21.983	0.395
29	86.226	0.092	3	16.959	0.419
28	85.053	0.098	2	11.629	0.444
27	83.816	0.103	1	5.983	0.470
26	82.496	0.110	0	0	0.499
25	81.100	0.116			

Notes

(1) *Formula* – Fraction of expenditure disallowed:

$$\frac{A - B}{A}$$

Where:

A is the percentage for duration of lease at acquisition or expenditure; and

B is the percentage for the duration of the lease at disposal.

(2) *Fraction of years* -– Add one-twelfth of the difference between the percentage for the whole year and the next higher percentage for each additional month. For a period of less than one month, odd days under 14 are not counted; 14 or more odd days are rounded up and treated as a month.

Short lease premiums

(ITTOIA 2005, s 277)

See **Chapter 6: Lease premiums** as to the calculation of the proportion of any premium received in respect of a lease of less than 50 years which is partly chargeable to capital gains tax, and that part which is chargeable to income tax as property business profits.

EXEMPT GILT-EDGED SECURITIES

(TCGA 1992, ss 16(2), 115, Sch 9)

2.50%	Treasury Stock 1986–2016
2.50%	Index-Linked Treasury Stock 2016
2.50%	Index-Linked Treasury Stock 2016 'A'
4.00%	Treasury Gilt 2016
2.00%	Treasury Gilt 2016
12.00%	Exchequer Stock 2013–2017
1.0%	Treasury Gilt 2017

continued

1.25%	Index-Linked Treasury Gilt 2017
1.75%	Treasury Gilt 2017
8.75%	Treasury Stock 2017
8.75%	Treasury Stock 2017 'A'
1.25%	Treasury Gilt 2018
5.00%	Treasury Gilt 2018
0.125%	Index-linked Treasury Gilt 2019
1.75%	Treasury Gilt 2019
3.75%	Treasury Gilt 2019
4.50%	Treasury Gilt 2019
2.50%	Index-linked Treasury Stock 2020
2.00%	Treasury Gilt 2020
4.75%	Treasury Stock 2020
3.75%	Treasury Gilt 2020
8.00%	Treasury Stock 2021
3.75%	Treasury Gilt 2021
1.5%	Treasury Gilt 2021
1.75%	Treasury Gilt 2022
1.875%	Index-Linked Treasury Gilt 2022
4.00%	Treasury Gilt 2022
0.50%	Treasury Gilt 2022
2.25%	Treasury Gilt 2023
0.75%	Treasury Gilt 2023
0.125%	Treasury Gilt 2023
0.125%	Index-linked Treasury Gilt 2024
1.00%	Treasury Gilt 2024
2.50%	Index-linked Treasury Stock 2024
2.75%	Treasury Gilt 2024
5.00%	Treasury Stock 2025
2.00%	Treasury Gilt 2025
0.625%	Treasury Gilt 2025
0.125%	Index-Linked Treasury Gilt 2026
1.5%	Treasury Gilt 2026
1.25%	Index-Linked Treasury Gilt 2027
1.25%	Treasury Gilt 2027
4.25%	Treasury Gilt 2027
6.00%	Treasury Stock 2028
1.625%	Treasury Gilt 2028
0.125%	Index-linked Treasury Gilt 2028
0.125%	Index-linked Treasury Gilt 2029
0.875%	Treasury Gilt 2029
4.125%	Index-Linked Treasury Stock 2030
4.75%	Treasury Gilt 2030
0.375	Treasury Gilt 2030

1.25%	Index-linked Treasury Gilt 2032
4.25%	Treasury Stock 2032
0.75%	Index-linked Treasury Gilt
4.50%	Treasury Gilt 2034
2.00%	Index-Linked Treasury Stock 2035
4.25%	Treasury Stock 2036
0.125%	Index-Linked Treasury Stock 2036
1.125%	Index-Linked Treasury Gilt 2037
1.75%	Treasury Gilt 2037
4.75%	Treasury Stock 2038
4.25%	Treasury Gilt 2039
0.625%	Index-linked Treasury Gilt 2040
4.25%	Treasury Gilt 2040
1.25%	Treasury Gilt 2041
0.125%	Index-linked Treasury Gilt 2041
0.625%	Index-linked Treasury Gilt 2042
4.50%	Treasury Stock 2042
0.125%	Index-linked Treasury Gilt 2044
3.25%	Treasury Gilt 2044
3.5%	Treasury Gilt 2045
4.25%	Treasury Gilt 2046
0.125%	Index-Linked Treasury Gilt 2046
0.75%	Index-Linked Treasury Gilt 2047
1.50%	Treasury Gilt 2047
0.125%	Index-linked Treasury Gilt 2048
4.25%	Treasury Gilt 2049
1.75%	Treasury Gilt 2049
0.50%	Index-linked Treasury Gilt 2050
0.25%	Index-linked Treasury Gilt 2052
3.75%	Treasury Gilt 2052
1.625%	Treasury Gilt 2054
1.25%	Indexed-linked Treasury Gilt 2055
4.25%	Treasury Gilt 2055
0.125%	Index-linked Treasury Gilt 2056
1.75%	Treasury Gilt 2057
0.125%	Index-linked Treasury Gilt 2058
4.00%	Treasury Gilt 2060
0.5%	Treasury Gilt 2061
0.375%	Index-linked Treasury Gilt 2062
0.125%	Index-Linked Treasury Stock 2065
2.50%	Treasury Gilt 2065
0.125%	Index-linked Treasury Gilt 2068
3.5%	Treasury Gilt 2068
1.625%	Treasury Gilt 2071

Notes

(1)   *No CGT* – Gains on the securities in the table above are not chargeable gains and any losses are not allowable losses.

(2)   *Further information* – For a full list of the gilt-edged securities with a redemption date on or after 1 January 1992 which are exempt from CGT see tinyurl.com/gvtglts.

IDENTIFICATION OF SECURITIES

(TCGA 1992, ss 104–109)

Disposals by individuals and trustees

Disposals on or after 6 April 2008 are to be identified with acquisitions in the following order:

(1)   Same day acquisitions (*TCGA 1992, s 105(1)(b)*) (subject to an election under *s 105A* (see below));

(2)   Acquisitions within the following 30 days on the basis of earlier acquisitions in that period, rather than later ones (a FIFO basis) (*TCGA 1992, s 106A(5)*); and

(3)   Securities within the expanded *TCGA 1994, s 104* holding, which specifically does not include acquisitions under (1) and (2) above, on the basis of later acquisitions before earlier ones (a LIFO basis) (*TCGA 1992, s 106A*).

Where the number of securities which comprise the disposal exceed those identified under the above rules, that excess is identified with subsequent acquisitions beyond the 30-day period referred to above, taking the earliest one first.

Disposals by companies

Order of identification:

(1)   Any acquisition on the same day (*TCGA 1992, s 105(1)(b)*);

(2)   Acquisitions within the previous 10 days (*TCGA 1992, s 107(3)*) (on a 'first in, first out' (FIFO) basis);

(3)   Acquisitions since 1 April 1982 ('the *s 104* holding', previously termed 'the new holding') (*TCGA 1992, s 107(7), (8)*);

(4)   Acquisitions in the period 6 April 1965 to 31 March 1982 ('the 1982 holding') (*TCGA 1992, s 107(7), (9)*), and

(5)   Those held on 6 April 1965, in respect of which no election has been made to include them in the pre-1982 pool; these will be identified on a last-in, first-out (LIFO) basis (*TCGA 1992, s 107(7), (9)*).

TIME LIMITS FOR ELECTIONS AND CLAIMS

The general time limit for claims and elections is four years from the end of the tax year or accounting period (*TMA 1970, s 43(1)*). HMRC may allow an extension of the normal time limit for certain elections and claims.

Provision	Time limit	References
Asset of negligible value	2 years from end of tax year (or accounting period, if a company) in which deemed disposal/reacquisition takes place	*TCGA 1992, s 24(2)*
Re-basing of all assets to 31 March 1982 values	For companies only: 2 years from end of accounting period of disposal	*TCGA 1992, s 35(6)*
50% relief if deferred charge on gains before 31 March 1982 (pre 06/04/08 disposals)	2 years from end of accounting period of disposal (if a company)	*TCGA 1992, s 36, Sch 4 para 9(1)*
Variation of a will so not to constitute a disposal for CGT purposes	Within 2 years of death; instrument of variation must contain a statement relying on *TCGA 1992, s 62(6)* (see *TCGA 1992, s 62(7)*)	*TCGA 1992, s 62(6)*
Employee share schemes – identifying disposals with acquisitions on "same day" transactions	Within 12 months from 31 January next following the tax year of the first disposal	*TCGA 1992, s 105B(2)*
Earn-out right to be treated as a security	Within 12 months from 31 January next following the tax year in which the right is conferred (or 2 years from end of accounting period, if a company)	*TCGA 1992, s 138A(5)*
Replacement of business assets (roll-over relief)	4 years from the end of the tax year (or accounting period) Replacement asset must be acquired in period: 1 year before to 3 years after disposal of old asset (*TCGA 1992, s 152(3)*)	*TCGA 1992, s 152(1)*
Asset appropriated to trading stock: trading profits to be adjusted by gain or loss on the deemed disposal at market value	Within 12 months from 31 January next following the year of assessment in which ends the period of account in which the asset is appropriated to trading stock (or 2 years from the end of the accounting period in which the asset is appropriated to trading stock, if a company)	*TCGA 1992, s 161(3A)*

continued

Provision	Time limit	References
Disapplication of incorporation relief under *TCGA 1992, s 162*	2 years from 31 January following the end of the year of assessment in which the business is transferred If all the new assets have been disposed of by the end of the year of assessment following the one in which the business transfer took place, the time limit is 12 months from 31 January next following the tax year of the business transfer	*TCGA 1992, s 162A(3), (4)*
Hold-over of relief for gifts of business assets	4 years from the end of the tax year	*TCGA 1992, s 165(1)*
Business Asset Disposal Relief	Within 12 months from 31 January following the tax year in which the qualifying business disposal is made	*TCGA 1992, s 169M(3)*
Deemed disposal/ reacquisition on expiry of mineral lease	4 years from the relevant date	*TCGA 1992, s 203(2)*
Main residence notification	2 years from date the second or subsequent property is occupied as the taxpayer's home. Non-resident taxpayers should give notice in the online return submitted within 30 days of disposal of the property	*TCGA 1992, ss 222(5)(5A), 222A(6)*
Small part disposals of land: consideration to be deducted from allowable expenditure on a subsequent disposal	Within 12 months from 31 January next following the tax year of disposal (or 2 years from end of accounting period of disposal, if a company)	*TCGA 1992, s 242(2A)*
Irrecoverable loan to a trader	4 years from the end of the tax year (or accounting period)	*TCGA 1992, s 253(3)*
Hold-over relief for gifts on which IHT is immediately chargeable etc	4 years from the end of the tax year.	*TCGA 1992, s 260(1)*
Trading losses relieved against gains	12 months from 31 January next following the tax year in which loss arose	*TCGA 1992, s 261B(8)*
Post-cessation expenses relieved against gains	12 months from 31 January next following the tax year in which expenses paid	*TCGA 1992, s 261D(6)*
Delayed remittances of foreign gains	4 years from the end of the tax year (or accounting period)	*TCGA 1992, s 279(5)*
Loss on disposal of right to deferred unascertainable consideration to be treated as accruing in an earlier year	Within 12 months from 31 January next following the year of the loss	*TCGA 1992, s 279D(8)*

Inheritance tax and estates

IHT THRESHOLDS

(IHTA 1984, s 7, Sch 1)

Period	Nil rate band £	Residence nil rate band £
2021/22 (note 2)	325,000	175,000
2020/21	325,000	175,000
2019/20	325,000	150,000
2018/19	325,000	125,000
2017/18	325,000	100,000
2009/10 to 2016/17	325,000	N/A
2008/09	312,000	
2007/08	300,000	
2006/07	285,000	
2005/06	275,000	
2004/05	263,000	
2003/04	255,000	
2002/03	250,000	
2001/02	242,000	
2000/01	234,000	
1999/2000	231,000	
1998/99	223,000	
1997/98	215,000	
1996/97	200,000	
1995/96	154,000	
10 March 1992 to 5 April 1995	150,000	
6 April 1991 to 9 March 1992	140,000	
1990/91	128,000	
1989/90	118,000	
15 March 1988 to 5 April 1989	110,000	
17 March 1987 to 14 March 1988	90,000	
18 March 1986 to 16 March 1987	71,000	

Notes

(1)   *Scope* – The above thresholds apply to cumulative lifetime transfers and transfers on death or within seven years before death.

(2)   *Nil rate band (NRB)* – Covers value of the estate and gifts made within seven years of death, IHT is paid on any excess value subject to RNRB and other reliefs (*FA 2010, s 8*). Unused proportion of NRB may be inherited from deceased spouse or civil partner. The NRB is now frozen for all tax years 2015/16 to 2025/26 (*FA 2014, Sch 25, para 2* and *F(No 2)A 2015, s 10*, https://tinyurl.com/hz9u9jfb).

(3)   *Residence nil rate band (RNRB)* – Where individual dies on or after 6 April 2017, and their estate is above the NRB, the RNRB may also be deducted if all the conditions apply.

(4)   *Conditions for RNRB* – The whole or a part share in the value of deceased's home is passed to a direct descendent on death. The maximum value of RNRB is the lower of: value of the home passed on, and the amount in the table above. RNRB is tapered away at £1 for every £2 by which the value of the total estate exceeds £2 million (*IHTA 1984, ss 8D–8M*).

(5)   *Liabilities* – For deaths occurring on or after 17 July 2013, a debt owed by the deceased may be deducted from the value of the estate only if it is actually discharged out of the estate on or after the death, unless certain conditions are satisfied (*IHTA 1984, s 175A*).

(6)   *Grossing up* – Applies at the rates of: 1/4 for net lifetime transfers and 2/3 for net transfers on death (not bearing own tax). Where the will specifies tax-free legacies and the estate residue passes to persons who are not eligible to receive the gift exempt of IHT, there is no requirement to gross-up to tax-free legacies.

(7)   *Death exemptions* – The following are exempt from IHT with no limit if the transfer of value is made on death:

- Estate of member of the Armed Forces who dies on active service or from their wounds/disease/accident inflicted on active service (*IHTA 1984, s 154*).

- Estate of member of the emergency service who dies from disease or accident acquired while working as an emergency responder (*IHTA 1984, s 153A*).

- Estate of constable or service personnel targeted because of their status (*IHTA 1984, s 155A*).

- Decorations for valour, if never transferred for money or money's worth (*IHTA 1984, s 6(1B)*).

- Compensation paid to victims of persecution during Second World War (*IHTA 1984, s 153ZA*).

Capital transfer tax (IHT thresholds) – 13 March 1975 to 17 March 1986

From	To	Limit
6 April 1985	17 March 1986	£67,000
13 March 1984	5 April 1985	£64,000
15 March 1983	12 March 1984	£60,000
9 March 1982	14 March 1983	£55,000
26 March 1980	8 March 1982	£50,000
27 October 1977	25 March 1980	£25,000
13 March 1975	26 October 1977	£15,000

Estate duty (IHT thresholds) – 16 August 1914 to 12 March 1975

England, Wales and Scotland

From	To	Limit
22 March 1972	12 March 1975	£15,000
31 March 1971	21 March 1972	£12,500
16 April 1969	30 March 1971	£10,000
4 April 1963	15 April 1969	£5,000
9 April 1962	3 April 1963	£4,000
30 July 1954	8 April 1962	£3,000
10 April 1946	29 July 1954	£2,000
16 August 1914	9 April 1946	£100

Northern Ireland

From	To	Limit
22 March 1972	12 March 1975	£15,000
5 May 1971	21 March 1972	£12,500
4 June 1969	4 May 1971	£10,000
22 May 1963	3 June 1969	£5,000
4 July 1962	21 May 1963	£4,000
1 November 1954	3 July 1962	£3,000
29 August 1946	31 October 1954	£2,000
16 August 1914	28 August 1946	£100

RATES OF IHT

(IHTA 1984, Sch 1A)

Period in which transfer occurs:	Life-time transfers	On death	Reduced rate on death
2012/13 to 2021/22	20%	40%	36%
18 March 1986 to 5 April 2012	20%	40%	N/A

Notes

(1)   *Reduced rate* – Available where at least 10% of the base-line net value of the estate is left to charities or CASCs on death (*IHTA 1984, Sch 1A, para 1*).

(2)   *Variations* – Where an Instrument of Variation is executed, leaving or increasing a legacy to charity, the variation will only be treated as being made by the deceased where it is shown that the charity has been notified of the variation (*IHTA 1984, s 142(3A)*).

(3)   *Further information* – For outline guidance on the reduced rate see: tinyurl. com/36rate. For detailed guidance, see HMRC's Inheritance Tax Manual at para IHTM45000+.

GIFT EXEMPTIONS

Annual and small gifts

(*IHTA 1984, ss 19, 20*)

Period	Annual exemption £	Small Gift exemption (to the same person) £
From 6 April 1981	3,000	250
6 April 1980 to 5 April 1981	2,000	250
6 April 1976 to 5 April 1980	2,000	100

Notes

(1)   *Carry forward* – To the extent that the annual exemption is unused for a particular tax year, it can be carried forward to the next tax year but not beyond.

(2)   *Priority* – The current year exemption must be used in priority over any brought forward exemption (*IHTA 1984, s 19(2)*).

In consideration of marriage or civil partnership

(*IHTA 1984, s 22*)

Donor	Limit
Parent of party to the marriage/civil partnership	£5,000
Remoter ancestor than parent of party to the marriage/civil partnership	£2,500
Party to the marriage/civil partnership	£2,500
Any other person	£1,000

Notes

(1)   *Before marriage* – The gift must be made on or before the date of the marriage, and it is not IHT free if the marriage does not take place.

(2) *Excess gifts* – If the value of the gift is greater than the amount of the available exemption, it is an exempt transfer up to the amount of the available exemption, and the excess is chargeable.

Non-UK domiciled spouse or civil partner

(IHTA 1984, s 18)

Transfers	Limit
From 6 April 2013 (Note 1)	£325,000
9 March 1982–5 April 2013	£55,000

Notes

(1) *Nil rate band alignment* – With effect for gifts made on and after 6 April 2013, the IHT-exempt amount that a UK-domiciled individual can transfer to their non-UK domiciled spouse or civil partner is increased to the prevailing nil rate band limit *(IHTA 1984, s 18(2))*

(2) *Election* – Individuals who are domiciled outside the UK and who have a UK-domiciled spouse or civil partner can elect to be treated as domiciled in the UK for IHT purposes. This election can be made at any time after marriage or civil partnership and within two years of the death where that occurs on or after 6 April 2013. The election can be back-dated up to seven years to the later of the date of the marriage or 6 April 2013 *(IHTA 1984, ss 267ZA–267ZB)*.

AGRICULTURAL AND BUSINESS PROPERTY RELIEF

(IHTA 1984, Pt V, Chs 1, 2)

Agricultural property (APR)		Business Property (BPR)	
Nature of property	**Relief %**	**Nature of property**	**Relief %**
Vacant possession or right to obtain it within 12 months	100	Business or interest in a business	100
Tenanted land with vacant possession value (note 4)	100	Quoted company: controlling shareholding	50
Agricultural land let on or after 1 September 1995	100	Unquoted company: any shareholding	100
Any other circumstances	50	Settled property used in life tenant's business: transferred with the business on death	100
		Settled property used in life tenant's business	50
		Land, buildings, machinery or plant used by a company controlled by transferor or by transferor's partnership	50

115

Notes

(1)   *Applies from* – The rates of relief in the tables above apply to disposals made on and after 6 April 1996.

(2)   *Location of land* – Agricultural property located in an EEA State, Channel Islands or Isle of Man, at the time of the chargeable event is eligible for relief (*IHTA 1984, s 115(5)*).

(3)   *Grazing land* – If land is let to graze animals or take grass from land for a season, and vacant possession reverts to the landowner within a year, any agricultural property relief due will be at the 100% rate (IHTM24142).

(4)   *Old tenancies* – Land let on a tenancy commencing before 10 March 1981 may qualify for relief at 100% in certain circumstances, ie broadly if the transferor owned the land before 10 March 1981, the land would have qualified for relief (under *FA 1975, Sch 8*) had it been transferred before that date, and the transferor did not have vacant possession (or entitlement to it) from then until the date of death/transfer (*IHTA 1984, s 116(2), (3)*).

(5)   *Liabilities* – Where a debt is incurred or refinanced on or after 6 April 2013 to acquire an asset on which relief is due under APR, BPR or woodlands relief, the debt must be first deducted from the value of that asset before application of APR/BPR with any excess debt deducted from the value of the total estate (*IHTA 1984, s 162B*).

(6)   *Further information* – See *Agricultural, Business and Heritage Property Relief* (Bloomsbury Professional)

QUICK SUCCESSION RELIEF

(*IHTA 1984, s 141*)

Years between transfers		Percentage (applied to formula – see below) %
More than	**Not more than**	
0	1	100
1	2	80
2	3	60
3	4	40
4	5	20

Formula:

$$\text{Percentage} \times \text{Tax charge on earlier transfer} \times \frac{\text{Increase in value of transferee's estate}}{\text{Value of earlier chargeable transfer}}$$

TAPER RELIEF

(IHTA 1984, s 7(4))

Period between gift and death	% of full charge at death rates
3 years or less	100
Over 3 years but not more than 4 years	80
Over 4 years but not more than 5 years	60
Over 5 years but not more than 6 years	40
Over 6 years but not more than 7 years	20

Notes

(1) *Lifetime gifts* – The relief provides for a reduced tax charge on gifts made within seven years before death. The amount of relief depends on the length of time the deceased survived following the transfer. The tax otherwise due at the death rates is reduced by applying the percentages in the preceding table.

(2) *Not applicable* – If IHT on a chargeable lifetime transfer is recalculated on death with taper relief and produces a lower IHT figure than originally calculated at lifetime rates, the original figure stands *(IHTA 1984, s 7(5))*.

PRE-OWNED ASSETS

(FA 2004, s 84, Sch 15)

Asset type	Chargeable amount calculated as:
Land	R x DV/V less actual rent paid under a legal obligation
Chattels	N x DV/ V less amounts paid for use of chattel under a legal obligation
Intangible property in settlor-interested settlements	N – T

Where: R is the rental value of the relevant land for the taxable period;

DV is the value at the valuation date of the interest in the relevant land or chattel that was disposed of by the chargeable person or, where the disposal was a non-exempt sale, the appropriate proportion of that value; and

V is the value of the relevant land or chattel at the valuation date.

N is the notional interest for the taxable period, at the official rate of interest at the start of the period, on the value of the property or chattel at the valuation date.

T is the amount of income tax or capital gains tax payable by the chargeable person in the taxable period by virtue of gains from contracts of life assurance, income from settlements where the settlor retains an interest, transfer of assets abroad, the charge on settlors with an interest in settlements and the attribution of gains to settlors with an interest in non-resident or dual resident settlements for capital gains tax purposes.

Notes

(1)   *The charge* – An income tax charge arises where a UK resident individual continues to benefit from property in the categories above, which was previously owned by them.

(2)   *Exemption* – No tax is payable if the chargeable amount does not exceed £5,000. If the chargeable benefits exceed £5,000, the tax is due on the full amount.

(3)   *Further Information* – HMRC's Inheritance Tax Manual at IHTM44000+.

DELIVERY OF IHT ACCOUNTS

Due dates

(IHTA 1984, s 216)

Type of transfer	Due Date
Chargeable lifetime transfer	Later of: – 12 months after end of month in which transfer occurred – 3 months after person became liable
Transfers on death	Later of: – 12 months after end of month in which death occurred – 3 months after personal representatives first act in that capacity
Potentially exempt transfers which have become chargeable	12 months after end of month in which the transferor died
Gifts subject to reservation included in donor's estate at death	12 months after end of month in which death occurred
National heritage property or woodlands (on disposal)	6 months after end of month in which chargeable event occurred
Relevant property trust IHT charges	6 months after end of month in which chargeable event occurred

Excepted transfers

From 6 April 2007

(SI 2008/605, reg 4)

For chargeable transfers from 6 April 2007, no account is necessary where:

•   the transfer is in cash or quoted shares or securities and the value of the transfer and other chargeable transfers made in the preceding seven years does not exceed the IHT threshold; or

•   the value of the transfer (ignoring business and agricultural property relief) and other chargeable transfers made in the preceding seven years does not exceed 80% of the

IHT threshold, and the value of the transfer does not exceed the net amount of the threshold available to the transferor at the time of the transfer.

Similar rules apply in determining whether the termination of an interest in possession in settled property is excepted from the requirement to deliver an account (*SI 2008/605, reg 5*).

Excepted estates

(SI 2004/2543; SI 2006/2141; SI 2011/214)

Deaths from	Before	Excepted estate limit	Assets held outside UK – limit	Total value of settled property	Specified transfers – limit	Specified exempt transfers – limit
6 April 2009	5 April 2022	325,000	100,000	150,000	150,000	1,000,000
6 April 2008	5 April 2009	312,000	100,000	150,000	150,000	1,000,000
6 April 2007	5 April 2008	300,000	100,000	150,000	150,000	1,000,000

Notes

(1) *General* – The regulations provide for three categories of excepted estate:

    (a)   The 'low value' estate;

    (b)   The 'exempt estate'; and

    (c)   The 'foreign domiciliaries' estate.

(2) *Transferable nil rate band* – For deaths on and after 6 April 2010, the low value and exempt estate categories are expanded to twice the nil rate band. This only applies if a claim is made for 100% of the nil rate band to be transferred from an earlier deceased spouse or civil partner, subject to other conditions being satisfied. The excepted estate return form IHT205, or C5 in Scotland, must be used (*SI 2011/214*).

(3) *Alternatively secured pension funds* – For deaths occurring from 6 April 2011 the conditions relating to the alternatively secured pension fund do not have effect (*SI 2004/2543, reg 4(10)*).

(4) *Further information* – See Chapter 8 of *Inheritance Tax 2021/22* (Bloomsbury Professional) and HMRC's IHT Manual at IHTM06011+.

Excepted settlements

(IHTA 1984, ss 216, 256; SI 2008/606)

No account is necessary of settled property in which no qualifying interest in possession subsists for chargeable events from 6 April 2007, broadly where:

Either:

●   Cash has always been the only property comprised in the settlement;

●   The settlor has added no further property to the settlement;

- The trustees have been UK resident since the settlement commenced;

- The gross value of settled property has not exceeded £1,000 since the settlement commenced; and

- There are no related settlements.

or

- The settlor was UK domiciled when the settlement was made, and remained so until the chargeable event, or until death (whichever is earlier);

- The trustees have been UK resident since the settlement commenced; and

- There are no related settlements; and *either*

- For ten-year anniversary IHT charge purposes, the value of the notional aggregate chargeable transfer (in *IHTA 1984, s 66(3)*) does not exceed 80% of the nil rate band; *or*

- On a chargeable event before the settlement's first ten-year anniversary, the value of the notional aggregate chargeable transfer (in *IHTA 1984, s 68(4)*) does not exceed 80% of the nil rate band; *or*

- On a chargeable event between ten-year anniversaries, the value of the notional aggregate chargeable transfer (in *IHTA 1984, s 66(3)*, taking account of *s 69*) does not exceed 80% of the nil rate band; *or*

- Where an IHT charge arises in respect of an 'age 18 to 25' trust (under *IHTA 1984, s 71E*), the value of the notional aggregate chargeable transfer (as adjusted in accordance with *IHTA 1984, s 71F(8)*) does not exceed 80% of the nil rate band.

Note

Further guidance – See HMRC's Inheritance Tax Manual at IHTM06120+.

Personal representatives' allowable expenses

(SP 2/04)

Gross value of estate	Allowable expenditure for deaths after 5 April 2004
Not exceeding £50,000	1.8% of the probate value of assets sold by the personal representatives.
Over £50,000 but not exceeding £90,000	£900, divided among all assets of the estate in proportion to their probate values and allowed in those proportions on assets sold by the personal representatives.
Over £90,000 but not exceeding £400,000	1% of the probate value of assets sold.
Over £400,000 but not exceeding £500,000	£4,000, divided among all assets of the estate in proportion to their probate values and allowed in those proportions on assets sold by the personal representatives.

Gross value of estate	Allowable expenditure for deaths after 5 April 2004
Over £500,000 but not exceeding £1,000,000	0.8% of the probate value of assets sold.
Over £1,000,000 but not exceeding £5,000,000	£8,000, divided among all assets of the estate in proportion to their probate values and allowed in those proportions on assets sold by the personal representatives.
Over £5,000,000	0.16% of the probate value of the assets sold, subject to a maximum of £10,000.

DUE DATES FOR PAYMENT OF IHT

(IHTA 1984, s 226)

Transfer	Due Date
Chargeable transfers other than death made between:	
6 April and 30 September	30 April in following year
1 October and 5 April	6 months after end of month in which transfer was made
Chargeable transfers which have conditional exemptions for heritage Charge to tax on disposals of trees or underwood	6 months after end of month in which chargeable event occurred
Transfers on death	Earlier of: – 6 months after end of month in which death occurs; or – delivery of account by personal representatives
Chargeable transfers and potentially exempt transfers within 7 years of death	6 months after end of month in which death occurs

Notes

(1) *Relevant property trusts* – For relevant property trust IHT charges arising on or after 6 April 2014, the IHT must generally be paid within six months after the end of the month in which the chargeable event occurs *(IHTA 1984, s 223(3C))*.

(2) *Penalties and interest* – For details of the penalties for late payment and interest that may be charged see **Chapter 17**.

DISTRIBUTION OF INTESTATE ESTATES

England and Wales

(Administration of Estates Act 1925, s 46; Inheritance and Trustees' Powers Act 2014)

See **Chapter 18** for Scottish estates

Distributions on and after 1 October 2014

Spouse or civil partner and issue survive	
Spouse or civil partner receives	*Issue receives*
• All personal chattels; • £250,000 absolutely (or the entire interest where this is less); and • One-half of residue (if any) in trust for the survivor absolutely.	• One half of residue (if any) on statutory trusts.
Spouse or civil partner survives without issue	
Spouse or civil partner receives: Residue in trust for the survivor absolutely.	

Notes

(1) *No Will* – The distribution of a deceased individual's estate, and the IHT liability in respect of the estate, can be affected if the individual died without having made a valid will.

(2) *Location* – The above tables only apply to deaths occurring in England, Wales and Northern Ireland. For deaths in Scotland see **Chapter 18**.

(3) *From 1 Oct 2014* – The fixed sum of £250,000 is determined by *AEA 1925, Sch 1A*, and is subject to possible future amendment by statutory instrument.

(4) *Civil partners* – The surviving civil partner effectively acquires the same rights as a surviving spouse in cases of intestacy.

(5) *Survivorship* – The above provisions in favour of the deceased's spouse or civil partner are subject to a 28-day survival period (*AEA 1925, s 46(2A)*).

(6) *No spouse or civil partner survives* – The estate is held in the following order in such cases, with no class beneficiaries participating unless all those in a prior class have predeceased. Statutory trusts may apply except under (b), (e) and (h):

    (a)   Issue of deceased.

    (b)   Parent(s).

    (c)   Brothers and sisters (or issue).

    (d)   Half-brothers and half-sisters (or issue).

    (e)   Grandparent(s).

    (f)   Uncles and aunts (or issue).

    (g)   Half-brothers and half-sisters of deceased's parents (or issue).

    (h)   The Crown, the Duchy of Lancaster or the Duke of Cornwall.

(7) *Further information* – See HMRC's Inheritance Tax manual at IHTM12101, and online tool to find out who is entitled: tinyurl.com/intesttool.

Capital Allowances

PLANT AND MACHINERY

(CAA 2001, Pt 2)

Annual investment allowance (AIA)

(CAA 2001, s 51A)

Expenditure incurred in period:	AIA cap £
From 1 January 2022	200,000
1 January 2019 to 31 December 2021	1,000,000
1 January 2016 to 31 December 2018	200,000
April 2014 to 31 December 2015	500,000
1 Jan 2013 to March/April 2014	250,000

Notes

(1) *Temporary increase* – The AIA cap is increased to £1m for three years to 31 December 2021 *(FA 2019, s 32)*.

(2) *Non-qualifying* – The AIA cannot be claimed by a trust or by a partnership where one or more members is a company, and there are restrictions to the amount of the AIA claimable by groups of companies and related companies *(CAA 2001, ss 38A, 51B–51N)*.

(3) *Exclusions* – The AIA cannot be claimed in respect of; the purchase of cars, for the final period of the trade, or where tax avoidance is the motive *(CAA 2001, s 38B)*.

(4) *Changes* – The changes at 31 December/1 January apply for both corporation tax and income tax. The changes in March/April were effective from 1 April for corporation tax and from 6 April for income tax. There are transitional rules for periods that straddle the dates of change (see notes (6) & (7)).

(5) *Chargeable periods* – The AIA is given for a chargeable period. As a general rule, the annual cap is proportionately increased or decreased for chargeable periods longer or shorter than 12 months.

(6)   *Periods straddling 1 January 2019* – The AIA cap is found by splitting the chargeable period at the dates of changes in the maximum AIA cap.

For example, a business with a chargeable period from 1 April 2018 to 31 March 2019 would calculate its AIA cap for that period in two parts:

(a)   nine months to 31 December 2018 = 9/12 × £200,000; and

(b)   three months to 31 March 2019 = 3/12 × £1,000,000

However, the calculation of the AIA cap is subject to additional transitional rules about the maximum allowance for expenditure actually incurred, which can restrict the available AIA for particular periods.

(7)   *Periods straddling 1 January 2022* – The AIA cap is the sum of the maximum cap as if the chargeable period was split at 31 December 2021 and the resulting periods were treated as separate chargeable periods:

(a)   the period from the first day of the chargeable period and ending with 31 December 2021, which is the proportion of the £1m cap;

(b)   the period beginning 1 January 2022 and ending with the last day of the chargeable period, which is based on the proportion of £200,000.

However, for expenditure incurred in that part of the chargeable period falling after 31 December 2021, the maximum AIA cap is the proportion of £200,000 calculated in b) above (*FA 2014, Sch 2*).

(8)   *Further information* – See: tinyurl.com/CAAIAgd or refer to *Capital Allowances: Transactions and Planning 2019/20* (Bloomsbury Professional), Chapter 14.

Super-deductions

(*Finance Bill 2021, cls 9–14*)

Expenditure incurred in period:	Qualifying for main pool %	Qualifying for special rate pool %
From 1 April 2021 to 31 March 2023	130	50

Notes

(1)   *Main pool* – FYA of 130% for the cost of new (not second hand) items of plant or machinery, or fixtures in properties, that qualify for inclusion in the main pool which are acquired in the period:1 April 2021 to 31 March 2023 inclusive.

(2)   *Special pool* – FYA of 50% for the cost of new and unused (not second hand) items of plant or machinery, including integral features, solar panels and thermal insulation.

(3)   *Disposals* – Where either FYA is claimed the items are not pooled. When an asset is sold in the period up to 31 March 2023, this could result in an immediate balancing charge, with part of the cost being clawed back and declared as taxable income

(4)   *Exclusions* – Items acquired under contracts entered into before 3 March 2021, long-life assets, cars.

(5) *Available to* – Companies within the charge to corporation tax.

(6) *Time apportioned* – Relief is time apportioned for accounting periods that straddle 1 April 2021 and 31 March 2023.

(7) *Further information* – See super-deduction factsheet: https://tinyurl.com/superdctFS

Writing down allowances (WDAs)

(CAA 2001, s 56)

	Main rate %	Special rate %
From April 2019	18	6
From April 2012 to April 2019	18	8
April 2008 to April 2012	20	10

Notes

(1) *Changes* – The changes in WDA rates apply from 1 April for corporation tax and from 6 April for income tax (*FA 2011, s 10*).

(2) *Straddling periods* – For chargeable periods which straddle the above relevant dates, the rate of WDA is a hybrid of the rates before and after the changes.

(3) *Further information* – Brief guidance is found here: tinyurl.com/CAwdwgd. For technical guidance see HMRC Capital Allowances manual at CA23200.

First year allowances (FYAs)

(CAA 2001, s 52)

FYAs at a rate of 100% are available for the following types of expenditure incurred by businesses of any size, subject to general exclusions listed below (see **First year allowances: general exclusions**).

Expenditure on	Section in CAA 2001
Energy-saving plant or machinery (note 1)	*s 45A*
Cars with low CO_2 emissions	*s 45D*
Goods vehicles with zero emissions (note 2)	*s 45DA*
Plant or machinery for gas refuelling stations (note 3)	*s 45E*
Plant or machinery for electric vehicle charging points (note 4)	*s 45EA*
Plant or machinery for use by a company wholly in a ring fence trade	*s 45F*
Environmentally beneficial plant or machinery (note 1)	*s 45H*
Certain new investment by companies in new plant or machinery in designated assisted areas in Enterprise Zones (see **Enterprise Zones**)	*s 45K*

Notes

(1)   *ECA* – Enhanced capital allowances are only available for items included on the Energy Technology List (tinyurl.com/ECAengtech) or the Water Technology List. ECA and environmentally beneficial allowances are abolished from 1 April 2020 for companies and 6 April 2020 for unincorporated businesses (*FA 2019, s 33*).

(2)   *Zero-emission goods vehicles* – The vehicle must be new and unused (not second hand), and must be acquired in the period from 1 or 6 April 2010 to 31 March 2021 or 5 April 2021 (*CAA 2001, s 45DA*). Firms in financial difficulty or in certain industrial sectors can't claim allowances for zero emissions vehicles (*CAA 2001, s 45DB*).

(3)   *Gas refuelling equipment* – FYAs for plant and machinery used in gas, biogas and hydrogen refuelling stations apply for acquisitions to 31 March 2021 (*CAA 2001, s 45E*).

(4)   *Electric charging points* – FYAs for plant and machinery used in electric vehicle charging points apply for expenditure from 23 November 2016 to 31 March 2023 (corporation tax), or 5 April 2023 (income tax) (*CAA 2001, s 45EA*).

First year allowances: general exclusions

(CAA 2001, s 46(2))

No first year allowances are available for the following types of expenditure:

- incurred in the chargeable period in which the qualifying activity is permanently discontinued;
- cars (other than those with low CO_2 emissions);
- certain ships (within *CAA 2001, s 94* but see *FA 2013, s 70*);
- certain railway assets (exclusion removed by *FA 2013, s 70*);
- expenditure that would be long-life asset expenditure but for transitional provisions (in *CAA 2001, Sch 3, para 20*);
- expenditure on the provision of plant or machinery for leasing (whether in the course of a trade or otherwise) (subject to exceptions in *CAA 2001, s 46(5)*);
- certain anti-avoidance cases where the obtaining of a FYA is linked to a change in the nature or conduct of a trade;
- plant and machinery that was initially acquired for purposes other than those of the qualifying activity;
- plant or machinery that was provided for long funding leasing but later starts to be used for other purposes; and
- plant and machinery that was acquired by way of gift.

CARS

(CAA 2001, ss 45D, 52, Pt 2, Ch 10A)

CO$_2$ emissions in g/km				Rate of capital allowance
2013/14 to 2014/15	2015/16 to 2017/18	2018/19 to 2020/21	2021/22 to 2024/25	
Up to 95	Up to 75	Up to 50	Zero	FYA at 100% (note 1)
96 to 130	76 to 130	51 to 110	Up to 50	Main rate pool
Over 130	Over 130	Over 110	Over 50	Special rate pool

Notes

(1)   100% FYA – The car must be new and unused (not second hand) *(CAA 2001, s 45D)*. For cars purchased from April 2021, FYA is only available where CO$_2$ emissions are zero g/km or the car is electric.

(2)   *Cars with private use* – The main or special rates apply as above (depending on CO$_2$ emissions) but the car is retained in a single asset pool (see HMRC's Capital Allowances Manual at CA23535). Allowances are restricted for private use.

(3)   *Leased cars* – CO$_2$ thresholds also changed from April 2021 see **Chapter 6: Business Profits**.

(4)   *Capital allowances rates* – For WDA rates in respect of the main rate pool and special rate pool, see **Writing down allowances** (WDAs) above.

BUILDINGS AND FIXTURES

Structures and Buildings (SBA)

(CAA 2001, Pt 2A, SI 2019/1087)

Costs included:	Rate of allowance:	
	2018/19 to 2019/20	From 2020/21
Construction or conversion	2% of qualifying expenditure.	3% of qualifying expenditure
Improvement, renovation or repair		
Demolition		
Preparing the land		
New and unused building acquired from developer or builder.		

Notes

(1)   *Covers* – Expenditure incurred on or after 29 October 2018 in the categories listed above, where the resulting building or structure starts to be used for a qualifying purpose within seven years of construction.

(2)   *Excluded costs* – Acquiring the land, associated SDLT (or other land taxes), professional fees and any planning permission costs are not covered.

(3)   *Excluded buildings* – Any building used as a dwelling house, or ancillary to a dwelling, or any building used for holiday or overnight accommodation of a prescribed kind. Where a building is partially used for a qualifying purpose an apportionment of costs may be allowed.

(4)   *How relief is given* – The cost of each building must be calculated separately. A flat percentage of the total cost is claimed as an allowance for each full year. The flat rate was increased for claims from 1 April 2020 (6 April for unincorporated businesses). This increase applies to all claims for SBA irrespective of when the expenditure was incurred (*FA 2020, s 29*).

(5)   *On sale of the building* – The flat rate allowance is claimed by the new owner for each year the building is used for a qualifying purpose. No balancing allowances or balancing charges accrue to the former owner.

(6)   *Further information* – See HMRC's Capital Allowances Manual CA90000-CA94810, and *Capital Allowances: Transactions and Planning 2019/20* (Bloomsbury Professional).

Integral Features

(CAA 2001, ss 33A, 33B, 104A(1), 104D)

Included:	Excluded:
Electrical and lighting systems.	Assets used to insulate or enclose the interior of a building, or to provide an interior wall, floor or ceiling intended to remain permanently in place.
Cold water systems.	
Space or water heating systems, powered systems of ventilation, air cooling or air purification, and any floor or ceiling comprised in such systems.	
Lifts, escalators and moving walkways.	
External solar shading.	

Notes

(1)   *Special rate pool* – Expenditure on integral features is included in the special rate pool, but can qualify for the AIA.

(2)   *Repairs* – The cost of repairs are treated as replacements of the integral feature if the expenditure exceeds 50% of the item's replacement cost in a 12 month period (*CAA 2001, s 33B*).

(3)   *Solar panels* – Expenditure on solar panels incurred on or after 1 April 2012 (corporation tax) or 6 April 2012 (income tax) must be included in the special rate pool whether integral or not (*CAA 2001, s 45AA*).

Fixtures

(CAA 2001, Pt 2, Ch 14)

The availability of capital allowances to a purchaser of fixtures on or after 1 April 2012 (for corporation tax) or 6 April 2012 (for income tax) is conditional on either:

(a)   the seller and purchaser using one of two pre-existing procedures (a joint election under *CAA 2001, ss 198–199* or determination by the First-tier Tribunal) to fix the value of the fixtures transferred within two years of the transfer, or

(b)   the past owner providing a written statement of the amount of the disposal value of fixtures which he had some time earlier been required to bring into account.

From April 2016 it is necessary to show that the business expenditure on qualifying fixtures had been pooled before a subsequent transfer on to another person *(CAA 2001, s 187A)*.

SHORT-LIFE ASSETS

Expenditure incurred	Period of short life
From April 2011	8 years
Before April 2011	4 years

Notes

(1)   *Why* – Where an asset is expected to have a short useful life the business can elect for the asset to be allocated to a single asset pool, so its value is not pooled with other assets. This ensures the full value of the asset is relieved for tax purposes over its useful life *(CAA 2001, s 83)*.

(2)   *Excluded assets* – Cars, ships, leased assets, and assets restricted to the special rate pool are all excluded from being treated as short life assets *(CAA 2001, s 84)*.

OTHER ALLOWANCES

(CAA 2001, ss 298–306, Pts 3A, 4A, 5–10)

Allowances	Date of expenditure	Initial allowance	Writing down allowance
Business premises renovation	From 11 April 2007 to 31 March 2017 or 5 April 2017	100%	25% (Notes 1, 2)
Dredging	From 1 April 1986	–	4% (Note 1)
Enterprise zones	Expenditure on industrial or commercial buildings if: (a) incurred within 10 years of site being included within the enterprise zone; or	100%	25% (Notes 1, 3)

continued

Allowances	Date of expenditure	Initial allowance	Writing down allowance
	(b) contracted within that 10-year period and incurred within 20 years after site being included in the zone.		
Know-how	From 1 April 1986	–	25% (Note 4)
Mineral extraction: acquisition of mineral asset	From 1 April 1986	–	10%
Mineral extraction: other expenditure	From 1 April 1986	–	25%
Patents	From 1 April 1986	–	25% (Note 4)
Research and development	From 5 November 1962	100%	

Notes

(1) *WDAs on straight line* – These WDAs are given on a 'straight line' basis rather than a 'reducing balance' basis.

(2) *Business Property Renovation Allowance (BPRA)* – From April 2014 the categories of expenditure that may qualify for BPRA are strictly defined (*CAA 2001, Pt 3A*).

(3) *Enterprise Zones* – Allowances for industrial and commercial buildings in 'old' ten-year enterprise zones were abolished with effect from 1 April 2011 (corporation tax) and 6 April 2011 (income tax) (*FA 2008, s 84*).

See **Enterprise Zones** as to 100% enhanced capital allowances in relation to designated assisted areas within enterprise zones.

(4) *Patents and know-how* – Replaced for most corporation tax purposes by the intangible assets regime with effect from 1 April 2002, but the allowances still apply for income tax.

TIME LIMITS FOR ELECTIONS AND CLAIMS

(FA 1998, Sch 18, Part IX; CAA 2001, ss 3, 85(2), 198, 201, 260(6), 266, 569–570)

Claim	Time Limit
Capital allowances: general (*CAA 2001, s 3; FA 1998, Sch 18, Part IX*)	Later of: • 12 months after the filing date for the return in respect of the tax year or accounting period to which the claim relates; • 30 days after a closure notice issued on completion of an enquiry;

Claim	Time Limit
	• 30 days after notice of amendment to a return issued following completion of an enquiry; or
	• 30 days after the determination of any appeal against an HMRC amendment.
'Short life' asset election (income tax) *(CAA 2001, s 85(2))*	12 months from 31 January next following the tax year in which the relevant chargeable period ends (ie generally the chargeable period in which the qualifying expenditure was incurred)
'Short life' asset election (corporation tax) *(CAA 2001, s 85(2))*	2 years from the end of the relevant chargeable period (ie generally the chargeable period in which the qualifying expenditure was incurred)
Purchase of interest in land that includes a fixture – election to fix apportionment of disposal proceeds *(CAA 2001, ss 198, 201)*	2 years from the date of purchase
Lease of interest in land that includes a fixture – election to fix apportionment of disposal proceeds *(CAA 2001, ss 199, 201)*	2 years from the date the lease is granted
Set-off of capital allowances on special leasing (corporation tax) *(CAA 2001, s 260(6))*	2 years from end of accounting period
Business successions – transfers between connected parties of plant and machinery at tax written down value *(CAA 2001, s 266)*	2 years from the date on which the succession took place
Connected parties and controlled sales treated as being at market value: election for sale to be treated as being for an alternative amount *(CAA 2001, s 570(5))*	2 years from the date of sale

Notes

(1) *Claims in return* – Capital allowances must generally be claimed in the tax return or as an amendment to the return *(CAA 2001, s 3(2))*.

(2) *Exceptions* – The following capital allowance claims may be made outside the tax return *(CAA 2001, s 3(4), (5))*:

   • Special leasing plant and machinery allowances; and

   • Patent allowances on non-trading expenditure (in income tax cases).

ENTERPRISE ZONES

(CA 2001, ss 45K–45N; SI 2018/485)

EZ location	EZ name	FYAs*
Anglesey (Wales)	Anglesey	N
Basingstoke & Deane, East Hampshire & Runnymede	Enterprise M3	Y
Birmingham (England)	Birmingham Curzon street	N
Black Country (England)	Black Country	Y
Buckinghamshire (England)	Aylesbury Vale	N
Cambridge (England)	Alconbury Enterprise Campus	N
Cambridge (England)	Cambridge Compass	N
Cardiff (Wales)	Central Cardiff	N
Cardiff (Wales)	Cardiff Airport and St. Athan	N
Cheshire & Warrington	Cheshire Science Corridor	Y
Cumbria	Carlisle Kingmoor Park	Y
Cornwall & Isles of Scilly (England)	Aerohub	Y
Derby & Nottingham	Nottingham and Derby	Y
Deeside (Wales)	Deeside	Y
Dorset	Dorset Green	N
Dundee (Scotland)	Dundee Claverhouse (Dundee City)	Y
Dundee (Scotland)	Dundee Port (Dundee City)	Y
Ebbw Vale (Wales)	Ebbw Vale	Y
Harlow (England)	Harlow	N
Haven Waterway (Wales)	Haven Waterway	Y
Hereford (England)	Hereford	N
Hertfordshire	Enviro-tech	N
Humber (England)	Humber	Y
Irvine (Scotland)	Irvine (N. Ayrshire)	Y
Kent (England)	Discovery Park	N
Samlesbury & Warton (England)	Lancashire	N
Lancashire	Blackpool Airport	Y
Leeds (England)	Leeds City region	Y
Leeds region	M62 Corridor	N
Leicester (England)	MIRA Technology Park	N
Liverpool (England)	Sci-Tech Daresbury	N
Liverpool (England)	Mersey Waters	N
London (England)	Royal Docks	N
Luton	Luton Airport	Y
Manchester (England)	Greater Manchester Life Science	N
Nigg (Scotland)	Nigg (Highland)	Y
Norfolk and Suffolk (England)	Great Yarmouth and Lowestoft	N

EZ location	EZ name	FYAs*
Northampton (England)	Northampton Waterside	N
Northern Ireland	Coleraine	Y
North East (England)	North East	Y
North West (England)	Hillhouse International	Y
Nottingham (England)	Nottingham	Y
Oxfordshire (England)	Science Vale UK	N
Oxfordshire	Didcot Growth Accelerator	N
Port Talbot (Wales)	Port Talbot	Y
Sheffield (England)	Sheffield City Region	Y
Snowdonia (Wales)	Snowdonia	N
South West England	Heart of South west	N
Stoke and Staffordshire	Ceramic Valley	Y
Gosport, Hampshire (England)	Solent	N
Tees Valley (England)	Tees Valley	Y
West of England	Bristol Temple Quarter & Bath & Somer valley	N
Yorkshire	York Central	N

*The FYAs may be restricted to designated areas within the Enterprise Zones.

Notes

(1) *Available to* – 100% FYAs are available to companies (not unincorporated businesses) for the cost of new and unused plant or machinery used primarily in designated assisted areas within Enterprise Zones. The expenditure must be incurred for the purposes of a qualifying activity, and must be new investment rather than replacement assets and not exceed £125 million for the investment project.

(2) *Limited period* – The relief is available for expenditure incurred in all enterprise zones on or before 31 March 2021, and otherwise in an 8 year period starting from the date the area is designated as an assisted area, as defined by the *Assisted Areas Orders 2014* and *2016, SI 2014/1508* and *SI 2016/751* (*CAA 2001, s 45K*). This legislative change took effect from April 2020 (*SI 2020/260*).

(3) *Exclusions* – Expenditure does not qualify for 100% FYAs if it is made by a firm in difficulty or in certain industrial sectors, incurred on means of transport or subject to grant finance (*CAA 2001, s 45M*).

(4) *Further information*:

- maps of English enterprise zones offering 100% FYA: tinyurl.com/EngEZFYA
- Wales: tinyurl.com/WalesEZ
- Scotland: tinyurl.com/ScotEZ
- Northern Ireland: tinyurl.com/NIrEZ

Stamp Taxes

STAMP DUTY LAND TAX (SDLT)

Residential property

(FA 2003, s 55; SDLTA 2015, SDLT(TR)A 2020)

Property value	From 1 October 2021 (notes 4, 6)		1 July 2021 to 30 September 2021 (notes 4, 5)		8 July 2020 to 30 June 2021 (notes 4, 5)	
	Main rates %	Higher rates %	Main rates %	Higher rates %	Main rates %	Higher rates %
Up to £125,000	0	3	0	3	0	3
£125,001–£250,000	2	5	0	3	0	3
£250,001–£500,000	5	8	5	8	0	3
£500,001–£925,000	5	8	5	8	5	8
£925,001–£1,500,000	10	13	10	13	10	13
Over £1,500,000	12	15	12	15	12	15

Notes

(1) *Calculation of duty* – SDLT is calculated as a percentage of the chargeable consideration (normally the purchase price) which lies in the appropriate band *(FA 2003, s 55(1B))*.

(2) *Location* – SDLT applies to property located in England and Northern Ireland, see **Chapter 18** for taxes relevant to purchases of property located in Scotland or Wales.

(3) *Main rates* – Apply to completions from 4 December 2014, *(SDLTA 2015, s 2)*.

(4) *Higher rates* – Apply to completions from 1 April 2016 where the conditions in note 7 apply. If contracts were agreed before 26 November 2015 and completed on or after 1 April 2016, the higher rates don't apply as long as the contract was not altered or assigned, see: tinyurl.com/asdlt3-rt *(FA 2003, Sch 4ZA)*.

(5) *Temporary rates* – Apply to completions in the period 8 July 2020 to 30 June 2021 inclusive *(Stamp Duty Land Tax (Temporary Relief) Act 2020)*. Different reduced rates apply from 1 July 2021 to 30 September 2021.

(6) *Reversion of rates* – From 1 October 2021, the SDLT rates and thresholds return to those that were in place before 8 July 2020.

(7) *Additional home* – Where the purchaser owns an interest in two or more homes at the end of the day of the transaction, and the property is not a replacement for their main home, the 3% supplement applies. A purchase by a company of a residential freehold for £40,000 or more, or leasehold with more than 21 years to run, is always subject to the higher rates. Separate rules apply to trustee purchasers.

(8) *Payment* – For completions on and after 1 March 2019 the SDLT must be paid within 14 days.

(9) *Refunds* – Where the higher rate has been paid a refund can be claimed if the previous home is disposed of within three years of acquiring the new home. If that sale has been delayed by coronavirus or other reasons outside the seller's control, that three-year period can be extended. The refund must be reclaimed within 12 months of the sale of the previous main residence, or within 12 months of the filing date of the return relating to the new residence, whichever is later (*FA 2019, s 44*).

(10) *First-time buyers* – From 22 November 2017 all purchasers must have never owned an interest in a residential property to qualify. SDLT on the first £300,000 is charged at 0%, if the total purchase price does not exceed £500,000. Also applies to buyers of shared ownership properties with effect for purchases from 22 November 2017 (*FA 2019, s 42; FA 2018, s 41*).

(11) *Mixed property* – Where the transaction consists of a mixture of residential and non-residential property the whole consideration is taxed as non-residential, see rates below.

(12) *Multiple dwellings* – Relief can be claimed for transactions which include the acquisition of interests in more than one dwelling. The rate of SDLT is determined by reference to the consideration divided by the number of dwellings, but subject to a minimum rate of 1%. Also a purchase in a single transaction of six or more dwellings is regarded as non-residential (*FA 2015, s 69; FA 2003, s 58D, Sch 6B*).

(13) *Flat rate* – SDLT is due at 15% on the entire consideration where a residential property is purchased by a non-natural person (corporate, mixed partnership or collective investment structure) for over £500,000, unless one of the exemptions in *FA 2003, Sch 4A* applies (*FA 2014, s 111*). There is no equivalent flat rate for LBTT or LTT.

(14) *Non-resident surcharge* – From 1 April 2021 purchasers who are not resident in the UK at the date of the transaction pay an additional 2% SDLT surcharge on the entire freehold or lease value of UK residential property, including on top of the flat 15% rate (*Finance Bill 2021, Sch 16 para 6*).

Non-residential or mixed property

(*FA 2003, s 55, Sch 5*)

Property value	Rates from 17 March 2016 %
Up to £150,000	0
£150,001–£250,000	2
Over £250,000	5

Notes

(1)   *Calculation of duty* – SDLT is calculated as a percentage of the amount of relevant consideration which lies in the appropriate band. Eg, a single purchase for over £250,000 will have portions of the consideration taxed at each of the three rates of SDLT (*FA 2003, s 55(1B)*).

(2)   *VAT inclusive* – Where VAT is due on disposal, SDLT is charged on the VAT inclusive price, as VAT is part of consideration (*VATA 1994, s 19*).

(3)   *Charities* – Exemption from SDLT applies to purchases by charities and where the property is intended to be held for charitable purposes (*FA 2003, Sch 8*).

(4)   *Penalties and interest* – See **Chapter 17**.

(5)   *Freeports* – *Finance Bill 2021* introduces SDLT relief for purchases of land and buildings within a Freeport tax site, subject to a 'control period' of up to three years and the land being acquired and used in a 'qualifying manner'. The relief applies to qualifying transactions with an effective date from the date the Freeport tax sites are designated until 30 September 2026 (*Finance Bill 2021, cl 111*).

Lease rentals

(FA 2003, s 56, Sch 5)

Effective Date	Residential property NPV of rents	Non-residential or mixed property NPV of rents	Rate %
From 1 July 2021 to 30 September 2021 (note 3)	Up to £250,000	Up to £150,000	0
	Over £250,000	£150,001 to £5m	1
	N/A	Over £5m	2
From 8 July 2020 to 30 June 2021	Up to £500,000	Up to £150,000	0
	Over £500,000	£150,001 to £5m	1
	N/A	Over £5m	2
From 17 March 2016	Up to £125,000	Up to £150,000	0
	Over £125,000	£150,001 to £5m	1
	N/A	Over £5m	2

Notes

(1)   *Calculation* – Where the chargeable consideration includes rent, SDLT is payable on the lease premium and on the 'net present value' (NPV) of the rent payable. SDLT calculators are available to work out the tax due for both leasehold and freehold transactions: tinyurl.com/SDLTCLT.

(2)   *Annual rent* – Where the annual rent for the lease of non-residential property amounts to £1,000 or more, the 0% SDLT band is unavailable in respect of any lease premium (*FA 2003, Sch 5, para 9A*).

(3)   *Reversion of rates* – From 1 October 2021, the temporary rates of SDLT will revert to the standard rates that were in place before 8 July 2020.

STAMP DUTY

(FA 1986, s 67; FA 1999, s 112, Schs 13, 15)

Transfers	Rate
Shares valued at no more than £1,000	Nil
Stocks or shares for more than £1,000	0.5%
Depository receipts	1.5%
Bearer instruments	1.5%

Notes

(1) *Rounding* – Stamp duty is rounded up to the nearest multiple of £5 (*FA 1999, s 112(1)(b)*).

(2) *Fixed duty* – This applies at the rate of £5 for certain instruments effecting land transactions (*FA 2008, Sch 32, para 22*).

(3) *Growth markets* – Stamp duty and SDRT does not apply to transfers of securities in recognised growth markets such as AIM and the ISDX with effect from 28 April 2014 (*FA 2014, Sch 24*).

(4) *Exemptions* – Exempt instruments for transfer of shares valued at no more than £1,000 and which are properly certified, do not need to be presented to HMRC stamping or adjudication.

(5) *Penalties and interest* – See **Chapter 17**.

(6) *Proposal* – Call for evidence on design of a new framework for Stamp Duty and SDRT (*Consultation 21 July 2020*).

(7) *Further information* – See *Stamp Taxes 2020/21* (Bloomsbury Professional).

STAMP DUTY RESERVE TAX (SDRT)

(FA 1986, Pt IV; FA 1999, Sch 19, Pt II)

Charge	Rate
Standard rate *(FA 1986, s 87)*	0.5%
Higher rate *(FA 1986, ss 93, 96)*	1.5%

Notes

(1) *Scope* – SDRT operates alongside the stamp duty charge on transfers of securities which are operated without a paper contract.

(2) *Standard rate* – Applies to transactions in securities (*FA 1986, s 87*).

(3) *Higher rate* – Applies to the transfer of securities into depository receipt schemes and clearance services (*FA 1986, ss 93, 96*).

(4)   *Rounding* – The above charges are rounded up to the nearest penny (*FA 1986, s 99(13)*).

(5)   *Unit trusts and OEICs* – Surrenders by investors of units or shares in unit trusts and open-ended investment companies are exempt from SDRT from 30 March 2014 (*FA 1999, Sch 19, Pt 2*). However, from that date the principal SDRT charge applies to non-pro rata in specie distributions (*FA 2014, s 114*).

VAT

REGISTRATION AND DEREGISTRATION LIMITS

UK taxable supplies

(VATA 1994, Sch 1 paras 1, 4; VAT Notices 700/1 and 700/11)

Effective date	Registration turnover: £	Registration exception: turnover not exceeding £	Deregistration turnover £
1 April 2017 to 31 March 2024	85,000	83,000	83,000
1 April 2016	83,000	81,000	81,000
1 April 2015	82,000	80,000	80,000
1 April 2014	81,000	79,000	79,000
1 April 2013	79,000	77,000	77,000
1 April 2012	77,000	75,000	75,000

Notes

(1) *Freezing of thresholds* – The VAT registration and deregistration thresholds will be frozen until 31 March 2024 (*Budget, 3 March 2021*).

(2) *'Turnover'* – Includes all taxable and zero-rated sales. It doesn't inlcude supplies that are exempt, non-business or outside the scope, capital assets, excluding any supplies of land on which the option to tax has been exercised (*VATA 1994, Sch 1, para 1(7)–(9)*).

(3) *Compulsory registration* – A trader becomes liable to be registered if the registration threshold has been exceeded in the last 12 months to date or is expected to be exceeded in the next 30-days, subject to the exception (note 5) (*VATA 1994, Sch 1, para 1*).

(4) *Going concern* – If all or part of a business is transferred as a going concern to a person who isn't VAT registered at the time of transfer, the transferee becomes liable to be registered if: the one-year or 30-day limits above are exceeded, subject to the exception (note 5) (*VATA 1994, Sch 1, para 2*).

(5) *Exception* – The exception threshold is the same as the deregistration limit: £83,000 until 2024. A person does not become liable to be registered under the mandatory (note 3) or the going concern (note 4) rules using the one-year turnover test, if HMRC are satisfied that the value of his taxable supplies in the one-year period

beginning when he would otherwise become liable to be registered doesn't exceed the exception threshold (*VATA 1994, Sch 1, para 3*).

(6)   *Non-UK established businesses* – From 1 January 2021, overseas sellers must register for UK VAT if they directly sell goods into Great Britain (GB) from abroad, or into Northern Ireland from outside GB and the EU, where the shipment value of the goods is £135 or less. From 1 December 2012, businesses without a UK establishment who make any UK taxable supplies must register for UK VAT, regardless of the value of taxable supplies they make in the UK (*VATA 1994, Sch 1A*).

(7)   *Deregistration* – The turnover threshold applies to the value of taxable supplies in the next 12 months.

(8)   *Voluntary deregistration* – A business can ask HMRC to cancel its VAT registration if its annual VAT taxable turnover falls, or is expected to fall in the next 12 months, below the deregistration threshold. Registration can't be cancelled if the reduction in turnover is due to the intention of the business to stop or suspend trading for 30 days or more in the next 12 months (VAT Notice 700/11, para 2.2).

(9)   *Compulsory deregistration* – A business which is registered due to making taxable supplies in the UK must cancel the registration in certain circumstances, eg ceasing to make taxable supplies, or if the business intended to make taxable supplies but no longer intends doing so (VAT Notice 700/11, para 2.1).

(10) *Making Tax Digital* – All VAT-registered businesses will have to submit VAT returns using MTD-compliant software for VAT periods beginning on and after 1 April 2022, those with turnover above the VAT registration limits are already mandated into MTD (see **Chapter 6**).

(11) *Payment deferral* – Businesses who deferred VAT payments payable between 20 March 2020 and 30 June 2020, must either pay the deferred VAT in full by 31 March 2021, or enter an agreement to pay by monthly instalments up to January 2022. No interest or default surcharges will be raised on late payment of deferred VAT paid within these deadlines (see: https://tinyurl.com/VATdfpp122).

RATES AND FRACTIONS

(VATA 1994, s 2(1))

Effective date	Standard rate %	Reduced rate %	VAT fraction
1 October 2021		12.5%	1/9
15 July 2020		5%	1/21
4 January 2011	20.0		1/6
1 January 2010	17.5		7/47
1 December 2008	15.0		3/23
1 April 1991	17.5		7/47

Notes

(1)   *VAT Fraction* – This is used to calculate the VAT element of VAT-inclusive goods and services at the appropriate rate.

(2) *5% rate* – Applies for certain supplies and acquisitions, in particular in hospitality sector on a temporary basis (*VATA 1994, s 29A, Sch 7A*), see **Reduced Rate Supplies** below.

(3) *12.5% rate* – Applies for certain supplies in hospitality and food sectors on a temporary basis (*VATA 1994, s 29A, Sch 7A*), see **Reduced Rate Supplies** below.

(4) *Penalties and interest* – See **Chapter 17**.

ZERO-RATED SUPPLIES

(*VATA 1994, Sch 8*)

Group Number	Subject matter
1	Food (note 1)
2	Sewerage services and water
3	Books, etc (note 2)
4	Talking books for the blind and handicapped and wireless sets for the blind
5	Construction of buildings, etc
6	Protected buildings
7	International services
8	Transport (note 3)
9	Caravans and houseboats (note 4)
10	Gold
11	Bank notes
12	Drugs, medicines, aids for the handicapped, etc
13	Imports, exports etc
15	Charities etc
16	Clothing and footwear for children and babies
18	Goods supplied to European Research Infrastructure Consortium
19	Womens sanitary products (note 5)
20	Personal protective equipment: *SI 2020/698* (note 6)
21	Online marketplaces (deemed supplies)

Notes

(1) *Hot food and sports drinks* – From 1 October 2012, standard rate VAT is imposed for hot food and sports drinks (if it didn't already apply). Baked hot products which are allowed to cool naturally on the premises are zero rated. A temporary 5% rate applies to food supplied in the course of catering see **Reduced Rate Supplies** below (see VAT Notices 701/14 and 709/1).

(2) *Books, etc* – From 1 May 2020 electronic publications are subject to zero-rating, with exceptions for publications which are predominately audio or video which remain standard rated (*SI 2020/459*).

(3) *'Qualifying aircraft'* – From 1 January 2011, zero-rating applies to supplies of aircraft used by an airline operating for reward chiefly on international routes (*VATA 1994, Sch 8, Group 8, Note A1(b)*).

(4) *Caravans* – From 6 April 2013, the rate of VAT applied to supplies of holiday caravans depends on the size of the caravan (over/under 7 metres) and whether it complies with standard BS 3632 (see VAT Notice 701/20).

(5) *Women's sanitary products* – From 1 January 2021 products designed to absorb or collect menstrual flow are zero-rated, incontinence products or any form of clothing are not included *(FA 2016, s 126(4))*.

(6) *PPE* – From 1 May 2020 to 31 October 2020 inclusive, supplies of personal protective equipment as defined by Public Health England are zero-rated (see VAT Notice 701/57, para 3.5).

REDUCED RATE SUPPLIES

(VATA 1994, Sch 7A)

Group Number	Subject matter
1	Supplies of domestic fuel or power
2	Installation of energy-saving materials (note 2)
3	Grant-funded installation of heating equipment or security goods or connection of gas supply.
4	Women's sanitary products (note 4)
5	Children's car seats (note 3)
6	Residential conversions
7	Residential renovations and alterations
8	Contraceptive products (from 1 July 2006: *SI 2006/1472*)
9	Welfare advice or information (from 1 July 2006: *SI 2006/1472*)
10	Installation of mobility aids for the elderly (from 1 July 2007: *SI 2007/1601*)
11	Smoking cessation products (from 1 July 2008: *SI 2008/1410*)
12	Caravans (from 6 April 2013)
13	Cable-suspended passenger transport systems (from 1 April 2013)
14	Food and drink in the course of catering (note 5)
15	Holiday accommodation, hotels and campsites (note 6)
16	Tourist attractions and certain entertainments (note 7)

Notes

(1) *Effective* – Reduced VAT rate (5%) applies with effect for certain supplies made, and acquisitions taking place, after 31 October 2001, or from the dates indicated, and for a temporary basis for groups 14,15 and 16 *(VATA 1994, s 29A)*.

(2) *Installation of energy-saving materials* – From 1 August 2013, buildings solely used for a relevant charitable purpose are removed from the scope of the reduced rate of VAT for the installation of energy-saving materials *(VATA 1994, Sch 7A, Pt 2, group 2,* see VAT Notice 708/6).

(3) *Children's car seats* – Extended to related base units from 1 July 2009 *(SI 2009/1359)*.

(4)   *Women's sanitary products* – From 1 January 2021 these products will be zero-rated, but until then the products carry VAT at 5% (*Budget OOTLAR para 2.23, 11 March 2020*).

(5)   *Food served and takeaways* – From 15 July 2020 to 30 September 2021 food and non-alcoholic drink served in cafés, restuarants, pubs and hot takeaway food and hot takeaway drinks (non-alcoholic) are subject to VAT at 5% (*SI 2020/728*, VAT Notice 709/1, VAT Notice 701/14). From 1 October 2021 to 31 March 2022 these supplies are subject to VAT at 12.5% (*Budget 3 March 2021*, https://tinyurl.com/VATrdr125).

(6)   *Hotels and holiday accommodation* – From 15 July 2020 to 30 September 2021 VAT is applied at 5% (*SI 2020/728*, VAT Notice 709/3). From 1 October 2021 to 31 March 2022 these supplies are subject to VAT at 12.5% (*Budget 3 March 2021*, https://tinyurl.com/VATrdr125).

(7)   *Tourist attractions and events* – From 15 July 2020 to 30 September 2021 VAT is applied at 5% to admission charges to: tourist attractions, shows, theatres, circuses, fairs, amusement parks, concerts, museums, zoos, cinemas, exhibitions and similar cultural events but NOT to sporting events (*SI 2020/728*, see tinyurl.com/VATgdadsh). From 1 October 2021 to 31 March 2022 these supplies are subject to VAT at 12.5% (*Budget 3 March 2021*, https://tinyurl.com/VATrdr125).

EXEMPT SUPPLIES

(*VATA 1994, Sch 9*)

Group Number	Subject matter
1	Land (note 5)
2	Insurance
3	Postal services (note 1)
4	Betting, gaming and lotteries
5	Finance
6	Education
7	Health and welfare
8	Burial and cremation
9	Subscriptions to trade unions, professional and other public interest bodies
10	Sport, sports competitions and physical education
11	Works of art etc
12	Fund-raising events by charities and other qualifying bodies
13	Cultural services etc (from 1 June 1996: *SI 1996/1256*)
14	Supplies of goods where input tax cannot be recovered (from 1 March 2000: *SI 1999/2833*)
15	Investment gold (from 1 January 2000: *SI 1999/3116*)
16	Supplies of services by groups involving cost sharing

Notes

(1)   *Postal services* – From 31 January 2011 postal services are supplies of public postal services and incidental goods made by a universal service provider (ie the Royal Mail) (*F(No 3)A 2010, s 22*).

(2)   *Cost sharing* – Exempts from VAT the supply of services by a group which consists of persons engaged in exempt or non-taxable activities so long as the services are supplied to group members at cost and for the purposes of those activities. The exemption aims to reduce a barrier that might otherwise prevent businesses and organisations that have exempt and/or non-business activities for VAT purposes from joining with others to share costs.

(3)   *Supplies by public bodies* – Government departments, local authorities and analogous institutions are not generally subject to VAT when making supplies of goods or services (*VATA 1994, s 41A*).

(4)   *Small packages* – Small non-commercial consignments can be sent into the UK from outside the UK or outside GB, or the EU into Northern Ireland, without VAT applied if the value of the goods does not exceed £39 (*SI 2016/1199*).

(5)   *Land* – There are many exceptions to this exemption, so VAT on the supply of land or buildings can apply at any rate of VAT (see VAT notice 742). For example the hire of hairdressers' chairs is standard rated, as are self-storage facilities (see VAT information sheet 10/13).

SUPPLIES BETWEEN EU MEMBER STATES

Supplies into Northern Ireland (distance selling)

(*VATA 1994, Sch 2;* VAT Notice 700/1, section 5, Notice 700/11, section 3)

Effective date	Registration threshold for goods £
1 January 1993	70,000

Notes

(1)   *Brexit* – Distance selling is no longer relevant to trading in Great Britain since 1 January 2021, but it remains relevant for traders in Northern Ireland.

(2)   *Goods only* – A taxable person in Northern Ireland or an EU state which supplies and delivers goods to non-VAT registered customers in the Northern Ireland or an EU member state (other than its own state), broadly becomes liable to register in that EU country if in a calender year the value of its relevant supplies exceeds the above limit.

(3)   *Excise goods* – Special rules apply to the sale of excise goods (eg alcohol and tobacco) sold in the UK (see VAT Notice 700/1, section 6.6).

(4)   *Cancel registration* – If the business was registered because it exceeded the distance sales threshold, it may apply to cancel its registration when:

    (a)   the value of its distance sales in the year ending 31 December did not exceed the threshold; and

(b)   the value of its distance sales in the year following, beginning 1 January, will not exceed the threshold.

(5)   *Compulsory deregistration* – The registration must be cancelled if either the business ceases to make distance sales, or if the business intended to make distance sales but no longer intends to do so and is not eligible or liable for registration as a result of any taxable supplies, acquisitions or relevant supplies (VAT Notice 700/11, para 3.1).

(6)   *Voluntary deregistration* – If the business was registered because the UK was the place of supply for its distance sales, and had made supplies, the business remains registered in the UK for at least two calendar years from the date of first supply following registration. However, if the business opted but did not start to make supplies, the business may apply for cancellation of registration (VAT Notice 700/11, para 3.2).

Digital services supplied to EU states

Transactions in:	Registration threshold for digital services £
2021 and later	Nil
2019 to 2020	8,818
2015 to 2018	Nil

(1)   *Digital services* – Traders who sell, broadcasting, telecoms or electronic services (BTE), to non-business customers in EU countries (B2C sales) must charge VAT at the rate applicable for the service in the country where the customer belongs (see **EU VAT Rates** below). The trader must either register for VAT in the country where the customer belongs or use the VAT Mini One Stop Shop (VAT MOSS) to comply with the EU VAT regulations and pay the VAT due.

(2)   *Thresholds* – If the annual supplies of digitial services, as defined in note (1), are less than the turnover thresholds given above, in the previous calendar year and expected to be so in the current year, the trader does not have to register for VAT MOSS.

(3)   *Exiting the EU* – The UK is not a member of the EU so UK traders can no longer use the EU MOSS, and cannot take advantage of the de-minimis registration threshold (*SI 2018/1194*).

(4)   *Non-Union MOSS* – From 1 January 2021 UK traders must use the non-Union MOSS, and must register for VAT in an EU country to be able to use that scheme. This registration must be made within 10 days of the end of the month in which sales of BTE services to EU consumers are first made in 2021 or later.

(5)   *EU-MOSS registration* – Before 2021 a UK trader had to be registered for VAT in the UK in order to register to use the EU MOSS. However, where the business turnover was under the UK VAT registration threshold the trader could register for VAT and EU-MOSS in one go and was NOT required to charge VAT to its UK customers until its UK turnover reaches the VAT registration threshold.

(6)   *VAT MOSS returns* – These must be submitted online by 20th of the month following the end of the calendar quarter; 20 April, 20 July, 20 October and 20 January. The VAT

due must be paid by the same date by electronic means, but not by direct debit. The deferral of VAT payments due in the period 20 March to 30 June 2020 does not apply to VAT due under VAT MOSS.

(7)   *Further information* – See **Place of Supply of Services** below and HMRC guidance at: tinyurl.com/VTMSS.

Acquisitions from EU member states

(*VATA 1994, Sch 3;* VAT Notice 700/1, Section 6; Notice 700/11, section 4.2)

Effective date	Registration threshold £
1 January 2021	85,000 (note 1)
1 April 2017	85,000
1 April 2016	83,000
1 April 2015	82,000
1 April 2014	81,000
1 April 2013	79,000
1 April 2012	77,000

Notes

(1)   *Threshold* – The registration threshold for relevant acquisitions from other EU Member States will remain at £85,000 until 31 March 2024 but will only be relevant for supplies of goods into Northern Ireland (*Budget, 3 March 2021*).

(2)   *No intended supply* – Where an unregistered business or organisation, which does not make or intend to make any taxable supplies in Northern Ireland, buys goods from a VAT registered supplier in another EU state to bring to Northern Ireland, these are known as relevant acquisitions. This would typically apply to a business making exempt supplies only or using the goods to make non-business supplies only.

(3)   *Annual measure* – The business must register for VAT where the value of relevant acquisitions exceeds the registration limit in the calendar year to 31 December, or if there are reasonable grounds for believing that the value of relevant acquisitions will exceed the registration limit in the next 30 days.

(4)   *Cancel registration* – The business may apply to cancel its registration where:

(a)   the value of its relevant acquisitions in the year ending 31 December did not exceed the threshold; and

(b)   the value of its relevant acquisitions in the year following, beginning 1 January, will not exceed the threshold.

(5)   *Compulsory deregistration* – The registration must be cancelled if the business ceases to make relevant acquisitions, or if the business intended to make relevant acquisitions but no longer intends doing so and is not eligible or liable for registration as a result of any taxable supplies, distance sales or relevant supplies (VAT Notice 700/11, para 4.1).

(6)   *Voluntary deregistration* – Where the value of relevant acquisitions in the year ending 31 December did not exceed the threshold, and the value of relevant acquisitions in the following year will not exceed the threshold. However, a business which voluntarily registered for relevant acquisitions will remain registered in the UK for at least two calendar years unless entitlement to be registered has ceased (VAT Notice 700/11, para 4.2).

ANNUAL ACCOUNTING SCHEME

(*VAT Regulations 1995, SI 1995/2518, regs 49–55*; VAT Notice 732)

Effective date	Joining threshold £	Leaving threshold £
1 April 2006	1,350,000	1,600,000

Notes

(1)   *Joining threshold* – A business can use this scheme if its estimated taxable supplies for the coming year are not expected to exceed the joining threshold, subject to certain other criteria (see *SI 1995/2518, reg 52;* VAT Notice 732, paras 2.1 and 2.6).

(2)   *Leaving threshold* – A business must leave the scheme if at the end of the current accounting year (or transitional accounting period) the value of taxable supplies in that year (or period) exceeds the leaving threshold (*SI 1995/2518, reg 53*).

(3)   *MTD regime* – Businesses which use the annual accounting scheme had their date for joining the MTD regime deferred until the first VAT period that began on or after 1 October 2019 (see **Chapter 6**).

CASH ACCOUNTING SCHEME

(*SI 1995/2518, regs 56–65*; VAT Notice 731)

Effective date	Joining threshold £	Leaving threshold £
1 April 2007	1,350,000	1,600,000

Notes

(1)   *Joining threshold* – A business can use the scheme if estimated taxable supplies in the next year are not expected to exceed the joining threshold, and subject to certain other criteria (see *SI 1995/2518, reg 58*; VAT Notice 731, para 2.1).

(2)   *Leaving threshold* – A business must leave the scheme if the value of taxable supplies for a 12-month period (ending at the end of a tax period) has exceeded the leaving threshold (*SI 1995/2518, reg 60*; VAT Notice 731, para 6.2).

(3)   *'One-off' sales increases* – A business may remain on cash accounting where it exceeds the leaving threshold because of a one-off increase in sales resulting from a genuine commercial activity, provided there are reasonable grounds for believing that the value of its taxable supplies in the next 12 months will be below the joining threshold (see VAT Notice 731, para 2.6).

FLAT-RATE SCHEME FOR SMALL BUSINESSES

(SI 1995/2518, regs 55A–55V; VAT Notice 733)

Category of business	From 15 July 2020 to 30 September 2021 %	From 1 April 2017 %
Limited cost trader (note 6)	16.5	16.5
Accountancy or book-keeping	14.5	14.5
Advertising	11.0	11.0
Agricultural services	11.0	11.0
Any other activity not listed elsewhere	12.0	12.0
Architect, civil and structural engineer or surveyor	14.5	14.5
Boarding or care of animals	12.0	12.0
Business services that are not listed elsewhere	12.0	12.0
Catering services including restaurants and takeaways	4.5	12.5
Computer and IT consultancy or data processing	14.5	14.5
Computer repair services	10.5	10.5
Dealing in waste or scrap	10.5	10.5
Entertainment or journalism	12.5	12.5
Estate agency or property management services	12.0	12.0
Farming or agriculture that is not listed elsewhere	6.5	6.5
Film, radio, television or video production	13.0	13.0
Financial services	13.5	13.5
Forestry or fishing	10.5	10.5
General building or construction services*	9.5	9.5
Hairdressing or other beauty treatment services	13.0	13.0
Hiring or renting goods	9.5	9.5
Hotel or accommodation	0	10.5
Investigation or security	12.0	12.0
Labour-only building or construction services (note 4)	14.5	14.5
Laundry or dry-cleaning services	12.0	12.0
Lawyer or legal services	14.5	14.5
Library, archive, museum or other cultural activity	9.5	9.5
Management consultancy	14.0	14.0
Manufacturing fabricated metal products	10.5	10.5
Manufacturing food	9.0	9.0
Manufacturing that is not listed elsewhere	9.5	9.5
Manufacturing yarn, textiles or clothing	9.0	9.0
Membership organisation	8.0	8.0
Mining or quarrying	10.0	10.0

Category of business	From 15 July 2020 to 30 September 2021 %	From 1 April 2017 %
Packaging	9.0	9.0
Photography	11.0	11.0
Post offices	5.0	5.0
Printing	8.5	8.5
Publishing	11.0	11.0
Pubs	1	6.5
Real estate activity not listed elsewhere	14.0	14.0
Repairing personal or household goods	10.0	10.0
Repairing vehicles	8.5	8.5
Retailing food, confectionery, tobacco, newspapers or children's clothing	4.0	4.0
Retailing pharmaceuticals, medical goods, cosmetics or toiletries	8.0	8.0
Retailing that is not listed elsewhere	7.5	7.5
Retailing vehicles or fuel	6.5	6.5
Secretarial services	13.0	13.0
Social work	11.0	11.0
Sport or recreation	8.5	8.5
Transport or storage, including couriers, freight, removals and taxis	10.0	10.0
Travel agency	10.5	10.5
Veterinary medicine	11.0	11.0
Wholesaling agricultural products	8.0	8.0
Wholesaling food	7.5	7.5
Wholesaling that is not listed elsewhere	8.5	8.5

Notes

(1) *Eligibility* – The flat-rate scheme is open to businesses who expect their taxable supplies (excluding exempt and outside the scope supplies) in the next year to be no more than £150,000 **excluding VAT** (VAT Notice 733, para 3.1). Admission to the scheme is also subject to certain other criteria (see *SI 1995/2518, reg 55L;* VAT Notice 733, para 3.6).

(2) *Withdrawal* – The business must leave the scheme when its annual flat rate turnover (excluding sales of capital assets but including all exempt and outside the scope income) exceeds £230,000 **including VAT** on the anniversary date of when it first joined the scheme. The business must also leave the scheme if its total turnover in the next 30 days alone can reasonably be expected to exceed £230,000 including VAT. A business may leave the scheme voluntarily on giving notice and when it becomes ineligible for other reasons. For the effective date of leaving the scheme see VAT Notice 733 para 12.2 (*SI 1995/2518, reg 55M*).

(3)   *Discount* – A business is entitled to a 1% discount on the normal flat rate percentage until the day before its first anniversary of becoming VAT registered. This also applies to limited cost traders see note (6) (*SI 1995/2518, reg 55JB*; VAT Notice 733, para 4.7).

(4)   *Labour only* – This means building or construction services where the value of materials supplied is less than 10% of relevant turnover from such services; any other building or construction services are 'general building or construction services'.

(5)   *Which category* – The business should use normal English to describe its activities and pick the category which is the best fit for the majority of its activities. See HMRC flat rate scheme manual paras FRS7200 and FRS7300.

(6)   *Limited cost trader* – From 1 April 2017 where the business has not acquired relevant goods in the VAT period equal to at least 2% of its gross sales, and at least £1,000 per year, it must use 16.5% as its flat rate percentage for that period. 'Relevant goods' excludes:

- goods not used entirely for business purposes;

- capital items of any value;

- motor fuel and parts, unless the business is in the transport sector and owns or leases a vehicle;

- food and drink for consumption by the business owner or staff;

- goods for resale, leasing, letting or hiring out if the main business activity doesn't ordinarily consist of selling, leasing, letting or hiring out such goods;

- goods intended for re-sell or hire out, unless selling or hiring is the main business activity; and

- goods for disposal as promotional items, gifts or donations.

(*SI 1995/2518, reg 55A(4)*; VAT Notice 733, para 4.4–4.6).

(7)   *Temporary reduced rates* – Due to the imposition of the reduced rate of 5% in the hospitality industry from 15 July 2020 to 30 September 2021, the flat rate precentages are reduced for three sectors for that period (*SI 2020/728 reg 6*).

PARTIAL EXEMPTION *DE MINIMIS* LIMITS

(*SI 1995/2518, regs 105A–107*; VAT Notice 706)

Exempt input tax not exceeding:
• £625 per month on average; and
• 50% of total input tax for the period concerned

Notes

(1)   *De-minimis threshold* – Businesses which have both taxable and exempt income can recover all their exempt input tax, provided that amount is below the *de minimis* limits in the table above. The input tax claimed in each tax period is provisional until any under or over recovery of input tax is accounted for in an annual adjustment.

(2)　*Simplified tests* – If the business passes either the original test in the table above or one of the optional tests in notes (3) to (5) below, it may treat itself as *de minimis* and provisionally recover input tax relating to exempt supplies, but it must still check its over/under recovery of input tax on an annual basis and make any annual adjustment as necessary (see *SI 1995/2518, reg 107*; VAT Information Sheet 04/10).

(3)　*Test 1* – Total input tax incurred is no more than £625 per month on average and the value of exempt supplies is no more than 50% of the value of all supplies.

(4)　*Test 2* – Total input tax incurred, less input tax directly attributable to taxable supplies, is no more than £625 per month on average and the value of exempt supplies is no more than 50% of the value of all supplies.

(5)　*Prior year test* – The business may treat itself as *de minimis* throughout a tax year if it was *de minimis* in the previous tax year.

CAPITAL GOODS SCHEME (CGS)

(*SI 1995/2518, Part XV*; VAT Notice 706/2)

Asset	No of intervals in adjustment period
Single items of computer equipment costing £50,000 or more excluding VAT	5
Ships boats and aircraft costing £50,000 or more excluding VAT	5
An interest in land, buildings or civil engineering works costing £250,000 or more excluding VAT	10

Notes

(1)　*Applies to* – Input tax recovered by partially exempt traders and businesses that have business/non-business use on property, computers, aircraft, ships and boats.

(2)　*Land and buildings* – Which includes; the purchase or construction of a building, alterations, constructions of extensions or annexes, refurbishments, and civil engineering works (*SI 1995/2518, reg 113*). Prior to 1 January 2011, building alterations and constructions of extensions or annexes were only included where additional floor space of 10% or more was created by the works.

(3)　*Adjustments* – Input tax is initially recovered under the normal partial exemption rules. Section 7 of VAT Notice 706/2 explains how to make subsequent adjustments under the scheme.

VAT INVOICES

(*SI 1995/2518, reg 14*)

In the UK a VAT invoice must show the following:

●　A sequential number based on one or more series which uniquely identifies the document.

●　The time of the supply.

- The date of the issue of the document.

- The name, address and registration number of the supplier.

- The name and address of the person to whom the goods or services are supplied.

- A description sufficient to identify the goods or services supplied.

- For each description, the quantity of the goods or the extent of the services, and the rate of VAT and the amount payable, excluding VAT, expressed in any currency.

- The gross total amount payable, excluding VAT, expressed in any currency.

- The rate of any cash discount offered.

- The total amount of VAT chargeable, expressed in sterling.

- The unit price.

- Where the VAT invoice includes zero-rated or exempt goods or services, the total of those values separately showing clearly that there is no VAT payable on them.

- Where a margin scheme is applied under *VATA 1994, s 50A* (see Note 3) or *53* (certain supplies made by a tour operator), a relevant reference or any indication that a margin scheme has been applied.

- Where a VAT invoice relates in whole or part to a supply where the reverse charge rules apply, an indication that the customer is liable to pay the tax.

- Where issued by the customer under a self-billing agreement it must say 'Self Billing' on the face of the invoice.

Notes

(1) *Retailers' invoices* – A retailer who makes a sale of goods or services for £250 or less (including VAT) can issue a simplified invoice (where the customer asks for a VAT invoice), if the supply is other than to a person in another member state. The VAT invoice need only contain the following particulars (*SI 1995/2518, reg 16*):

- The name, address and registration number of the retailer;

- The time of the supply;

- A description sufficient to identify the goods or services supplied;

- The total amount payable including VAT; and

- For each rate of VAT chargeable, the gross amount payable including VAT, and the VAT rate applicable.

(2) *Overseas customers* – Where a VAT invoice is provided for a person in another EU member state (see EU VAT rates below), separate requirements apply, unless HMRC allow otherwise (*SI 1995/2518, reg 14(2)*).

(3) *Margin schemes* – VATA 1994, s 50A applies to supplies of works of art, antiques or collectors' items, motor vehicles, second-hand goods, and any supply of goods through a person who acts as an agent, but in his own name, in relation to the supply. An invoice in relation to such supplies must include a relevant reference. Similar provisions apply to certain supplies made by tour operators (*VATA 1994, s 53*).

(4) *Relevant reference* – Examples of relevant references or indications that a margin scheme has been applied are if the invoice includes: 'This invoice is for a second-hand margin scheme supply' or 'This is a tour operators' margin scheme supply' (*SI 1995/2518, reg 14(8)*).

(5) *Electronic invoices* – Invoices sent electronically must include the same information as paper invoices. When an invoice is attached as a document to an email, HMRC recommend using PDF or XML format for the invoice.

(6) *Further information* – HMRC guidance: tinyurl.com/vrkvin.

PRIVATE FUEL SCALE CHARGES

(VATA 1994, ss 56(7), 57)

All the following tables show figures on a VAT-inclusive basis.

Fuel scale charge from 1 May 2020

Description of vehicle: vehicle's CO_2 emissions figure (Note 2)	12-month period £	3-month period £	1-month period £
120 or less	581	144	48
125	870	218	72
130	930	231	76
135	986	246	81
140	1,047	261	87
145	1,103	275	91
150	1,163	290	96
155	1,219	305	101
160	1,279	319	106
165	1,335	334	111
170	1,396	348	115
175	1,452	362	120
180	1,512	377	125
185	1,568	392	130
190	1,628	406	135
195	1,684	421	140
200	1,745	436	144
205	1,801	450	149
210	1,861	464	154
215	1,917	479	159
220	1,977	493	164
225 or more	2,033	508	168

Fuel scale charge from 1 May 2019 to 30 April 2020

Description of vehicle: vehicle's CO_2 emissions figure (Note 2)	12-month period £	3-month period £	1-month period £
120 or less	592	147	49
125	886	222	73
130	947	236	78
135	1,004	250	83
140	1,066	265	88
145	1,123	280	93
150	1,184	295	98
155	1,241	310	103
160	1,303	325	107
165	1,360	340	113
170	1,421	354	117
175	1,478	369	122
180	1,540	384	128
185	1,597	399	132
190	1,658	414	137
195	1,715	429	143
200	1,777	444	147
205	1,834	458	152
210	1,895	473	157
215	1,952	487	162
220	2,014	502	167
225 or more	2,071	517	172

Fuel scale charge from 1 May 2018 to 30 April 2019

Description of vehicle: vehicle's CO_2 emissions figure (but see Note 2 below)	12-month period £	3-month period £	1-month period £
120 or less	562	140	46
125	842	210	70
130	900	224	74
135	954	238	79
140	1,013	252	84
145	1,067	266	88
150	1,125	280	93
155	1,179	295	98
160	1,238	309	102
165	1,292	323	107

Description of vehicle: vehicle's CO_2 emissions figure (but see Note 2 below)	12-month period £	3-month period £	1-month period £
170	1,350	336	111
175	1,404	351	116
180	1,463	365	121
185	1,517	379	125
190	1,575	393	130
195	1,630	407	135
200	1,688	421	140
205	1,742	436	145
210	1,801	449	149
215	1,855	463	154
220	1,913	477	159
225 or more	1,967	491	163

Fuel scale charge from 1 May 2017 to 30 April 2018

Description of vehicle: vehicle's CO_2 emissions figure (but see Note 2 below)	12-month period £	3-month period £	1-month period £
120 or less	563	140	46
125	842	211	70
130	901	224	74
135	955	238	79
140	1,013	252	84
145	1,068	267	88
150	1,126	281	93
155	1,180	295	98
160	1,239	309	102
165	1,293	323	107
170	1,351	337	111
175	1,405	351	116
180	1,464	365	121
185	1,518	379	125
190	1,577	393	131
195	1,631	408	136
200	1,689	422	140
205	1,743	436	145
210	1,802	449	149
215	1,856	463	154
220	1,914	478	159
225 or more	1,969	492	163

Fuel scale charge from 1 May 2016 to 30 April 2017

Description of vehicle: vehicle's CO$_2$ emissions figure (but see Note 2 below)	12-month period £	3-month period £	1-month period £
120 or less	497	116	38
125	699	175	58
130	747	186	61
135	792	197	65
140	841	209	69
145	886	221	73
150	934	233	77
155	979	245	81
160	1,028	256	85
165	1,073	268	89
170	1,121	279	92
175	1,166	291	96
180	1,214	303	101
185	1,259	314	104
190	1,308	326	108
195	1,353	338	112
200	1,401	350	116
205	1,446	362	120
210	1,495	373	123
215	1,540	384	128
220	1,588	396	132
225 or more	1,633	408	135

Notes

(1) *How to use the tables* – If a business pays for any fuel used for private motoring by its owners, directors or employees, it has to pay VAT on the VAT-inclusive fuel scale charge listed above at the rate applicable at the time the charge is due. To calculate standard rate VAT from the VAT inclusive amount, multiply the VAT inclusive scale charge by the appropriate VAT fraction.

(2) *Not for car benefits* – The tables above are not the same as those used to calculate car benefit charge for income tax purposes. See **Chapter 2: Expenses and Benefits** for the latest advisory fuel rates for use by company car drivers. A business can reclaim the VAT element on the amount attributable to fuel of mileage allowances paid to employees or subcontractors.

(3) *Rounding down* – Where the CO$_2$ emissions figure of a vehicle is not a multiple of five, the figure is rounded down to the next multiple of five to determine the level of the charge. For a bi-fuel vehicle which has two CO$_2$ emissions figures, the lower of the two figures should be used. For cars which are too old to have a CO$_2$ emissions

figure, HMRC have prescribed a level of emissions by reference to the vehicle's engine capacity (VAT Notice 700/64, para 9.3).

(4)   *Further information* – For information on fuel scale charges and motor expenses see VAT Notice 700/64 and tinyurl.com/VTFLSCS.

EU VAT RATES FOR CROSS-BORDER SALES

(SI 1995/2518, reg 2)

EU country	Country code	Standard rates %	VAT MOSS rates %	Other reduced rates %	B2C invoice required?
Austria	AT	20	10	13, 5 & 0	No
Belgium	BE	21	6	12 & 0	No
Bulgaria	BG	20	20 (10)	9 & 0	No R
Croatia	HR	25	5	13 & 0	Yes Alt
Cyprus	CY	19	5	9 & 0	Yes
Czech Republic	CZ	21	10	15 & 0	No
Denmark	DK	25	25	0	No
Estonia	EE	20	20	9 & 0	No
Finland	FI	24	10	14 & 0	No
France	FR	20	5.5	10 & 2.1 & 0	No Alt
Germany	DE	19 (16)	7 (5)	0	No
Greece	EL	24	24	6 &13 & 0	No Alt
Hungary	HU	27	27 & 5	18 & 0	No R
Ireland	IE	23 (21)	9	4.8 & 13.5 & 0	No
Italy	IT	22	4	10 & 5 & 0	No
Latvia	LV	21	21	12 & 5 & 0	No R
Lithuania	LT	21	21	5 & 9 &0	No
Luxembourg	LU	17	3	8 & 14 & 0	No
Malta	MT	18	5	7 & 0	No
Netherlands	NL	21	9	0	No
Poland	PL	23	5	8 & 0	No R
Portugal	PT	23	6	13 & 0	No
Romania	RO	19	19	0 & 5 & 9	No Alt
Slovak Republic	SK	20	20	10 & 0	No
Slovenia	SI	22	5	9.5 & 0	Yes
Spain	ES	21	4	10 & 0	Yes
Sweden	SE	25	6	12 & 0	No
United Kingdom	GB	20	0	5 & 0	No

Notes

(1) *Rates* – Electronic services, broadcasting and telecommunications services are generally subject to VAT at the standard rate, but many countries apply lower rates for certain electronic services such as e-books. The UK reduced the rate for electronic publications to zero on 1 May 2020. VAT rates change frequently, check the rates menu on the VATMOSS return page (see tinyurl.com/VATMOSSrts).

(2) *Cyprus* – Those areas under the control of the Government of the Republic of Cyprus and including the UK Sovereign Base Areas of Akrotiri and Dhekelia.

(3) *Italy* – Excludes: Livigno, Campione d'Italia, the Italian waters of Lake Lugano, San Marino, and the Vatican City.

(4) *France* – Includes Monaco but excludes overseas departments: Guadeloupe, Martinique, Reunion, St. Pierre and Miquelon, and French Guiana. Excludes Andorra. Reduced rates apply to digital newspapers: 2.1%.

(5) *Bulgaria* – Rates for educational items such as textbooks and music scores are reduced to those shown in brackets from 1 July 2020 to 31 December 2021.

(6) *Germany* – Excludes Büsingen and the Isle of Heligoland. The rates are reduced to those shown in brackets from 1 July to 31 December 2020

(7) *Ireland* – The main rate is reduced to 21% from 1 September 2020 to 28 February 2021

(8) *Not in EU* – The following are not part of the EU VAT area:

- The Åland Islands

- Liechtenstein

- Mount Athos (Agion Poros).

(9) *Portugal* – Includes the Azores and Madeira.

(10) *Spain* – Includes the Balearic Islands but excludes Ceuta, Melilla and the Canary Islands. Excludes Gibraltar and Andorra which are not part of the EU.

(11) *United Kingdom* – The UK and the Isle of Man were part of the EU VAT area until 31 December 2020. Sales to the UK and/or the Isle of Man should not be included on the EC Sales List (ESL). The Channel Islands are not part of the EU. The rate on electronic publications, but not music, was reduced to 0% from 1 May 2020.

(12) *Further information* – For the VAT number formats for each EU country and links to foreign language enquiry letters see: tinyurl.com/VATNFMT.

(13) *Invoices* – 'R' means must be supplied on request, 'Alt' means alternatives to a VAT invoice may be accepted.

PLACE OF SUPPLY – SERVICES

(VATA 1994, s 7A, Sch 4A)

Customers within the EU

From 1 January 2010, the general rule for the place of supply of services where the customer is within the EU is:

- *For business to business (B2B) supplies* – where the customer belongs (EC Sales List needs to be completed).

- *For business to customer (B2C) supplies* – where the supplier belongs, except for digital services – see last line of exceptions table below.

From 1 January 2021, for most B2B and B2C supplies, the place of supply is where the customer belongs, but no EC Sales List will be required (see below).

Customers outside the UK

Where the customer belongs outside the UK the place of supply is where the customer belongs for most B2B and B2C services.

Exceptions

Exceptions to the above general rules are as follows:

	Place of supply of services	
Category of service:	**B2B supplies**	**B2C supplies**
Relating to land and property	Where the land is situated	Where the land is situated
Physical performances eg: artistic, cultural, educational, training, sporting, entertainment, exhibitions, conferences, meetings; and any ancillary services.	Subject to the general rule for B2B services – where the customer belongs	Where the event actually takes place
Admission to cultural, artistic, sporting, scientific, educational, entertainment, fairs and exhibitions; and any ancillary services relating to admission to such events	Where event takes place	Where the event takes place
Work on, or valuation of moveable goods and ancillary transport services	Subject to the general rule for B2B services – where the customer belongs	Where the services are physically performed
Restaurant and catering	Where the services are physically carried out	Where the services are physically carried out

continued

	Place of supply of services	
Category of service:	**B2B supplies**	**B2C supplies**
Passenger transport	Where it takes place, (Note 3)	Where it takes place, (see Note 3)
Freight transport	Subject to the general rule for B2B services – where the customer belongs	
B2C international freight transport (between the EC and non-EC countries, or wholly outside the EC)		Where the transport takes place
B2C intra-EC freight transport		The Member State in which the transportation begins
Short-term hire of means of transport (see Note 4)	Where the means of transport is put at the disposal of the hiree	Where the means of transport is put at the disposal of the hiree
Long-term hire of means of transport	Subject to the general rule for B2B services – where the customer belongs	Where the recipient/customer belongs, unless the hire is long-term hire of a pleasure boat where it will be the place where the pleasure boat is put at the disposal of the customer
Supplies of telecommunications, broadcasting and e-services (digital services)	Taxed where the supplier belongs.	Where the consumer is located (see note 5).

Notes

(1) *Place of supply: 'Use and enjoyment'* – There are additional rules for the letting on hire of goods, electronically supplied services, telecommunications services and radio and television broadcasting services in either of the following situations:

- the place of supply would be the UK (because the supplier or customer belongs in the UK) but the services are effectively used and enjoyed outside the UK, or

- the place of supply would be outside the UK (because the supplier or customer belongs outside the UK) but the services are effectively used and enjoyed in the UK.

In these circumstances, the place of supply is where their effective use and enjoyment takes place. Where this is the UK, the services are subject to UK VAT.

(2) *Use and enjoyment: Accounting procedures* – The accounting procedures taking account of the use and enjoyment provisions are:

If your B2B supply is:	You are:
to a customer belonging in the UK	not required to account for UK VAT to the extent that the customer uses and enjoys the services outside the UK
to a customer belonging outside the UK	required to account for UK VAT to the extent that the customer uses and enjoys the services in the UK
to a customer belonging outside the UK and the customer uses and enjoys the services in an EU Member State	not required to account for UK VAT as those services are supplied in that Member State but you may be required to register and account for VAT in that Member State

(3) *Passenger transport* – To the extent that the transport takes place outside the UK, it is outside the scope of UK VAT. However, if a journey involves travel through an EU Member State, the supply of passenger transport will be made in that Member State to the extent that the transport takes place there. In effect VAT is due in each member state the transport passes through in proportion to the total length of the journey.

(4) *'Short-term hire'* – Means for a continuous period not exceeding 90 days if the means of transport is a vessel and not exceeding 30 days for any other means of transport.

(5) *Digital Services* – Traders who sell B2C digital services in EU countries can use VAT MOSS non-union scheme to make a single return of the VAT due in all other EU countries on those B2C sales of digital services, see **Services supplied to other EU states** above.

INTRASTAT REPORTING

(Council Regulation (EC) No 638/2004)

Effective date	Arrivals £	Dispatches £	Delivery terms £
1 Jan 2015	1,500,000	250,000	24,000,000
1 Jan 2014	1,200,000	250,000	24,000,000

Notes

(1) *Reporting* – VAT registered businesses are required to submit an Intrastat declaration or Supplementary Sales Declaration (SSD) each month if their purchases from other EU Member States exceed the thresholds above. The SSD must be submitted online by 21st day following the month to which it relates.

(2)   *Exiting the EU* – In 2021 UK traders will still be required to make intrastat reports of arrivals in the UK for HMRC statistical purposes, but they will not be required to report dispatches of goods to the EU. In Northern Ireland movements of goods to and from the EU will be required to be recorded on Intrastat until at least 2025.

(3)   *Further information* – For detailed guidance see: www.uktradeinfo.com and HMRC Notice 60

EC SALES LIST (ESL)

(SI 1995/2518, Part IV)

Effective date	Goods to other EU countries £	Services £
1 January 2014	35,000	No upper limit
1 January 2010	70,000	No upper limit

Notes

(1)   *Reporting* – All VAT registered businesses in the EU are required to submit regular ESLs if they sell goods or services to VAT registered businesses in other EU countries.

(2)   *Northern Ireland only* – From 1 January 2021 traders in Great Britain are not required to submit an ESL (form VAT101) as the UK is no longer a member of the EU and the transitional period ended on 31 December 2020. However, traders in Northern Ireland are still required to submit ESLs.

(3)   *Further information* – Outline guidance https://tinyurl.com/ESL101NI. For detailed guidance see VAT Notice 725.

13

Other taxes and duties

ANNUAL TAX ON ENVELOPED DWELLINGS (ATED)

(FA 2013, ss 94–174, Schs 33–35; SI 2016/1244)

Property value £	2017/18 £	2018/19 £	2019/20 £	2020/21 £	2021/22 £
500,001–1,000,000	3,500	3,600	3,650	3,700	3,700
1,000,0001–2,000,000	7,050	7,250	7,400	7,500	7,500
2,000,001–5,000,000	23,550	24,250	24,800	25,200	25,300
5,000,001–10,000,000	54,950	56,550	57,900	58,850	59,100
10,000,001–20,000,000	110,100	113,400	116,100	118,050	118,600
Over £20,000,000	220,350	226,950	232,350	236,250	237,400

Notes

(1) *Who pays* – Non-natural persons (NNP) who hold a beneficial interest in a UK dwelling valued within the above bands. If the NNP owns the property interest for only part of the year, or a relief or exemption applies (see note 4).

(2) *Valuations* – For 2018/19 to 2023/24 the value of a property for ATED purposes is its market value on 1 April 2017, or when acquired, if later. For ATED due for 2013/14 to 2017/18 the valuation point was 1 April 2012, or the later acquisition date within that period. HMRC's 'pre-return banding check' service can be used to check which valuation band the property falls into (*FA 2013, s 102*).

(3) *Returns and payments* – The charge is payable annually by 30 April within the chargeable year (from 1 April), but may be proportionately reduced where a relief applies and a refund can be claimed (*FA 2013, ss 99, 101*). ATED is self-assessed by submitting an ATED return by 30 April within the chargeable year. For dwellings first falling within ATED, returns and payments are due within 30 days of the acquisition date, 90 days from completion where the dwelling is a new build (*FA 2013, ss 158–161*).

(4) *Reliefs and exemptions* – These are similar to, but not identical to those reliefs that apply for the flat 15% rate of SDLT (see **Chapter 11**).The NNP must make relief declaration return to claim the relevant reliefs from ATED, but one relief return can cover an entire property portfolio (*FA 2013, ss 132–150*).

(5) *Gains* – For disposals made before 6 April 2019, where the property has been subject to the ATED, all or part of any gain arising is subject to the ATED-related CGT charge (see **Chapter 8**).

(6)   *Further information* – HMRC guidance is available at: tinyurl.com/ATEDgd.

(7)   *Housing co-operatives* – From 3 March 2021 qualifying housing co-operatives owning or purchasing residential property valued over £500,000 can claim relief from ATED for chargeable periods beginning on or after 1 April 2020. Similar relief is introduced for the flat 15% rate of SDLT (*Finance Bill 2021, cl 89, 90, 91*).

MACHINE GAMES DUTY (MGD)

(FA 2012, s 191, Sch 24; SI 2012/2500)

Rates

(FA 2012, Sch 24, para 9)

Description	Cost to play	Highest prize	Rate
Lower rate – type 1 games	20p or less	£10 or less	5%
Standard rate – type 2 games	21p to £5	more than £10	20%
Higher rate – all other games	More than £5	Any amount	25%

Notes

(1)   *Calculated on* – Total net takings from the playing of 'dutiable' machine games in the UK (ie broadly games which offer cash prizes, the value of which exceeds the cost of playing the game). Takings on which MGD is payable are exempt from VAT (*VATA 1994, Sch 9, Group 4, Item 1A*).

(2)   *Commencement* – From 1 February 2013 for the standard and lower rates. The higher rate applies from 1 March 2015 (*FA 2012, Sch 24*).

(3)   *Games type* – If the machine has games of more than one type, the rate for all games is set at the highest rated game (*FA 2012, Sch 24, para 5*).

(4)   *Returns and payments* – MGD accounting periods are normally quarterly. Returns and payments must be made by the 30th day following the end of every accounting period (*SI 2012/2500, regs 12, 13*). Penalties and interest can be charged for errors in returns, failure to register, and failure to make payments on time.

(5)   *Registration* – The person who is responsible for premises where dutiable gaming machines are provided for play is required to register for MGD with HMRC, either online or by paper (see VAT Notice 452, para 6.6).

(6)   *Further guidance* – Outline guidance: www.gov.uk/machine-games-duty. For detailed guidance see HMRC Notice 452.

INSURANCE PREMIUM TAX (IPT)

(FA 1994, Pt III, Schs 6A–7A; SI 1994/1774)

Rates of IPT

(FA 1994, ss 51, 51A)

Period	Standard Rate %	Higher Rate %
From 1 June 2017	12.0	20.0
1 October 2016 to 31 May 2017	10.0	20.0
1 November 2015 to 30 September 2016	9.5	20.0
4 January 2011 to 31 October 2015	6.0	20.0

Notes

(1) *Effective from* – Insurance premium tax (IPT) is charged on premiums received by insurers under taxable insurance contracts from 1 October 1994.

(2) *Higher rate of IPT* – This applies to insurance sold in certain circumstances relating to motor cars or motorcycles, certain electrical or mechanical domestic appliances and travel insurance *(FA 1994, Sch 6A)*.

LANDFILL TAX

(FA 1996, Pt III, Sch 5; FA 2011, s 25; SI 1996/1527; SI 2011/1017)

Rates

(FA 1996, s 42; SI 2016/376)

Disposals made or treated as made in year beginning:	Standard rate per tonne £	Lower rate per tonne £	Maximum credit %
1 April 2022	98.60	3.15	5.3
1 April 2021	96.70	3.10	5.3
1 April 2020	94.15	3.00	5.3
1 April 2019	91.35	2.90	5.3
1 April 2018	88.95	2.80	5.3
1 April 2017	86.10	2.70	5.3
1 April 2016	84.40	2.65	4.2
1 April 2015	82.60	2.60	5.7

Notes

(1)   *Applies to* – Waste disposals by way of landfill at a licensed site in England or Northern Ireland, and at licensed sites in Wales before April 2018, unless specifically exempted. Landfill site operators are taxed on disposals of waste by reference to the weight and type of waste concerned.

(2)   *Which rate* – The lower rate of landfill tax relates to inactive (or inert) wastes, as listed in the *Landfill Tax (Qualifying Material) Order 2011, SI 2011/1017*. The standard rate applies to all other taxable waste.

(3)   *Tax credits* – Registered landfill site operators can claim a tax credit worth 90% of any qualifying contributions made to approved environmental bodies, subject to a maximum percentage of their landfill tax liability during the contribution year (*Landfill Tax Regulations 1996, SI 1996/1527, reg 31*).

(4)   *Scottish landfill* – From 1 April 2015 Scottish landfill tax applies to waste disposal at registered sites in Scotland, see **Chapter 18**.

(5)   *Welsh landfill* – From 1 April 2018 Welsh landfill disposal tax applies to waste disposal at registered sites in Wales, see **Chapter 18**.

(6)   *Further information* – See www.gov.uk/topic/business-tax/landfill-tax and HMRC Notice LFT1.

AGGREGATES LEVY

(*FA 2001, Pt 2, Schs 4–10; FA 2011, s 24; SI 2002/761*)

Rates

(*FA 2001, s 16*)

Aggregate exploited in period:	Rate per tonne £
1 April 2009–31 March 2022	2.00
1 April 2008–31 March 2009	1.95
1 April 2002–31 March 2008	1.60

Notes

(1)   *Charged on* – Aggregates levy is charged on aggregate (broadly rock, sand and gravel) subjected to commercial exploitation.

(2)   *How much* – The levy is charged at a rate per tonne, and the amount of levy charged on a part of a tonne of aggregate shall be the proportionately reduced amount (*FA 2001, s 16(4)*).

(3)   *Tax credit* – HMRC may pay a tax credit in relation to aggregates levy paid in Northern Ireland under the aggregates levy credit scheme (*FA 2001, ss 30B–30D*).

(4)   *Further information* – See www.gov.uk/topic/business-tax/aggregates-levy and HMRC Notice AGL1.

CLIMATE CHANGE LEVY (CCL)

(FA 2000 s 30, Sch 6; SI 2001/838)

Rates

(FA 2000, Sch 6, para 42; FA 2011, s 23)

Taxable commodity supplied from:	Main rate at which CCL payable					
	1 April 2023	1 April 2022	1 April 2021	1 April 2020	1 April 2019	1 April 2018
Electricity	0.775p/kWh	0.775p/kWh	0.775p/kWh	0.811p/kWh	0.847p/kWh	0.583p/kWh
– reduced rate of above	8%	8%	8%	8%	7%	10%
Natural gas	0.672p/kWh	0.568p/kWh	0.465p/kWh	0.406p/kWh	0.339p/kWh	0.203p/kWh
– reduced rate of above	12%	14%	17%	19%	22%	35%
Liquefied petroleum gas	2.175p/kg	2.175p/kg	2.175p/kg	2.175p/kg	2.175p/kg	1.304p/kg
– reduced rate of above	23%	23%	23%	23%	35%	35%
Any other taxable commodity	5.258p/kg	4.449p/kg	3.640p/kg	3.174p/kg	2.653p/kg	1.591p/kg
– reduced rate of above	12%	14%	17%	19%	22%	35%

Notes

(1) *Chargeable on* – Industrial and commercial supply of taxable commodities for lighting, heating and power for consumers in specified business sectors.

(2) *Reduced rate supplies* – CCL is charged at a percentage of the main rate for energy intensive industries that have entered into a negotiated energy efficiency Climate Change Agreement *(FA 2010, s 18; FA 2016, s 148; FA 2000, Sch 6, para 42(1))*.

(3) *Renewable sources* – Exemption for electricity from renewable sources is removed from 1 August 2018 *(FA 2016, s 144)*.

(4) *Further information* – See www.gov.uk/topic/business-tax/climate-change-levy.

167

ROAD FUEL DUTY

(Hydrocarbon Oil Duties Act 1979 (HODA 1979); FA 2011, ss 19, 20; FA 2009, ss 15, 16; FA 2010, ss 12, 13)

Description	From 23 March 2011	1 January 2011 to 22 March 2011	1 October 2010 to 31 December 2010	1 April 2010 to 30 September 2010	1 September 2009 to 31 March 2010
Unleaded petrol and bio-ethanol *(HODA 1979, s 6(1A)(a))*	57.95p	58.95p	58.19p	57.19p	56.19p
Heavy oil and bio-diesel *(HODA 1979, s 6(1A)(c))*	57.95p	58.95p	58.19p	57.19p	36.19p
Natural road fuel gas (including bio-gas) *(HODA 1979, s 8(3)(a))*	24.70p per kg	26.15p per kg	25.05p per kg	23.60p per kg	22.16p per kg
Other road fuel gas (eg liquefied petroleum gas) *(HODA 1979, s 8(3)(b))*	31.61p per kg	33.04p per kg	31.95p per kg	30.53p per kg	27.67p per kg

Notes

(1)   *Per litre* – Figures shown in pence per litre (unless otherwise stated).

(2)   *Reliefs* – There are reliefs dependant on how the fuel is used (for aviation, marine voyages, or to generate electricity), for horticultural producers, and for retailers who sell fuel in remote parts of the UK (rural duty relief). For more information see: tinyurl.com/FDutyR.

(3)   *Aqua Methanol* – A fuel which is 95% methanol and 5% water used as a greener alternative for petrol and diesel. Duty of 7.9p/litre applies from 1 October 2016.

VEHICLE EXCISE DUTY (VED)

(Vehicle Excise and Registration Act 1994 (VERA 1994), ss 2, 4, Sch 1; FA 2008, s 17; FA 2009, ss 13, 14; FA 2011, ss 21, 22)

Older cars – standard rates

(VERA 1994, Sch 1, para 1B)

Cars registered on or after 1 March 2001 and before 1 April 2017

VED Band	CO$_2$ (g/km)	From 1 April:				
		2021 £	2020 £	2019 £	2018 £	2017 £
A	Up to 100	0	0	0	0	0
B	101 to 110	20	20	20	20	20
C	111 to 120	30	30	30	30	30
D	121 to 130	130	125	125	120	115
E	131 to 140	155	150	145	140	135
F	141 to 150	170	165	160	155	150
G	151 to 165	210	205	200	195	190
H	166 to 175	250	240	235	230	220
I	176 to 185	275	265	260	250	240
J	186 to 200	315	305	300	290	280
K	201 to 225	340	330	325	315	305
L	226 to 255	585	565	555	540	520
M	Over 255	600	580	570	555	535

Newer cars – standard rates

(F(No 2)A 2015, Pt 5)

Cars registered on or after 1 April 2017

List price of vehicle	2021/22			2020/21			2019/20		
	Petrol or diesel £	Electric £	Alternative fuel £	Petrol or diesel £	Electric £	Alternative fuel £	Petrol or diesel £	Electric £	Alternative fuel £
Up to £40,000	155	0	145	150	0	140	145	0	135
Over £40,000	490	335	480	475	325	465	465	320	455

Notes

(1)   *First year* – The VED due for the first year a car is registered is based on its CO$_2$ omissions – see below. The VED for years other than the first year is not affected by the vehicle's omissions.

(2) *Period of duty* – The above rates apply for 12 month VED. The rate for a six-month VED is 55% of the annual rate, but these are not applicable to vehicles with a standard rate of less than £50 (*VERA 1994, s 4(2)*).

(3) *Over £40,000* – This higher rate applies to cars with a list price of over £40,000 for the next five standard rate years – ie years 2 to 6 of registration.

(4) *Alternative fuels* – For cars that run on alternative fuels (tax class 59).

(5) *Further information* – A full list of VED rates for all vehicles can be found at: www.gov.uk/vehicle-tax-rate-tables.

Cars – First year rates

Cars registered on or after 1 April 2017

(VERA 1994, Sch 1, para 1B)

Tax year:	2021/22 £	2021/22 £	2020/21 £	2020/21 £	2019/20 £	2019/20 £
CO_2 emissions	Diesel (note 3)	Other cars	Diesel (note 3)	Other cars	Diesel (note 3)	Other cars
0	0	0	0	0	0	0
1 to 50	25	10	25	10	25	10
51 to 75	115	25	110	25	110	25
76 to 90	140	115	135	110	130	110
91 to 100	160	140	155	135	150	130
101 to 110	180	160	175	155	170	150
111 to 130	220	180	215	175	210	170
131 to 150	555	220	540	215	530	210
151 to 170	895	555	870	540	855	530
170 to 190	1345	895	1305	870	1280	855
191 to 225	1910	1345	1850	1305	1815	1280
226 to 255	2245	1910	2175	1850	2135	1815
Over 255	2245	2245	2175	2175	2135	2135

Notes

(1) *First year rates* – The above rates of vehicle excise duty apply for the first 12 months of duty, with effect from the date of first registration. From the second year onwards, the standard or reduced rate of vehicle excise duty applies, see tables above.

(2) *Six month duty* – VED can be paid for half year periods when the annual VED is more than £50 (*VERA 1994, s 3(2)*).

(3) *Diesel* – These rates apply to diesel cars which don't meet real driving emissions step 2 (RDE2) standard.

(4) *Alternative fuels* – There is a £10 discount on the "other cars" rate for cars that run on alternative fuels (tax class 59).

(5) *Vintage* – Cars built before 1 January 1980 are exempt from VED from 1 April 2020.

Other vehicles

(VERA 1994, Sch 1, paras 1, 1J, 2)

Category	From 1 April					
	2021	**2020**	**2019**	**2018** £	**2017** £	**2016** £
Vans *(Sch 1, para 1J)*	275	265	260	250	240	230
Lower-emissions vans *(Sch 1, para 1J)*	140	140	140	140	140	140
Motor-cycles *(VERA 1994 Sch 1, para 2)*						
Not over 150cc	21	20	20	19	18	17
151 to 400cc	45	44	43	42	41	39
401 to 600cc	69	67	66	64	62	60
Over 600cc	96	93	91	88	85	82
Motor-tricycles						
Not over 150cc	21	20	20	19	18	17
Any other case	96	93	91	88	85	82

Notes

(1) *Vans* – Lower rate of VED applies to models which Euro 4 emissions standards *(VERA 1994, Sch 1, para 1K)* and were registered on or after 1 March 2003 and before 1 January 2007, or that meet the Euro 5 emissions standards and were registered on or after 1 January 2009 and before 1 January 2011 *(VERA 1994, Sch 1, para 1M)*.

(2) *Medical couriers* – Motorcycles and cars used by medical courier charities for the transportation of medical products, and marked with 'Blood' on both sides, are exempt from VED from 1 April 2020 *(FA 2020, s 87)*.

AIR PASSENGER DUTY (APD)

(FA 1994, ss 28–30, Sch 5A; FA 2010, s 14)

Band (approximate distance in miles from London to the capital city of the destination country)	From 1 April 2022			From 1 April 2021			From 1 April 2020		
	H £	**S** £	**L** £	**H** £	**S** £	**L** £	**H** £	**S** £	**L** £
Band A (0–2,000)	78	26	13	78	26	13	78	26	13
Band B (over 2,000)	554	185	84	541	180	82	528	176	80

Notes

(1) *Charged on* – Air passenger duty (APD) is chargeable on the carriage of each chargeable passenger on the approximate distance travelled allocated to bands *(FA 1994, s 30(1))*.

(2) *Rates of duty* – The rates of duty (higher: H standard: S and lower: L) depend upon the class of travel. The higher rate (H) applies to passengers in business jets that carry fewer than 19 passengers, and have take-off weight of 20 tonnes or more (*FA 2012, s 190, Sch 23*).

(3) *Lower or reduced rate* – Applies to 'Standard class travel' which is:

    (a) in the case of an aircraft on which only one class of travel is available, that class of travel;

    (b) in any other case, the lowest class of travel available on the aircraft (*FA 1994, s 30(10)*).

(4) *Seat space* – Where a seat pitch exceeds 1.016 metres (40 inches), whether the flight has a single class or more than one class, the standard rate S of APD applies (*FA 1994, s 30(11)*; HMRC Notice 550, para 2.6.5).

(5) *Northern Ireland* – The APD for direct long-haul routes (band B) departing from Northern Ireland is nil (*FA 2012, s 190, Sch 23*).

(6) *Child passengers* – No APD is due for children under 16 (*SI 2015/942*).

(7) *Further information* – see https://www.gov.uk/air-passenger-duty.

BANK LEVY

(FA 2011, s 73, Sch 19)

Period	Short-term chargeable liabilities	Long-term chargeable equity and liabilities
2021	0.10%	0.05%
2020	0.14%	0.07%
2019	0.15%	0.075%
2018	0.16%	0.080%
2017	0.17%	0.085%
2016	0.18%	0.09%
1 April 2015–31 Dec 2015	0.21%	0.105%
1 Jan 2014–31 March 2015	0.156%	0.078%
1 Jan 2013–31 Dec 2013	0.130%	0.065%
1 Jan 2012–31 Dec 2012	0.088%	0.044%

Notes

(1) *Commencement* – The bank levy applies to periods of account ending on or after 1 January 2011 (*FA 2011, Sch 19, paras 4(8), 5(4)*). Periods falling wholly before 1 January 2011 are ignored for these purposes.

(2) *Chargeable on* – The total chargeable equity and liabilities as reported in the relevant balance sheets of banks and banking groups, building societies and building society groups operating in the UK and UK banks in non-banking groups, at the end of a chargeable period.

(3) *Threshold* – The bank levy is nil if the amount of chargeable equity and liabilities is £20 billion or less. If this limit is exceeded, the first £20 billion (on which no levy is charged) is apportioned between long term equities and liabilities and short term liabilities, in accordance with the proportion of chargeable equity and liabilities of each (*FA 2011, Sch 19, para 6*).

(4) *Payment* – Payment of the bank levy is treated as a payment of corporation tax (*FA 2011, Sch 19, Pt 6*). It is subject to corporation tax payment procedures, including the quarterly instalment payments system (see **Chapter 7: Taxation of companies**).

(5) *Surcharge* – From 1 January 2016 a 8% corporation tax surcharge applies to banking profits above £25 million per year per group (*F(No 2)A 2015, Schs 2, 3*).

(6) *Credits* – For periods ending on and after 1 January 2016, where the bank pays EU single resolution fund levy (SRFL) and UK bank levy, the SRFL can be set as a credit against the bank levy, but it may not reduce the levy below zero (*SI 2016/1212*).

PLASTIC PACKAGING TAX

Notes

(1) *Commencement* – From 1 April 2022. It is designed to encourage the use of recycled plastic instead of new plastic within packaging.

(2) *Chargeable on* – The charge to plastic packaging tax arises when a chargeable plastic packaging component is produced in the UK by a person acting in the course of a business, or imported into the UK on behalf of such a person.

(3) *Plastic packaging component* – A plastic packaging component is chargeable if the proportion of recycled plastic in the component, when measured by weight, is less than 30% of the total amount of plastic in the component, and it is finished.

(4) *Rate* – Plastic packaging tax is charged at the rate of £200 per metric tonne of chargeable plastic packaging components of a single specification.

(5) *Exemption* – An exemption will apply for businesses who manufacture and/or import less than 10 tonnes of plastic packaging in a 12-month period. There are other exemptions, eg where the plastic packaging is manufactured or imported for use as immediate packaging of licensed human medicines.

(6) *Further information* – See *Finance Bill 2021, Pt 2*.

National Insurance Contributions (NIC)

CLASS 1 CONTRIBUTIONS

Primary (employee) contributions

(SSCBA 1992, ss 5(1), 8, 19(4); SI 2001/1004, regs 10, 131; Pension Schemes Act 1993, ss 41, 42A; SI 2006/1009, art 3)

Class 1 NIC rates and thresholds	2021/22 £	2020/21 £	2019/20 £	2018/19 £	2017/18 £
Lower earnings limit (LEL)	120 per week 520 per month 6,240 per year	120 per week 520 per month 6,240 per year	118 per week 512 per month 6,136 per year	116 per week 503 per month 6,032 per year	113 per week 490 per month 5,876 per year
Primary threshold (PT)	184 per week 797 per month 9,568 per year	183 per week 792 per month 9,500 per year	166 per week 719 per month 8,632 per year	162 per week 702 per month 8,424 per year	157 per week 680 per month 8,164 per year
Upper earnings limit (UEL)	967 per week 4,189 per month 50,270 per year	962 per week 4,167 per month 50,000 per year	962 per week 4,167 per month 50,000 per year	892 per week 3,863 per month 46,350 per year	866 per week 3,750 per month 45,000 per year
Not contracted out	12% on earnings between PT and UEL 2% on excess over UEL	12% on earnings between PT and UEL 2% on excess over UEL	12% on earnings between PT and UEL 2% on excess over UEL	12% on earnings between PT and UEL 2% on excess over UEL	12% on earnings between PT and UEL 2% on excess over UEL

Class 1 NIC rates and thresholds	2021/22 £	2020/21 £	2019/20 £	2018/19 £	2017/18 £
Reduced rate (note 4)	5.85% on earnings between PT and UEL 2% on excess over UEL	5.85% on earnings between PT and UEL 2% on excess over UEL	5.85% on earnings between PT and UEL 2% on excess over UEL	5.85% on earnings between PT and UEL 2% on excess over UEL	5.85% on earnings between PT and UEL 2% on excess over UEL

Class 1 Primary (employee) contributions (continued)

(SSCBA 1992, ss 5(1), 8, 19(4); SI 2001/1004, regs 10, 131; Pension Schemes Act 1993, ss 41, 42A; SI 2006/1009, art 3)

Class 1 NIC rates and thresholds	2016/17 £	2015/16 £	2014/15 £
Lower earnings limit (LEL)	112 per week 486 per month 5,824 per year	112 per week 486 per month 5,824 per year	111 per week 481 per month 5,772 per year
Primary threshold (PT)	155 per week 672 per month 8,060 per year	155 per week 672 per month 8,060 per year	153 per week 663 per month 7,956 per year
Upper accrual point	N/A	770 per week 3,337 per month 40,040 per year	770 per week 3,337 per month 40,040 per year
Upper earnings limit (UEL)	827 per week 3,583 per month 43,000 per year	815 per week 3,532 per month 42,385 per year	805 per week 3,489 per month 41,865 per year
Not contracted out	12% on earnings between PT and UEL 2% on excess over UEL	12% on earnings between PT and UEL 2% on excess over UEL	12% on earnings between PT and UEL 2% on excess over UEL
Contracted out	N/A	10.6% on earnings between PT and UAP 12% on earnings between UAP and UEL 2% on excess over UEL	10.6% on earnings between PT and UAP 12% on earnings between UAP and UEL 2% on excess over UEL
Contracted out rebate (note 3)	N/A	1.4%	1.4%
Reduced rate (note 4)	5.85% on earnings between PT and UEL 2% on excess over UEL	5.85% on earnings between PT and UEL 2% on excess over UEL	5.85% on earnings between PT and UEL 2% on excess over UEL

Notes

(1)   *Nil band* – No Class 1 contributions are payable on earnings between the lower earnings limit and primary threshold, but the employee is treated as having paid such contributions for the purposes of establishing or protecting entitlement to certain state benefits (*SSCBA 1992, s 6A*).

(2)   *'Upper Accrual Point' (UAP)* – This is the point from which entitlement to contributory related benefits ceases to accrue.

(3)   *Contracting out* – This was abolished for defined contribution (money purchase) pension schemes from 6 April 2012, and for defined benefit (final salary) pension schemes from 6 April 2016 (*FA 2013, s 52*).

(4)   *Reduced rate* – This applies to women who were married before 6 April 1977 who have elected to pay a reduced rate of Class 1 contributions.

(5)   *UEL frozen* – As announced in the Budget on 3 March 2021, in line with the freeze on income tax rates (see **Chapter 1**) the Upper Earnings Limit will remain at £50,270 between 2021/22 and 2025/26.

Class 1 Secondary (employer) contributions

(SSCBA 1992, ss 6(1)(b), 9; SI 2001/1004, reg 10; Pension Schemes Act 1993, ss 41, 42A; SI 2006/1009, arts 2, 3)

Class 1 NIC rates and thresholds	2021/22 £	2020/21 £	2019/20 £	2018/19 £	2017/18 £
Secondary threshold (ST)	170 per week 737 per month 8,840 per year	169 per week 732 per month 8,788 per year	166 per week 719 per month 8,632 per year	162 per week 702 per month 8,424 per year	157 per week 680 per month 8,164 per year
Upper & Apprentice secondary threshold (UST) & (AUST)	967 per week 4,189 per month 50,270 per year	962 per week 4,167 per month 50,000 per year	962 per week 4,167 per month 50,000 per year	892 per week 3,863 per month 46,350 per year	866 per week 3,750 per month 45,000 per year
Not contracted out rate	13.8% on earnings above ST	13.8% on earnings above ST	13.8% on earnings above ST	13.8% on earnings above ST	13.8% on earnings above ST

Class 1 NIC rates and thresholds	2016/17 £	2015/16 £	2014/15 £
Secondary threshold (ST)	156 per week 676 per month 8,112 per year	156 per week 676 per month 8,112 per year	153 per week 663 per month 7,956 per year
Upper & Apprentice secondary threshold (UST) & (AUST)	827 per week 3,583 per month 43,000 per year	815 per week 3,532 per month 42,385 per year	N/A
Not contracted out rate	13.8% on earnings above ST	13.8% on earnings above ST	13.8% on earnings above ST
Contracted out rates salary related (note 6)	N/A	10.4%	10.4%
Contracted out rebate rates salary related (note 6)	N/A	3.4%	3.4%

Notes

(1) *Age limits* – Class 1 contributions are not payable in respect of individuals under the age of 16 at the time of payment of the earnings. Employees who have achieved state pension age (SPA) at the time of payment are not liable to pay primary Class 1 contributions, but employers must continue to pay secondary Class 1 contributions for employees over their SPA (*SSCBA 1992, s 6(3)*; see NIM1001).

(2) *Under 21* – From 6 April 2015 employers' Class 1 NIC is not payable in respect of employees aged under 21 on earnings up to the upper secondary threshold (*SSCBA 1992, s 9A*).

(3) *Apprentices* – From 6 April 2016 employers' Class 1 NIC is not payable in respect of apprentices aged under 25 on earnings up to the Apprentice upper secondary threshold (*SSCBA 1992, s 9B*).

(4) *Disguised remuneration* – Class 1 NIC for employees and employers can arise on 'disguised remuneration' from Employee Benefit Trusts (EBTs), unapproved pension schemes (EFRBS) and other third party intermediaries where such income would not otherwise be within the charge to NIC (see *ITEPA 2003, ss 554A–554Z20*; *Social Security (Contributions) Regulations, SI 2001/1004*).

(5) *Apprenticeship levy* – From 6 April 2017 employers with annual pay costs of £3 million or more must pay 0.5% of their annual pay bill as the Apprenticeship Levy (see **Chapter 3**).

(6) *Contracting out* – This was abolished for defined contribution (money purchase) pension schemes from 6 April 2012, and for defined benefit (final salary) pension schemes from 6 April 2016 (*FA 2013, s 52*).

(7) *Veterans* – With effect from 6 April 2021 employers who employ ex-members of the armed forces in their first civilian role will be able to claim relief from employers' Class 1 NIC up to the UST for 12 months (https://tinyurl.com/7zfm85au).

EMPLOYMENT ALLOWANCE

(NICA 2014, ss 1, 2, 4, 8, SI 2020/218)

Tax Year	Maximum claim per employer or group £
2021/22	4,000
2020/21	4,000
2019/20	3,000
2018/19	3,000
2017/18	3,000
2016/17	3,000
2015/16	2,000

Notes

(1)   *Eligible employers* – Private sector employers, charities and community amateur sports (*NICA 2014, s 8*).

(2)   *Excluded from April 2020* – Where the Class 1 NIC liability of the employer and any connected organisation was £100,000 or more in the previous tax year. Employers are only eligible to claim if the Employment Allowance plus any other state aid they receive does not breach the state aid de-minimis threshold for their industry sector (*SI 2020/218*).

(3)   *Excluded from April 2016* – Companies where the director is the sole employee. Also public authorities which are not charities and businesses that carry out functions of a public nature such as NHS services (*SI 2016/344*).

(4)   *Set against* – Secondary Class 1 NIC liability. NIC on the deemed salary payment under IR35 cannot be set against the allowance (*NICA 2014, s 2*).

(5)   *Excluded workers* – The allowance can't be set against Class 1 NIC paid on the wages of domestic workers who work in the employer's own home, unless they are care workers who personally assist the employer or household due to old age, disability, illness or other dependency (*NICA 2014, s 2*).

(6)   *How to claim* – Tick a box on the first EPS submitted for the first tax year in which the allowance is claimed. From 2020/21 the employer must make a declaration that state aid thresholds have not been breached and indicate which trade sector the employer operates in (*NICA 2014, s 4*).

(7)   *Further information* – Detailed guidance is found at: tinyurl.com/EAdgd4emps.

CLASS 1A CONTRIBUTIONS

(SSCBA 1992, s 10)

(1) *Payable by* – Employers (and certain third parties) on taxable benefits provided to employees.

(2) *Charge calculated as* – A percentage of the cash equivalent of the benefits, that percentage is equal to rate of secondary Class 1 NIC for the tax year in question (13.8% for 2021/22).

(3) *Termination payments* – From 6 April 2020 where a termination payment exceeds the £30,000 tax free threshold the excess is subject to Class 1A NIC *(SI 2020/285)*.

(4) *Sporting testimonials* – From 6 April 2020 where a sporting testimonial payment exceeds £100,000 the excess is subject to Class 1A NIC *(SI 2020/285)*.

(5) *Payment due by* – 22 July in the tax year following the tax year for which the benefit was paid (19 July for cheque payments), except for payments due on termination payments and sporting testimonials when payment is due within the tax year.

(6) *Not payable on* – Benefits which are (see HMRC leaflet CWG5, Pt 2):

- exempt from income tax *(SSCBA 1992, s 10(1)(a))*;

- exempt from Class 1A NIC *(SI 2001/1004, Pt 3)* (see CWG5, pt 5);

- covered by an Extra-Statutory Concession (as listed in *SI 2001/1004, reg 40(7)*);

- included in a PAYE Settlement Agreement (see Class 1B contributions) *(SSCBA 1992, s 10(6))*;

- provided for business use, where any private use is not significant *(ITEPA 2003, s 316)*;

- already liable to Class 1 NIC *(SSCBA 1992, s 10(1)(c))*;

- also exempt from Class 1 NIC *(SI 2001/1004, reg 40)*.

CLASS 1B CONTRIBUTIONS

(SSCBA 1992, s 10A)

- *Payable by* – Employers who enter into a PAYE Settlement Agreement (PSA) with HMRC, which allows the employer to account for tax on certain expense payments and benefits in one payment.

- *Charge applies to* – Items contained within a PSA that would normally attract a liability for Class 1 or Class 1A NICs, and to the total tax payable under the PSA.

- *Calculated as* – A percentage of the total amount chargeable, that percentage is equal to the rate of secondary Class 1 NIC for the tax year in question (13.8% for 2021/22).

- *Payment due by* – 22 October in the tax year following the tax year to which the PSA applies (19 October for cheque payments) *(SI 2003/2682, reg 109(2))*.

CLASS 2 CONTRIBUTIONS

(SSCBA 1992, ss 11, 12, 117(1); NICA 2015; SI 2001/1004, regs 46(a), 125(c), 152(b))

Tax year	Flat rate per week £	Share fishermen per week £	Volunteer development workers per week £	Small earnings exception/small profits threshold £
2021/22	3.05	3.70	6.00	6,515
2020/21	3.05	3.70	6.00	6,475
2019/20	3.00	3.65	5.90	6,365
2018/19	2.95	3.60	5.80	6,205
2017/18	2.85	3.50	5.65	6,025
2016/17	2.80	3.45	5.60	5,965
2015/16	2.80	3.45	5.60	5,965

Notes

(1) *Age limits* – Class 2 NIC contributions are payable by self-employed persons aged between 16 and state pension age (SPA).

(2) *Payments due* – From 2015/16 Class 2 NIC is collected as part of the taxpayer's self-assessment by 31 January following the tax year. For earlier years the contributions were due on 31 July and 31 January, but payments could be made by direct debit for each month in arrears.

(3) *Small profits* – From 2015/16 a Class 2 liability does not arise if the self-employed profits for the year don't exceed the small profits threshold. For earlier years the taxpayer could claim exception from liability to pay Class 2 NIC if profits weren't expected to exceed the small earnings exception limit.

(4) *Voluntary contributions* – Class 2 contributions can be paid voluntarily if a liability does not arise due to low earnings *(SI 2001/1004, reg 46(b))*. Alternatively, an individual may pay Class 3 contributions if entitled to do so *(NIM21044)*.

CLASS 3 CONTRIBUTIONS

(SSCBA 1992, s 13)

Tax Year	Weekly Rate £
2021/22	15.40
2020/21	15.30
2019/20	15.00
2018/19	14.65
2017/18	14.25
2016/17	14.10
2015/16	14.10

Notes

(1) *Eligibility* – Individuals wishing to pay Class 3 contributions in order to meet the conditions for entitlement to certain benefits must be over the age of 16 and be resident in Great Britain or Northern Ireland in the relevant tax year (*SSCBA 1992, s 1(6)(b); SI 2001/1004, regs 48(1), 145(1)(e)*).

(2) *Earnings factor* – An individual is entitled to pay Class 3 contributions if his or her earnings factor (EF) derived from Class 1, 2 and/or 3 NICs is less than the qualifying earnings factor for the relevant tax year, subject to certain restrictions on the right to pay. A qualifying earnings factor is an amount equal to 52 times that year's lower earnings limit for Class 1 contributions (*SSCBA 1992, s 14; SI 1979/676, Sch 1, Pt 2*) (see *NIM25001*).

CLASS 4 CONTRIBUTIONS

(*SSCBA 1992, s 15(3), (3ZA)*)

Tax Year	Main rate	Additional rate	Lower profits limit	Upper profits limit
	%	%	£	£
2021/22	9	2	9,568	50,270
2020/21	9	2	9,500	50,000
2019/20	9	2	8,632	50,000
2018/19	9	2	8,424	46,350
2017/18	9	2	8,164	45,000
2016/17	9	2	8,060	43,000
2015/16	9	2	8,060	42,385

Notes

(1) *Payable on* – Class 4 NIC are payable on profits from UK trades, professions or vocations, which exceed the lower profits limit and are chargeable to income tax under *ITTOIA 2005, Pt 2, Ch 2*. The additional rate is payable on profits that exceed the upper profits limit.

(2) *Payable by* – Individuals who are aged between 16 and state pension age, at the beginning of the relevant tax year (*SI 2001/1004, regs 91, 93*).

(3) *Annual maximum* – Class 4 NIC are subject to an annual maximum (*SI 2001/1004, reg 100*). The liability for contributions at the main rate is broadly limited to a maximum of 53 times the appropriate weekly amount of Class 2 NIC, plus the maximum amount of Class 4 contributions payable at the main rate, less any Class 2 NIC and any Class 1 NIC paid at the main rate. However, Class 4 NIC remain payable at the additional rate.

(4) *Refund* – An application to HMRC for a refund of Class 4 NIC (if appropriate) can be made online by an individual or by post on form CA5610, see: www.hmrc.gov.uk/forms/ca5610.pdf.

(5) *Upper Profits Limit frozen* – As announced in the Budget on 3 March 2021, in line with the freeze on income tax rates (see **Chapter 1**) the Upper Profits Limit will remain at £50,270 between 2021/22 and 2025/26.

State benefits

TAX CREDITS

Child tax credit (CTC)

(Child Tax Credit Regulations 2002, SI 2002/2007, reg 7)

Maximum amounts per year	2021/22 £	2020/21 £	2019/20 £
Family element (note 4)	545	545	545
Child element	2,845	2,830	2,780
Disabled child element	3,435	3,415	3,355
Severely disabled child element (addition)	1,390	1,385	1,360

Notes

(1) *Eligibility* – CTC is paid to the main carer for children up to 16 years old, or 18 in full-time education. CTC is separate from, and additional to, Child Benefit.

(2) *Claims* – Tax Credits claims are made provisionally for the coming year based on the previous year's income (2020/21 income forms the basis of 2021/22 claims). A Tax Credits claim must be renewed by 31 July, but estimated figures can be provided, which must be finalised by the following 31 January.

(3) *Disabled or severely disabled* – As to what constitutes disability or severe disability for these purposes, see *SI 2002/2007, reg 8*.

(4) *Family element* – From 6 April 2017 the family element is restricted to families with a child born before 6 April 2017.

(5) *Two child policy* – CTC is not awarded for a third or subsequent child born on or after 6 April 2017. There are exceptions for; multiple births, adopted children, non-parental care arrangements, child conceived by rape and claimant's grandchild.

(6) *Disabled children* – The disabled child elements remain payable even if those children are third or subsequent children (*Parliamentary statement, 20 July 2016*).

(7) *Further information* – Guidance for advisers including access to all the Tax Credits legislation can be found here: www.revenuebenefits.org.uk.

Working Tax Credit (WTC)

(SI 2002/2005, reg 20(1), Sch 2, para 1)

Maximum amounts per year	2021/22 £	2020/21 £	2019/20 £
Basic element (*reg 4*)	2,005	3,040	1,960
Couple and lone parent element (*regs 11, 12*)	2,060	2,045	2,010
30 hour element (*reg 10*)	830	825	810
Disabled worker element (*reg 9*)	3,240	3,220	3,165
Severe disability element (*reg 17*)	1,400	1,390	1,365

Notes

(1) *Eligibility* – To be eligible for WTCs the person must be in qualifying remunerative work, either employed 'or self-employed as defined (*SI 2015/605*).

(2) *Self-employed* – The claimant must be trading on a commercial basis with a view to a profit, and be registered with HMRC as self-employed (*SI 2015/605*).

(3) *Online tools* – An online tax credits calculator is available: https://www.gov.uk/qualify-tax-credits.

Childcare element

(SI 2002/2005, reg 20(2), (3))

Maximum amounts for weekly costs	2021/22 £	2020/21 £	2019/20 £
Maximum eligible cost for one child	175	175	175
Maximum eligible cost for two or more children	300	300	300
Percentage of eligible costs covered	70%	70%	70%

Notes

(1) *Entitlement* – The childcare element applies where the claimant pays for registered or approved childcare (*SI 2001/2005, regs 13, 14*).

(2) *Employer-supported childcare* – Employees who joined employer-provided childcare support or childcare voucher schemes before 4 October 2018 need to understand how this affects their tax credit entitlement (see **Chapter 2**). An online calculator helps Tax Credit claimants decide whether it would be beneficial to accept the employer-provided childcare vouchers (https://www.gov.uk/childcare-vouchers-better-off-calculator).

INCOME THRESHOLDS AND WITHDRAWAL RATES

(Tax Credits Act 2002, ss 7, 13(2); Tax Credits (Income Thresholds and Determination of Rates) Regulations 2002, SI 2002/2008, regs 3, 7, 8)

Annual Rates and thresholds	2021/22 £	2020/21 £	2019/20 £
Income threshold	6,565	6,530	6,420
Withdrawal (or taper) rate	41%	41%	41%
First threshold for those entitled to CTC only	16,480	16,385	16,105
Income rise disregard	2,500	2,500	2,500
Income fall disregard	2,500	2,500	2,500

Notes

(1)   *Withdrawal rate* – Entitlement of a claimant of both WTC and CTC (or WTC only) is reduced at the first withdrawal rate on each £1 by which their income exceeds the first income threshold.

(2)   *Income disregards* – Claimants' awards are initially based on their previous year's income. Once they report their current year's income, the award can be finalised.

(3)   *Further information* – Detailed guidance concerning Tax Credits can be found at: www.revenuebenefits.org.uk.

UNIVERSAL CREDIT

(Welfare Reform Act 2012, Pt 1; SI 2017/260)

Rates per monthly assessment:	2021/22 £		2020/21 £	2019/20 £
	Oct 2021 to March 2022	April 2021 to Sept 2021		
Standard Allowance				
Single claimant under 25	257.33	344.00	342.72	251.77
Single claimant 25 and over	324.84	411.51	409.89	317.82
Joint claimants, both under 25	403.93	490.60	488.59	395.20
Joint claimants, either/both 25 and over	509.91	596.58	594.04	498.89
Child Element				
1st child	282.50		281.25	277.08
2nd and subsequent child	237.08		235.83	231.67
Additional amount for disabled child				
Lower rate	128.89		128.25	126.11
Higher rate	402.41		400.29	392.08
Capacity for work				
Limited capability for work	128.89		128.25	126.11
Limited capability for work and work-related activity	343.63		341.92	336.20

Rates per monthly assessment:	2021/22 £		2020/21 £	2019/20 £
	Oct 2021 to March 2022	April 2021 to Sept 2021		
Carer element	163.73		162.92	160.20
Childcare costs (maximum)				
One child	646.35		646.35	646.35
Two or more children	1108.04		1108.04	1108.04
Work allowance				
If claim includes housing costs	293.00		292.00	287.00
Claim doesn't include housing support	515.00		512.00	503.00

Notes

(1) *Replaces benefits* – Universal Credit (UC) is a means tested benefit designed to replace the following working age benefits:

- Working and Child Tax Credits;

- Income support;

- Income-related employment and support allowance;

- Income based jobseekers allowance; and

- Housing benefit.

(2) *Rollout* – UC is being rolled out gradually across Great Britain. To check if a postcode area is covered by UC see: http://universalcreditinfo.net/.

(3) *Payment* – UC claims are paid monthly based on the reported income in the monthly assessment period. The above rates are an indication of amounts payable.

(4) *Taper rates* – UC benefits are withdrawn at the rate of 63% above higher and lower work allowances.

(5) *Assessment period* – Starts on the day of the month the claim is first made, and ends on that day minus 1 in the next month (eg, if a UC claim is first received on 4 November, the assessment period for that claimant will run to the 3rd of each month).

(6) *Claims* – Couples living in the same household must make a joint claim.

(7) *Cash basis reporting* – Self-employed claimants must report their net income for the month online every month using a version of a cash basis for trading businesses. A minimum income floor would normally apply after the first 12 months of self-employment, but this minimum income floor is not applied during the period of the coronavirus (*SI 2020/371, reg 2*).

(8) *Use of RTI* – The Department of Work and Pensions adjusts UC awards based on information reported through RTI, or self-reported by the claimant, in the assessment period.

(9) *Further information* – Guidance for advisers on UC can be found here: www. revenuebenefits.org.uk/universal-credit/.

SOCIAL SECURITY BENEFIT RATES

(ITEPA 2003, Pts 9, 10)

Benefit (weekly rates unless stated)	April 2021 £	April 2020 £	April 2019 £
Attendance allowance (N)			
• Higher rate	89.60	89.15	87.65
• Lower rate	60.00	59.70	57.70
Bereavement Support (note 10)			
Standard lump sum	2500.00	2500.00	2500.00
Higher rate lump sum	3500.00	3500.00	3500.00
Standard rate monthly payments	100.00	100.00	100.00
Higher rate monthly payments	350.00	350.00	350.00
Widowed parent's allowance (T)	122.55	121.95	119.90
Carer's Allowance (T)	67.60	67.25	66.15
Employment and Support Allowance (ESA) (T)			
Personal Allowances			
Single under 25	59.20	58.90	57.90
Single 25 or over	74.70	74.35	73.10
Lone parent under 18	59.20	58.90	57.90
Lone parent 18 and over	74.70	74.35	73.10
Couple			
• Both under 18	59.20	58.90	57.90
• Both under 18 – with child	89.45	89.00	87.50
• Both under 18 (main phase)	74.70	74.35	73.10
• One under 18, or both over 18	117.40	116.80	114.85
• Claimant under 25 partner under 18	59.20	58.90	57.90
Components			
• Work-related activity	29.70	29.55	29.05
• Support	39.40	39.20	37.65
Income support (note 8) **Personal Allowances**			
• Single under 25	59.20	58.90	57.90
• Single 25 or over	74.70	74.35	73.10
• Lone parent under 18	59.20	58.90	57.90
• Lone parent 18 or over	74.70	74.35	73.10

Benefit (weekly rates unless stated)	April 2021 £	April 2020 £	April 2019 £
Couple			
● Both under 18 – higher rate	89.45	89.00	87.50
● Both 18 or over	117.40	116.80	114.85
● Dependent children	68.60	68.27	66.90
Premiums			
Family	17.65	17.60	17.45
Family lone parent	22.20	22.20	22.20
Disability			
● Single	35.10	34.95	34.35
● Couple	50.05	49.80	48.95
Enhanced disability (also for ESA)			
● Single	17.20	17.10	16.80
● Disabled child	26.67	26.60	26.04
Severe disability (also for ESA)			
● Single – one qualifies	67.30	66.95	65.85
● Couple – two qualify	134.60	133.90	131.70
Disabled child	65.94	65.52	64.19
Carer (also for ESA claims)	37.70	37.50	36.85
Jobseeker's Allowance (JSA) (T)			
Contribution-based JSA – Personal rates			
● Under 25	59.20	58.90	57.90
● 25 or over	74.70	74.35	73.10
Income-based JSA – Personal allowances			
● Under 25	59.20	58.90	57.90
● 25 or over	74.70	74.35	73.10
● Lone parent under 18	59.20	58.90	57.90
● Lone parent 18 or over	74.70	74.35	73.10
Couple			
● Both under 18	59.20	58.90	57.90
● Both under 18 – higher rate	89.45	89.00	87.50
● One under 18, one under 25	59.20	58.90	57.90
● One under 18, one 25 and over	74.70	74.35	73.10
● Both 18 or over	117.40	116.80	114.85
Dependent children	68.60	68.27	66.90
Premiums (see Income Support rates)			
Maternity Allowance (N)			
● Standard rate	151.97	151.20	148.68
● Maternity Allowance threshold	30.00	30.00	30.00

continued

Benefit (weekly rates unless stated)	April 2021 £	April 2020 £	April 2019 £
Personal Independence payment (Note 9)			
• Daily living – enhanced	89.60	89.15	87.65
• Daily living – standard	60.00	59.70	58.70
• Mobility – enhanced	62.55	62.25	61.20
• Mobility – standard	23.70	23.60	23.20
Pension Credit (N)			
Standard minimum guarantee			
• Single	177.10	173.75	167.25
• Couple	270.30	265.20	255.25
Additional amount for severe disability			
• Single	67.30	66.95	65.85
• Couple (one qualifies)	67.30	66.95	65.85
• Couple (both qualify)	134.60	133.90	131.70
Additional amount for carers	37.70	37.50	36.85
Savings credit			
• Threshold – single	153.70	150.47	144.38
• Threshold – couple	244.12	239.17	229.67
• Maximum – single	14.04	13.97	13.72
• Maximum – couple	15.71	15.62	13.35
Amount for claimant and first spouse in polygamous marriage	270.30	265.20	255.25
Additional amount for additional spouse	93.20	91.45	88.00
Severe Disablement Allowance (N)			
Basic rate	81.25	80.85	79.50
Age-related addition			
• Higher rate	12.15	12.10	11.90
• Middle rate	6.75	6.70	6.60
• Lower rate	6.75	6.70	6.60
Widow's Benefit (T)			
Widowed Mother's Allowance	122.55	121.95	119.90
Widow's Pension (Standard rate)	122.55	121.95	119.90

Notes

(1) *Eligibility* – The above list represents a selection of state benefit rates. More comprehensive guidance of who is entitled to which benefit can be found at: www.entitledto.co.uk.

(2) *Commencement* – The benefit rates for 2021/22 apply from 6 April 2021.

(3) *Uprating of benefits* – The annual uprating of benefits takes place for state pensions and most other benefits in the first full week of the tax year (*SI 2020/234*).

(4) *Taxable or not* – In the table above, (**T**) indicates a taxable benefit and (**N**) indicates a non-taxable benefit. Only those UK social security benefits that are specified in Table A at *ITEPA 2003, s 660(1)* are taxable as social security income under *ITEPA 2003, Pt 10*. Some other social security benefits, specified at *ITEPA 2003, s 577*, are taxable as pension income under *ITEPA 2003, Pt 9*.

(5) *Foreign benefits* – Certain foreign social security payments are exempt from UK tax (see *ITEPA 2003, Pt 10, Ch 7*).

(6) *Statutory payments* – Details of statutory sick pay, maternity pay, paternity pay and adoption pay are given in **Chapter 16**.

(7) *ESA* – Replaced Incapacity Benefit and Income Support paid on incapacity grounds for claims starting from 27 October 2008. Existing recipients of Incapacity Benefit or Income Support continue to receive that benefit until they are moved to ESA (EIM76180).

(8) *Income support* – For further information on taxable and non-taxable parts of income support, see EIM76190.

(9) *Personal Independence Payment (PIP)* – Replaced Disability Living Allowance for people aged 16 to 64 from 8 April 2013. For further guidance, see: www.gov.uk/pip.

(10) *Bereavement support payment* – Applies for deaths on and after 6 April 2017, at the higher rate for those with children, or the lower rate for those without children. The monthly payments continue for 18 months.

NON-TAXABLE SOCIAL SECURITY BENEFITS

(ITEPA 2003, Pt 10)

- Attendance Allowance
- Bereavement Payment
- Child Benefit (but see HICBC in **Chapter 1**)
- Child Tax Credit
- Cold Weather Payments
- Council Tax Benefit
- Constant Attendance Allowance (see Industrial Injuries Benefits)
- Disability Living Allowance
- Employment and Support Allowance (income related)
- Exceptionally Severe Disablement Allowance (see Industrial Injuries Benefits)
- Guardian's Allowance
- Housing Benefit
- Income Support (certain payments)

- Industrial Injuries Benefits (ie industrial injuries pension, reduced earnings allowance, retirement allowance, constant attendance allowance and exceptionally severe disablement allowance)

- Maternity Allowance

- Payments to reduce under-occupation by housing benefit claimants (aka 'bedroom tax')

- Pensioner's Christmas Bonus

- Pension Credit

- Severe Disablement Allowance

- Social Fund Payments

- Universal credit

- War Widow's pension

- Winter Fuel payment

- Working Tax Credit

- Young person's bridging allowance

(Sources – *ITEPA 2003, s 677 (Table B);* EIM76100; tinyurl.com/txntxstbn)

Notes

(1) *Industrial injuries benefits* – The above excludes industrial death benefit, which is taxable (*ITEPA 2003, ss 577(1), 677(2)*).

(2) *Payments out of the social fund* – Payments are made to people on low incomes to help with maternity expenses, funeral costs, financial crises and as community care grants. The fund also makes interest-free loans.

(3) *War Widow's pension* – Where a pension or allowance is not paid or only a reduced amount is paid because the claimant gets a different benefit (eg widowed mother's allowance or widow's pension), the amount of that other benefit that equals the amount of pension withheld, is exempt from income tax (*ITEPA 2003, s 640*; see EIM76103).

With regard to wounds and disability pensions for service with the forces, see EIM74302. For allowances payable to civilians in respect of war injuries, see EIM74700.

(4) *Foreign benefits* – Certain foreign social security payments are exempt from UK tax (see *ITEPA 2003, Pt 10, Ch 7*).

CHILD BENEFIT AND GUARDIAN'S ALLOWANCE

(Child Benefit (Rates) Regulations 2006, SI 2006/965)

Weekly rates	First child rate £	Additional children rate £	Guardian/'s allowance £
2021/22	21.15	14.00	18.00
2020/21	21.05	13.95	17.90
2019/20	20.70	13.70	17.60
2018/19	20.70	13.70	17.20
2017/18	20.70	13.70	16.70
2016/17	20.70	13.70	16.55
2015/16	20.70	13.70	16.55

Notes

(1)   *Payment* – Child benefit is not income related and is paid to the claimant (usually the mother) after a single claim, until the child is no longer eligible, or until the claimant opts out of receiving the payments (see note 3).

(2)   *Not taxable* – Child benefit is not taxable, and it does not form part of the recipient's taxable income. However, child benefit can be clawed back from the highest earner in the family, even if that person is not the claimant (see **Chapter 1: High Income Child Benefit Charge**).

(3)   *Election not to receive* – The child benefit claimant may opt to stop receiving child benefit payments, while retaining an entitlement to the benefit and the associated rights to NI credits (see tinyurl.com/stpCBpyt).

(4)   *NI credits* – Where the child who is the subject to the child benefit claim is under 12 years and the claimant earns no more than LEL, the claimant will automatically receive national insurance credits, which can help make up qualifying years for the State pension.

(5)   *Guardian's allowance* – This is a tax-free payment for people who are bringing up children whose parents have died.

(6)   *Further information* – For child benefit and guardian's allowance, see www.gov.uk/browse/benefits/child.

STATE PENSION

(Pensions Act 2011)

Weekly rates	Flat rate state pension £	Basic single person: category A £	Spouse/'s pension: category B £	Non-contributory: category C or D £
2021/22	179.60	137.60	82.45	82.45
2020/21	175.20	134.25	80.45	80.45
2019/20	168.60	129.20	77.45	77.45
2018/19	164.35	125.95	75.50	75.50
2017/18	159.55	122.30	73.30	73.30
2016/17	155.65	119.30	71.50	71.50
2015/16	N/A	115.95	69.50	69.50

Notes

(1)   *Payable from* – An individual is eligible to draw the state retirement pension when they reach state pension age (SPA), which is now age 65 for both men and women. The SPA is gradually increasing to 68, and is dependent on the taxpayer's birth date, so needs to be calculated individually for each person at: www.gov.uk/state-pension-age.

(2)   *Deferment* – An individual who qualifies for the state pension may choose to defer claiming the pension. Where the claim is deferred for 12 months or more, that pensioner may opt to receive either the pension foregone as a lump sum or as a higher pension.

(3)   *Taxable* – The state pension is taxable, as is any state pension lump sum received due to deferment (*F(No 2)A 2005, ss 7–10*; see EIM74650).

(4)   *Qualifying years* – An individual who reaches SPA on or after 6 April 2016 must have 35 qualifying years to receive the full flat rate state pension. A qualifying year is achieved when the person has paid sufficient NI contributions, or received sufficient NI credits, in a tax year.

(5)   *Age bonus* – A person who qualifies for the old state pension receives an additional payment of 25p per week from age 80.

(6)   *Pension forecast* – An individual can request a forecast of their state pension through their personal tax account online or by completing DWP form BR19: www.gov.uk/check-state-pension.

(7)   *Flat rate state pension* – This replaces pension credit, the old state pension and second state pension (see: www.gov.uk/new-state-pension).

Statutory payments

NATIONAL MINIMUM WAGE (NMW)

(NMWA 1998, s 2; SI 2015/621)

Hourly rate from	Living wage £/hr	Adult £/hr	Youth development £/hr	Under 18 £/hr	Apprentice £/hr	Accommodation daily off-set £/day
1 April 2021	8.91	8.36	6.56	4.62	4.30	8.36
1 April 2020	8.72	8.20	6.45	4.55	4.15	8.20
1 April 2019	8.21	7.70	6.15	4.35	3.90	7.55
1 April 2018	7.83	7.38	5.90	4.20	3.70	7.00
1 April 2017	7.50	7.05	5.60	4.05	3.50	6.40
1 October 2016	7.20	6.95	5.55	4.00	3.40	6.00
1 April 2016	7.20	6.70	5.30	3.87	3.30	5.35

Notes

(1) *Living Wage* – Payable to employees aged 23 and over from 1 April 2021, to those aged 25 and over for pay periods starting on and after 1 April 2016 *(SI 2021/329)*.

(2) *Adult rate* – Applies to workers aged 21 and 22 from 1 April 2021, for earlier periods this rate applies to workers who have reached age 21 but not 25 *(SI 2015/621)*.

(3) *Development rate* – Applies to workers who have reached the age of 18, but not 21 *(SI 1999/584, reg 13(1))*.

(4) *Apprentice rate* – Applies to apprentices who are either aged under 19, or in the first year of their apprenticeship *(SI 2015/621, Pt 2)*.

(5) *Under 18 rate* – Applies from school leaving age, which varies in the different countries within the UK.

(6) *Accommodation off-set* – The maximum daily rate of accommodation charge permitted to be set against wages by the employer. If the charge for accommodation is greater, the difference is deducted from the employee's pay as calculated for NMW. If accommodation is provided for free the off-set rate is added to the worker's pay to calculate the deemed amount for NMW (*SI 2015/ 621 reg 16*).

(7) *Penalties* – Where an employer fails to pay correct NMW, it must pay the back wages at the correct level, plus a penalty of 100% of the underpayment capped at £20,000. The employer will also be 'named and shamed' for failing to pay correct NMW where underpaid amount is £500 or more for entire payroll. Tax penalties may be due on any unpaid tax and NICs (*SI 2014/547*).

(8) *Records* – Employers are required to keep records for six years to prove correct NMW has been paid (*SI 2021/329*).

(9) *Furloughed employees* – The NMW or NLW does not have to be paid to employees for periods they are on furlough, but it must be paid to employees for any periods spent training while not working in a furlough period.

(10) *Further information* – Guidance for employers, see: www.gov.uk/national-minimum-wage.

STATUTORY SICK PAY (SSP)

(SSCBA 1992; SI 1982/894; SI 2006/799; SI 2020/287)

Tax year	Weekly earnings threshold £	Weekly rate £
2021/22	120	96.35
2020/21	120	95.85
2019/20	118	94.25
2018/19	116	92.05
2017/18	113	89.35
2016/17	112	88.45
2015/16	112	88.45

Notes

(1) *Two systems* – From 13 March 2020 there are two versions of statutory sick pay: SSP, and coronavirus sick pay (CSSP). They are alternatives and are paid at the same rate, based on the same qualifying earnings. Employers may also pay employees higher rates of sick pay under a corporate scheme. SSP is the minimum level of sick pay a qualifying employee must receive.

(2) SSP – Payable from the fourth day of absence due to sickness, if the employee's average weekly earnings in the relevant period are at least equal to the earnings threshold. SSP cannot be recovered by any employer.

(3)   *Coronavirus SSP* – Payable from the first day the employee is absent from work where the individual meets any of these conditions from the dates indicated:

- has symptoms of coronavirus (13 March 2020);

- lives with or is in a linked or extended household with someone who has symptoms (13 March 2020);

- has been informed by NHS track and trace (or similar in Scotland or Wales) that they have had contact with a person who was, at the time of the contact, infected with coronavirus (28 May 2020);

- shielding in accordance with public health guidance (16 April 2020);

- has tested positive for coronavirus (30 July 2020);

- lives with someone who has tested positive for coronavirus (30 July 2020);

- isolating at home prior to being admitted to hospital (26 August 2020).

(4)   *Recovery* – Up to 14 days of CSSP per employee per coronavirus absence may be recovered by eligible employers from 26 May 2020. Eligible employers are those with fewer than 250 employees on the payroll at 28 February 2020, who were not in financial difficulty on 31 December 2019, and are within the state aid limit for their trade sector.

(5)   *Treatment* – Employers can pay up to £500 for recommended medical treatment for employees to help them back to work (see **Chapter 2**).

(6)   *Further information* – For guidance on SSP see: www.gov.uk/employers-sick-pay. For coronavirus SSP see: tinyurl.com/s6xdspq.

STATUTORY MATERNITY PAY (SMP)

(SI 1994/1882)

Tax year	Weekly earnings threshold £	Weekly flat rate £
2021/22	120	151.97
2020/21	120	151.20
2019/20	118	148.68
2018/19	116	145.18
2017/18	113	140.98
2016/17	112	139.58
2015/16	112	139.58

Notes

(1)   *Rates* – SMP is paid at 90% of average weekly earnings for the first six weeks and at the lower of the flat rate above and 90% of average weekly earnings for the next 33 weeks.

(2) *No SMP* – Where average weekly earnings for the relevant period do not exceed the weekly earnings threshold, no SMP is payable.

(3) *Recovery of SMP* – Employers can recover SMP from HMRC at 92% of the amount paid if their total Class 1 NIC liability for the previous tax year was more than £45,000. The recovery amount is set a 103% if the total Class 1 NIC liability for the employer was no more than £45,000 in the previous tax year. Recovery is achieved by showing the recoverable amounts on the EPS for each pay period.

(4) *Shared parental pay* – For babies due on and after 5 April 2015 working parents can share parental leave and pay. A maximum of 37 weeks of SMP can be shared or 35 weeks for factory workers. All shared pay is paid at the lower flat rate unless the employer chooses to pay a contractually higher amount.

(5) *Further information* – For guidance for employers on SMP see: www.gov.uk/employers-maternity-pay-leave.

STATUTORY ADOPTION PAY (SAP)

(*SI 2002/2818*)

Tax year	Weekly earnings threshold £	Weekly flat rate £
2021/22	120	151.97
2020/21	120	151.20
2019/20	118	148.68
2018/19	116	145.18
2017/18	113	140.98
2016/17	112	139.58
2015/16	112	139.58

Notes

(1) *Rates* – SAP is paid at the lower of the flat rate above and 90% of average weekly earnings for up to 39 weeks.

(2) *No SAP* – If average weekly earnings for the relevant period do not exceed the weekly earnings threshold, no SAP is payable.

(3) *Recovery of SAP* – Employers can recover SAP from HMRC at the rate of 92% of SAP paid out, or at the rate of 103% of the SAP paid, if the employer's total Class 1 NIC liability was no more than £45,000 in the previous tax year. Recovery is achieved by showing the recoverable amounts on the EPS for each pay period.

(4) *Further information* – For guidance for employers on SAP see: www.gov.uk/employers-adoption-pay-leave.

STATUTORY PATERNITY PAY (SPP)

(SSCBA 1992, Pt 12ZA; SI 2011/678; SI 2010/1060)

Tax year	Weekly earnings threshold £	Weekly flat rate £
2021/22	120	151.97
2020/21	120	151.20
2019/20	118	148.68
2018/19	116	145.18
2017/18	113	140.98
2016/17	112	139.58
2015/16	112	139.58

Notes

(1)   *SPP Rates* – Statutory Paternity Pay (SPP) is paid at the lower of the flat rate above and 90% of average weekly earnings for up to two weeks.

(2)   *No SPP* – If the employee's average weekly earnings do not exceed the weekly earnings threshold no SPP is payable.

(3)   *Recovery of SPP* – Employers can recover SPP from HMRC at the rate of 92% of such payments, or at the rate of 103%, if the total Class 1 NIC liability for the previous year was no more than £45,000. Recovery is achieved by showing the recoverable amounts on the EPS for each pay period.

(4)   *Further information* – For guidance on paternity pay see: www.gov.uk/employers-paternity-pay-leave.

STATUTORY PARENTAL BEREAVEMENT PAY (SPBP)

(SI 2020/233; SI 2020/240; SI 2020/246)

Tax year	Weekly earnings threshold £	Weekly flat rate £
2021/22	120	151.97
2020/21	120	151.20

Notes

(1)   *Who is eligible* – Parents who had a child aged under 18 die, or a stillbirth after 24 weeks of pregnancy, on or after 6 April 2020.

(2)   *SPBP rates* – Statutory Paternal Bereavement Pay (SPBP) is paid at the lower of the flat rate above and 90% of average weekly earnings for up to two weeks.

(3) *No SPBP* – If the employee's average weekly earnings in the relevant period do not exceed the weekly earnings threshold no SPBP is payable.

(4) *Recovery of SPBP* – Employers can recover SPBP from HMRC at the rate of 92% of such payments, or at the rate of 103%, if the total Class 1 NIC liability for the previous year was no more than £45,000. Recovery is achieved by showing the recoverable amounts on the EPS for each pay period.

(5) *Further information* – For guidance on paternal bereavement pay see: www.gov.uk/ employers-parental-bereavement-pay-leave.

Penalties and interest

STRUCTURE OF PENALTIES

HMRC may impose penalties on taxpayers in the following circumstances:

- Late payment of tax or duty;
- Late filing of returns;
- Failure to notify chargeability to tax;
- Errors on returns and documents;
- Failure to keep or retain records;
- VAT and excise wrong-doing; and
- Failure to submit returns online.

Notes

(1) *Scope* – The structure of tax penalties is now generally the same across all the taxes administered by HMRC, but there are different regimes for late filing and late payment of VAT and PAYE.

(2) *Effective from* – This penalty regime came into force for income tax, CGT, CT, VAT and direct tax claims not included in a return, from 1 April 2009, and for failure to pay CIS or PAYE from 6 April 2010.

(3) *Other taxes* – The new penalty regime came into effect for IPT, SDLT, aggregates levy, climate change levy and landfill tax from 1 April 2010 or 1 April 2012. Record keeping requirements apply to bank payroll tax from 8 April 2010, and excise duties from 1 April 2011.

(4) *GAAR penalty* – For arrangements entered into on or after 15 September 2016 a penalty of 60% of the counteracted tax can apply when an arrangement is counteracted by application of the general anti-abuse rule (GAAR) (*FA 2016, s 158*).

UK matters

The amount of penalty that can be imposed is determined according to the behaviour of the taxpayer, the degree of disclosure the taxpayer has made to HMRC, and whether that disclosure was prompted or unprompted (the *quality* of the disclosure). The penalty is charged as a percentage of the potential lost revenue (PLR), as set out on the following grid.

Behaviour of taxpayer:	Unprompted disclosure		Prompted disclosure	
	Max. Penalty	Min. Penalty	Max. Penalty	Min. Penalty
Reasonable care taken	0%	0%	0%	0%
Careless	30%	0%	30%	15%
Deliberate but not concealed	70%	20%	70%	35%
Deliberate and concealed	100%	30%	100%	50%

Notes

(1)   *Applicable to* – this grid applies to penalties imposed for the following:

- Errors in returns and documents (*FA 2007, s 97, Sch 24*);

- Failures to notify (*FA 2008, s 123, Sch 41*);

- Late submission (see **Late filing**, *FA 2009, s 106, Sch 55*); and

- Under-assessment by HMRC (*FA 2007, Sch 24, paras 2, 4C*).

(2)   *Commencement* – The penalty provisions generally apply to assessments for tax periods commencing from 1 April 2008, where the filing date is on or after 1 April 2009 (see **Structure of Penalties**) (*SI 2008/568, art 2(b)*).

(3)   *Potential lost revenue (PLR)* – This is the amount of tax which is payable as a result of correcting the error, or notifying HMRC of the liability. Where inflated losses have been claimed, but not yet utilised, the PLR is 10% of the unused loss (*FA 2007, Sch 24, paras 5–8*).

(4)   *Failure to notify* – If HMRC become aware of the failure to notify less than 12 months after the tax first becomes unpaid due to the failure, the penalty for careless behaviour ranges from 0% to 30% for unprompted disclosure, and from 10% to 30% for prompted disclosure. Otherwise, the penalty ranges stated above apply (*FA 2008, Sch 41, para 13(3)*).

(5)   *Error by another person* – A penalty can also apply to an error in a taxpayer's document which is attributable to another person (*FA 2007, Sch 24, para 1A*).

(6)   *Late returns: Penalty aggregation* – The penalty regime for late returns applies both fixed and tax-geared penalties (see **Late filing** below). A taxpayer may become liable to more than one category of penalty in respect of the same return, etc (*FA 2009, Sch 55, para 1(3)*). However, where more than one tax-geared penalty arises, the aggregate must not exceed a statutory maximum (*FA 2009, Sch 55, para 17(3)*).

(7)   *Reasonable excuse* – No penalty arises if there is a 'reasonable excuse' throughout the period of default for a failure to notify or late filing (*FA 2008, Sch 41, para 20, FA 2009, Sch 55, para 23*).

(8)   *Errors: Under-assessment* – A penalty can be charged on a person if an HMRC assessment understates the tax payable, and the person fails to take reasonable steps to notify HMRC of the under-assessment within 30 days from the date of the assessment (*FA 2007, Sch 24, para 2*).

(9)   *Special reductions* – HMRC may reduce a penalty for errors in returns or documents, failure to notify, or late returns, because of 'special circumstances' (*FA 2007, Sch 24, para 11, FA 2008, Sch 41, para 14, FA 2009, Sch 55, para 16*).

(10) *Enablers of avoidance* – Individuals and entities who enable the use of tax avoidance arrangements, which are shown to fail, by court judgment or agreement with HMRC, can be subject to a penalty of 100% of the fee charged for the advice or scheme *(F(No 2)A 2017, Sch 16 para 5)*.

(11) *Failure to keep and preserve records* – Applies to direct taxes and VAT from 1 April 2009 for all other taxes and duties generally from 1 April 2010. Maximum penalty: £3,000 per tax year or accounting period *(TMA 1970, s 12B(5); FA 1998, Sch 18, para 23; SI 2009/402; SI 2010/815)*.

(12) *Coronavirus support schemes* – Where a taxpayer has incorrectly claimed a payment under CJRS (see **Chapter 3**), SEISS (see **Chapter 6**) or CSPP (see **Chapter 16**), the amount over-claimed will be clawed-back as a tax charge. Where the overpayment is not declared to HMRC within the later of: 90 days of the claim and 20 October 2020, a penalty may be applied under the failure to notify rules on the basis that the error was deliberate and concealed *(FA 2020, Sch 16)*.

(13) *Further information* – See HMRC's compliance factsheets: tinyurl.com/y8dp55u5, and overview of penalties: tinyurl.com/PovtAA.

Offshore matters

(1) The *Criminal Finances Act 2017* introduced these offences:

- a criminal offence for individual offshore tax evaders;
- a corporate criminal offence for failure to prevent tax evasion.

(2) *Enabling off-shore tax evasion* – Tax Advisers can be subject to a penalty as enablers of offshore tax evasion from 1 January 2017. The person enabled by the adviser must be liable to a civil tax penalty or have committed a criminal tax offence, both in relation to offshore matters. The penalty for the enabler is the higher of £3,000 and 100% of the PLR *(SI 2016/1249)*.

Classification of territories

Territories are classified in accordance with the penalty regime for errors *(FA 2007, Sch 24, para 21A; FA 2015, Sch 20 para 2)*.

There are different levels of penalty for failure to notify or in accuracies which apply only for income tax, IHT and CGT for periods from April 2016. If HMRC become aware of the failure to notify less than 12 months after the tax first becomes unpaid due to the failure, the minimum penalty for a non-deliberate action is reduced for an unprompted disclosure.

CATEGORY 1 TERRITORY

Reason behind inaccuracy or error	Unprompted disclosure		Prompted disclosure	
	Maximum penalty	Minimum penalty	Maximum penalty	Minimum penalty
Careless	30%	0%	30%	15%
Deliberate, not concealed	70%	30%	70%	45%
Deliberate and concealed	100%	40%	100%	60%

Reason behind the failure to notify or disclose	Unprompted disclosure		Prompted disclosure	
	Maximum penalty	Minimum penalty	Maximum penalty	Minimum penalty
Non-deliberate failure within 12 months of tax due	30%	0%	30%	10%
Non-deliberate failure over 12 months of tax due	30%	10%	30%	20%
Deliberate but not concealed within 12 months of tax due	70%	30%	70%	45%
Deliberate but not concealed over 12 months of tax due	70%	30%	70%	45%
Deliberate and concealed	100%	40%	100%	60%

Notes

(1)   *Category 1 information* – This is information involving:

   (a)   A UK domestic matter; or

   (b)   An offshore matter, where the territory is in Category 1 or the tax at stake is income tax or CGT (or IHT from April 2017).

(2)   *Failure to notify* – The penalties for failure to notify only relate to matters connected with income tax or CGT from 2016/17, and for IHT for transfers from 1 April 2017.

(3)   *Which countries* – A list of Category 1 and Category 3 territories is available at: tinyurl.com/tcosp0713. All countries which are not Category 1 or 3 are Category 2.

CATEGORY 2 TERRITORY

(*FA 2007, Sch 24, para 10*)

Reason behind inaccuracy or error	Unprompted disclosure		Prompted disclosure	
	Maximum penalty	Minimum penalty	Maximum penalty	Minimum penalty
Careless	45%	0%	45%	22.5%
Deliberate but not concealed	105%	40%	105%	62.5%
Deliberate and concealed	150%	55%	150%	85%

Reason behind the failure to notify or disclose	Unprompted disclosure		Prompted disclosure	
	Maximum penalty	Minimum penalty	Maximum penalty	Minimum penalty
Non-deliberate failure within 12 months of tax due	45%	0%	45%	15%
Non-deliberate failure over 12 months of tax due	45%	15%	45%	30%
Deliberate but not concealed	105%	40%	105%	62.5%
Deliberate and concealed	150%	55%	150%	85%

Notes

(1) *Category 2 information* – This is information involving an offshore matter, in a Category 2 territory, which would enable or assist HMRC to assess an income tax or CGT liability.

(2) *Failure to notify* – The penalties for failure to notify only relate to matters connected with income tax or CGT from 2016/17, and for IHT for transfers from 1 April 2017.

(3) *Further information* – See HMRC Compliance Handbook CH11660 and HMRC factsheets CC/FS17 and CC/FS17a.

CATEGORY 3 TERRITORY

(*FA 2007, Sch 24, para 10*)

Reason behind inaccuracy or error	Unprompted disclosure		Prompted disclosure	
	Maximum penalty	Minimum penalty	Maximum penalty	Minimum penalty
Careless	60%	0%	60%	30%
Deliberate but not concealed	140%	50%	140%	80%
Deliberate and concealed	200%	70%	200%	110%

Reason behind the failure to notify or disclose	Unprompted disclosure		Prompted disclosure	
	Maximum penalty	Minimum penalty	Maximum penalty	Minimum penalty
Non-deliberate failure within 12 months of tax due	60%	0%	60%	20%
Non-deliberate failure over 12 months of tax due	60%	20%	60%	40%
Deliberate but not concealed	140%	50%	140%	80%
Deliberate and concealed	200%	70%	200%	110%

Notes

(1) *Category 3 information* – This is information involving an offshore matter, in a Category 3 territory, which would enable or assist HMRC to assess an income tax or CGT liability.

(2) *Failure to notify* – The penalties for failure to notify only relate to matters connected with income tax or CGT from 2016/17, and for IHT for transfers from 1 April 2017.

(3) *Further information* – See HMRC Compliance Handbook CH116700.

Requirement to correct

(F(No 2)A 2017, Sch 18 para 15(2))

	Unprompted disclosure	**Prompted disclosure**
Minimum	50% of standard penalty	80% of standard penalty
Maximum	100% of standard penalty	100% of standard penalty

Notes

(1) *Applies when* – A failure to correct (FTC) penalty will apply where an offshore inaccuracy or omission existed at 6 April 2017, and the correction was not made before 30 September 2018.

(2) *Reasonable excuse* – If the taxpayer can demonstrate they had a reasonable excuse the FTC penalty will not apply but the tax and interest will be payable.

(3) *Further information* – See tinyurl.com/RTCTDOA.

LATE FILING OR LATE PAYMENT

Late filing

(FA 2009, s 106, Sch 55)

Period	Penalty	Notes
Up to 3 months late	£100	Automatic fixed penalty
More than 3 months late	£10 per day	Maximum of 90 days ie £900.
		Payable only if HMRC give notice of the penalty, and the notice specifies the date from which the penalty is payable.
More than 6 months late	Greater of: • 5% of tax liability; and • £300	'Tax liability' is any tax which would have been shown in the return in question.
More than 12 months late, except where taxpayer withholds information deliberately (see below).	Greater of: • 5% of tax liability; and • £300	
12 months + late and information withheld deliberately **but not** concealed	Greater of: • Relevant % of tax liability; and • £300	See **Structure of penalties** above
12 months + late and information withheld deliberately **and** concealed	Greater of: • Relevant % of tax liability; and • £300	See **Structure of penalties** above

Notes

(1) *Applies to* – Income Tax, CGT, ATED, SDRT, Bank Payroll Tax and Registered Pensions Schemes. There are slightly different penalty models for other taxes.

(2) *Effective from* – For returns due for 2010/11 and later tax years (*FA 2009, s 106, Sch 55; SI 2011/702*).

(3) *New points-based regime* – *Finance Bill 2021* introduces a new points-based penalty regime (announced at Budget 2020) for regular tax return filing obligations. Occasional submissions will continue to be covered by the current relevant penalty regime.

The new regime comes into effect:

- For accounting periods beginning on or after 6 April 2023, for MTD ITSA taxpayers (see **Chapter 6**).

- For accounting periods beginning on or after 6 April 2024, for all other ITSA taxpayers.

See https://tinyurl.com/pnts4plt for further information (*Finance Bill 2021, cl 112*).

(4) *Further information* – See HMRC's Compliance Handbook at CH61000.

Late payment

(*FA 2009, s 107, Sch 56*)

Length of delay	Penalty
30 days	5% of the unpaid tax
6 months	5% of the unpaid tax (additional)
12 months	5% of the unpaid tax (additional)

Notes

(1) *Applies to* – Income tax, CGT, PAYE, NIC, Student Loan deductions, CIS, ATED, MGD, Bank Payroll Tax and Registered Pension Schemes. For income tax under self-assessment these penalties only apply to late balancing payments (ie based on tax returns for individuals or trustees etc).

(2) *Effective from* – In relation to 2010/11 and later tax years (*SI 2011/702, art 3*).

(3) *Assessments and appeals* – HMRC must assess the late payment penalty, and notify the person liable as to the period to which the penalty relates. The penalty is payable within 30 days from the day on which the penalty notice is issued. There is a right of appeal against both the imposition of a penalty, and the amount involved (*FA 2009, Sch 56, paras 11, 13*).

(4) *Reduction and suspension* – HMRC may reduce a late payment penalty in 'special circumstances', which does not include inability to pay (*FA 2009, Sch 56, para 9*). In addition, a defence of 'reasonable excuse' may be available (*Sch 56, para 16*).

(5) *Payments on account* – The maximum penalty for fraudulent or negligent claims by taxpayers to reduce payments on account is the difference between the correct

amount payable on account and the amount of any payment on account made by him (*TMA 1970, s 59A(6)*).

(6)   *New regime – Finance Bill 2021* introduces a new two-tiered penalty model for individuals and businesses that fail to pay their tax liabilities on time. The new regime will initially replace existing penalties for VAT and ITSA, with plans to expand to other taxes in the future.

The new regime comes into effect:

- For all MTD ITSA taxpayers who join MTD in the 2023/24 tax year, to all late payments relating to the 2023/24 year onward;

- For all other ITSA taxpayers, to all late payments relating to the 2024/25 tax year onward.

See https://tinyurl.com/pntltpplty for further information (*Finance Bill 2021, cl 113*).

(7)   *Further information* – See HMRC's Compliance Handbook at CH150500.

CORPORATION TAX PENALTIES

(*FA 1998, Sch 18; FA 2007, s 97, Sch 24; FA 2008, s 113, Sch 36, s 123, Sch 41*)

Offence	Maximum penalty
Failure to notify chargeability (*FA 2008, s 123, Sch 41, paras 1, 6, 6A; SI 2009/511*)	
Deliberate and concealed act or failure	100% of potential lost revenue
Deliberate but not concealed act or failure	70% of potential lost revenue
Any other case	30% of potential lost revenue
Failure to deliver a return (*FA 1998, Sch 18, paras 17, 18*)	
Up to 3 months after filing date	£100 third successive failure: £500
More than 3 months after filing date	A further £100 plus third successive failure: £1000
At least 18 months but less than 24 months after end of return period	10% of tax unpaid at 18 months after end of return period
24 months or more after end of return period	A further 10% of tax unpaid at 18 months after end of return period
Errors in returns etc (*FA 2007, s 97, Sch 24, para 4; SI 2008/568*)	
Reasonable care taken	No penalty liability
Careless inaccuracy	30% of potential lost revenue
Deliberate but not concealed inaccuracy	70% of potential lost revenue
Deliberate and concealed inaccuracy	100% of potential lost revenue
Quarterly instalment payments	
Deliberate or reckless failure to pay the correct amount on an instalment date;	Up to twice the amount of interest charged on any unpaid amount
Fraudulent or negligent claim for repayment (under *reg 6(2)* of the instalment regulations) (*TMA 1970, s 59E(4); SI 1998/3175, reg 13*)	in respect of the company's total liability for the accounting period

Notes

(1) *Failure to notify* – These provisions took effect from 1 April 2010. For earlier periods penalties were charged under *FA 1998, Sch 18, para 2(3)*, up to a maximum of 100% of tax payable for the accounting period and remaining unpaid 12 months after the end of the period.

(2) *Failure to make returns etc* – A fixed and tax related penalty regime applies for the late filing of corporation tax returns from 6 October 2011 (*FA 2009, s 106, Sch 55; SI 2011/2391*).

(3) *Failure to deliver a return* – The above flat rate penalties do not apply if the return period is one for which the company must deliver accounts under the *Companies Act 2006*, and the return is filed by the date allowed by Companies House (*FA 1998, Sch 18, para 19*). This has no effect on the tax geared penalties which may arise.

VAT PENALTIES

Default surcharge

(*VATA 1994, ss 59–59B, 71*; VAT Notice 700/50)

Number of defaults during rolling 12 month period	Surcharge where turnover less than £150,000 (VAT Notice 700/50, para 4.2)	Surcharge if turnover is £150,000 or more
1st	No surcharge, but if default within 12 months will enter surcharge default period. Help letter issued	No surcharge, but enter a surcharge period. Surcharge Liability Notice issued
2nd	No surcharge but enter a surcharge period	2% (no surcharge issued if charge is under £400)
3rd	2% (no surcharge issued if charge is under £400)	5% (no surcharge issued if charge is under £400)
4th	5% (no surcharge issued if charge is under £400)	greater of 10% or £30
5th	greater of 10% or £30	greater of 15% or £30
6th	greater of 15% or £30	greater of 15% or £30

Notes

(1) *Applies to* – Failure to submit a return or pay amount of VAT payable on time, or pay the amount due under the payment on account scheme on time. The surcharge is calculated as a percentage of the unpaid VAT in default.

(2) *Reasonable excuse* – A surcharge liability does not arise if HMRC or the Tax Tribunal are satisfied that there is a reasonable excuse for the return or VAT payment being late (*VATA 1994, s 59(7)*). As to circumstances which cannot constitute a 'reasonable excuse' for these purposes, see *VATA 1994, s 71(1)*.

(3) *Payments on account* – Surcharges can apply to late payments on account; see *VATA 1994, s 59A* and VAT Notice 700/50, para 4.4.

(4)   *Payment deferral* – VAT debts due between 20 March and 30 June 2020, which were deferred, need to be paid in full by 31 March 2021, or paid under an instalment agreement with HMRC so the full amount is paid by January 2022. No interest or default surcharges will be raised on late payment of deferred VAT paid within these deadlines (see: https://tinyurl.com/VATdfpp122).

(5)   *New regime – Finance Bill 2021* introduces a new penalty regime for the late submission of regular VAT obligations, as well as new penalties relating to the late payment of VAT.

For all VAT taxpayers, the new regime comes into effect for accounting periods beginning on or after 1 April 2022.

See https://tinyurl.com/pnts4plt and https://tinyurl.com/pntltpplty for further information (*Finance Bill 2021, cls 112, 113*).

(6)   *Further information* – For default surcharges and VAT penalties see www.gov.uk/vat-returns/surcharges-and-penalties.

Unauthorised issue of VAT invoice

(*FA 2008, Sch 41, paras 2, 6*)

● *General* – A penalty is payable by a person who makes an unauthorised issue of a VAT invoice, ie where an 'unauthorised person' (eg a person not registered under *VATA 1994*) issues an invoice showing an amount of VAT or a VAT inclusive amount).

● *Commencement* – The provisions apply to any unauthorised issue of an invoice taking place from 1 April 2010 (*SI 2009/511, art 3*).

● *Level of penalty* – The same penalties apply as for failure to notify (see **UK matters** above), except that the lower penalties for non-deliberate behaviour do not apply.

● *Special reductions and reasonable excuse* – HMRC may reduce a penalty in 'special circumstances' and penalties do not arise if HMRC or the tribunal are satisfied that there is a 'reasonable excuse' for the act or failure (*FA 2008, Sch 41, paras 14, 20*).

Incorrect certificates as to zero-rating etc

(*VATA 1994, s 62*)

● *General* – The penalty is charged in respect of incorrect certificates within *VATA 1994, s 62(1)*, or in respect of acquisitions of goods from other member states within the fiscal warehousing regime; see *s 62(1A)*.

● *Person liable* – The person giving or preparing the certificate is liable to the penalty.

● *Level of penalty* – The penalty is equal to the difference between the VAT chargeable if the certificate had been correct and any VAT actually charged, or (in respect of acquisitions from other member states within the fiscal warehousing regime) the amount of VAT actually chargeable on the acquisition.

Breach of walking possession agreements

(*VATA 1994, s 68*)

- *General* – A penalty can be imposed for the breach of an undertaking contained in a walking possession agreement (NB a penalty under *VATA 1994, s 68* does not extend to Scotland).

- *Amount of penalty* – The person in default is liable to a penalty equal to 50% of VAT due or any amount recoverable as if it were VAT due.

Breaches of regulatory provisions

(*VATA 1994, s 69;* VCP11100 et seq)

Failures in the two year period	Prescribed rate	Late payment or late submission of return
First failure	£5 per day	1/6th of 1% of VAT due
Second failure	£10 per day	1/3rd of 1% of VAT due
Any other case	£15 per day	1/2 of 1% of VAT due

Notes

(1) *Who it applies to* – A penalty for a failure to comply with any regulatory requirement is determined according to the number of occasions in the previous two years on which the person has failed to comply with that requirement.

(2) *Amount of penalty* – Greater of £50 and the prescribed daily rate for up to 100 days.

(3) *Late payments or late filing* – Where the breach is a late payment failure or the late filing of a VAT return, the prescribed penalty rate is the greater of the penalty in note 2, and the amounts shown in the table above (*VATA 1994, s 69(5)*).

(4) *Double penalties* – A late payment or filing penalty cannot be assessed if a default surcharge is to be assessed for the same failure (VCP11134).

Failure to preserve records

(*VATA 1994, ss 69(2), 69B, Sch 11, para 6A(1), (6)*)

Failure to keep records:	Penalty
Under requirement imposed by VATA *Sch 11, para 6(3)*	£500
As required by HMRC direction	£200 per day up to 30 days
As required by HMRC to preserve records for up to 6 years	£500

Notes

(1)   *General failure* – HMRC may require records to be preserved for a period specified in writing, but not exceeding 6 years (*VATA 1994, Sch 11, para 6(3)*).

(2)   *Amount of penalty* – As shown in table above, unless there is a reasonable excuse for the failure.

(3)   *Breach of direction* – Penalties as shown in table above unless HMRC or the tribunal is satisfied that there is a reasonable excuse for the failure.

Evasion of import VAT (and other relevant duties)

(FA 2003, ss 24(2)(d), 25)

- *General* – A penalty can be imposed where a person engages in conduct to evade import VAT, or by which he contravenes a legislative duty, obligation, requirement or condition in relation to import VAT.

- *Penalty* – The penalty for evasion involving dishonesty is an amount equal to the import VAT evaded or sought to be evaded.

- *Other relevant duties* – The same penalty provisions that apply to import VAT apply to other relevant duties.

Contravention of relevant rules

(FA 2003, ss 26, 27, 29; SI 2003/3113)

- *General* – A penalty can arise for contravening a 'relevant rule' (see *FA 2003, s 26(8); SI 2003/3113, reg 3, Sch*).

- *Penalty* – A penalty of up to £2,500 (or other amount prescribed by Treasury Order) can be imposed, unless HMRC or the tribunal are satisfied that there is a reasonable excuse for the failure, or unless the penalty is reduced or cancelled by HMRC or the tribunal.

Failure to file VAT returns online

(SI 1995/2518, reg 25A)

Annual VAT exclusive turnover	Penalty	Annual VAT exclusive turnover	Penalty
Over £22.8m	£400	£100,001 to £5.6m	£200
£5.6m to £22.8m	£300	£100,000 and under	£100

Notes

(1) *Commencement* – VAT traders can be liable to penalties in relation to returns made for prescribed accounting periods ending on or after 31 March 2011 (*SI 1995/2518, reg 25A(15)*).

(2) *Online submission* – All VAT registered traders are required to submit VAT returns through the HMRC online form (the portal) from 1 April 2012, unless they qualify for exemption (see note 4).

(3) *Penalties* – Are charged for paper VAT returns submitted for VAT periods ending on or after 31 March 2013, unless the taxpayer qualifies for exemption, or the person has a reasonable excuse for failing to file online.

(4) *Exemptions* – Businesses run by individuals who have a religious conscience objection to the use of computers, and those who find it impossible or impractical to use computers due to age, disability or location, can apply to HMRC for an exemption to online filing. In those cases, arrangements can be made with HMRC to submit the VAT figures by phone.

(5) *MTD* – Most VAT registered traders are required to submit VAT returns via MTD-compatible software for periods beginning on and after 1 April 2019 (see **Chapter 6**). Under the soft-landing for compliance with the MTD, penalties for non-compliance are unlikely to be applied until April 2021. The penalties for non-compliance with MTD regulations are to be revised from April 2021.

EC SALES LIST (ESL) PENALTIES

(*VATA 1994, ss 65, 66*)

Defaults	Inaccuracy in return	Late or non-submission (up to 100 days)
First default	–	£5 per day
Second default	–	£10 per day
Any other case	£100 (see note 1)	£15 per day

Notes

(1) *Inaccuracies* – The error must be a material inaccuracy included on statement submitted within two years after a penalty notice has been issued by HMRC. A penalty will only be imposed where the third ESL containing an inaccuracy has been submitted (see VCP11044).

(2) *Late filing* – Penalties are only charged if HMRC has served a default notice and the ELS is not submitted within 14 days. The penalty is the greater of: £50 and up to 100 days of the daily penalties.

SDLT PENALTIES

(FA 2003, Schs 10, 11; FA 2007, Sch 24)

Offence	Penalty
Failure to deliver a return by the filing date *(FA 2003, Sch 10, paras 3, 4)*	Up to 3 months late – £100
	Over 3 months late – £200
	Over 12 months – tax related penalty not exceeding the tax chargeable

Notes

(1)   *Short filing period* – From 1 March 2019 the SDLT return and payment must reach HMRC within 14 days of the completion date (see **Chapter 11**).

(2)   *Errors* – For penalties relating to errors or mistakes in SDLT and SDRT returns, see **Structure of penalties** above.

Stamp duty penalties – late stamping

(SA 1891, s 15B)

Document late by:	Penalty
Up to 12 months	10% of duty, capped at £300
12 to 24 months	20% of duty
More than 24 months	30% of duty

Notes

(1)   *Effective for* – Instruments submitted for stamping from 1 October 2014.

(2)   *Interest* – In addition to the above penalty for late filing, if the stamp duty was not paid on time, interest will also be due on the late payment at the official rate (see below).

(3)   *Further information* – See https://www.gov.uk/stamp-duty-penalties-appeals-and-interest.

INTEREST RATES

Income tax, NICs, CGT and stamp duties

(SA 1891, s 15A; FA 1999, s 110; FA 2003, ss 87, 89; SI 1986/1711, regs 13, 14)

Period from	Rate payable %	Repayment Rate %
7 April 2020	2.60	0.50
30 March 2020 to 6 April 2020	2.75	0.50

Period from	Rate payable %	Repayment Rate %
21 August 2018 to 29 March 2020	3.25	0.50
21 Nov 2017 to 20 Aug 2018	3.00	0.50
23 Aug 2016 to 20 Nov 2017	2.75	0.50
29 Sept 2009 to 22 Aug 2016	3.00	0.50

Notes

(1) *Interest payable* – The interest regime in *FA 2009, ss 101–103* ('Late payment interest on sums to be paid by HMRC', 'Repayment interest on sums to be paid by HMRC' and 'Rates of interest') applies with effect from 31 October 2011, for the purposes of self-assessment payments and repayments (*SI 2011/701*).

(2) *Unified rates* – From 29 September 2009, the rates of interest charged and paid by HMRC for all the main taxes and duties are aligned (*SI 2009/2032*).

(3) *Stamp duty* – Interest on unpaid stamp duty applies from the end of 30 days after the date on which the document was executed until the duty is paid. The interest is rounded down to the nearest multiple of £5, and no interest is payable (or repayable) on amounts of less than £25.

(4) *SDLT* – Interest on unpaid SDLT runs from the end of 14 days after the 'relevant date' (generally the effective date of the transaction) until the tax is paid. The relevant dates for repayment of overpaid SDLT are from the date on which the payment is lodged with HMRC until the date when the repayment order is issued.

(5) *SDRT* – Interest on SDRT is charged from the 'accountable date' to the date of payment. If SDRT is overpaid then any repayment of SDRT will be made with interest from the date that it was paid. However, no interest is added to SDRT repayments under £25.

(6) *Earlier years* – Interest rates on late payments and repayments for earlier years can be found here: tinyurl.com/HMINTRS.

VAT, APD, IPT, customs duties, etc

Period from	Statutory interest %	Default interest %
7 April 2020	0.5	2.60
30 March 2020 to 6 April 2020	0.5	2.75
21 August 2018	0.5	3.25
21 Nov 2017 to 20 Aug 2018	0.5	3.00
23 Aug 2016 to 20 Nov 2017	0.5	2.75
29 Sept 2009 to 22 Aug 2016	0.5	3.00

Notes

(1) *Default interest* – This is charged where due on any amount of VAT which has been underdeclared or overclaimed, from the time the amount should have been paid to the time it is assessed (VAT Notice 700/43, para 1.2).

(2) *Payment of interest* – If all the VAT liable to interest is not paid within 30 days of a notification from HMRC, further interest is chargeable. Interest continues to be charged on a monthly basis until all the VAT liable to interest is paid (VAT Notice 700/43, para 2.8).

(3) *Statutory interest* – This is paid by HMRC, where errors have been made or if the mistake meant that the recipient had to wait an unreasonable time before receiving payment of an amount related to VAT.

(4) *Claiming interest* – A separate claim must be made for any interest from HMRC, as it is not paid automatically. The claim must be made not more than four years after the end of the applicable period to which it relates (*VATA 1994, s 78(11)*).

(5) *VAT interest harmonisation* – *Finance Bill 2021* amends *FA 2009* regarding late payment and repayment interest for VAT to generally bring them in line with the rules for ITSA, to ensure that interest is charged and paid to customers consistently. The measures are to come into effect by way of regulations (*Finance Bill 2021, cl 116*).

(6) *Further information* – For rates in earlier periods see: tinyurl.com/dfstint.

Companies – general

(TMA 1970, ss 87, 87A, 109; SI 1998/3175, reg 7)

Description	Interest runs from
Corporation tax	Due and payable date
Corporation tax payable in instalments	Date instalment is due to be paid
Overdue income tax deducted from certain payments	14 days after end of return period
Overdue tax on loans to participators of close companies	Due and payable date

Notes

(1) *Historical interest rates* – The rates of interest charged on underpaid quarterly instalments are found here: tinyurl.com/HMINTRS.

(2) *Surrender of tax refund within a group* – A group company which is due a tax refund for an accounting period may surrender it to another group member, if both companies give notice to HMRC. The effect is that the recipient company is generally treated as having paid the tax when the surrendering company paid it (or on the due and payable date for the surrendering company, if paid earlier) (*CTA 2010, ss 963, 964*).

Corporation tax not paid by instalments (CTSA)

From	Under-paid %	Over-paid %
7 April 2020	2.60	0.50
30 March 2020 to 6 April 2020	2.75	0.50
21 August 2018 to 29 March 2020	3.25	0.50
21 Nov 2017 to 20 Aug 2018	3.00	0.50
23 Aug 2016 to 20 Nov 2017	2.75	0.50
29 Sept 2009 to 22 Aug 2016	3.00	0.50

Corporation tax paid by instalments (Periods ending from 1 July 1999)

From	Under-paid %	Over-paid or early paid not by instalments %
30 March 2020	1.10	0.50
23 March 2020 to 29 March 2020	1.25	0.50
13 August 2018 to 22 March 2020	1.75	0.50
13 Nov 2017 to 12 Aug 2018	1.50	0.50
15 Aug 2016 to 12 Nov 2017	1.25	0.50
21 Sept 2009 to 14 Aug 2016	1.50	0.50

Corporation tax pay and file

From	Under-paid %	Over-paid %
7 April 2020	2.60	0.50
30 March 2020 to 6 April 2020	2.75	0.50
21 August 2018 to 29 March 2020	3.25	0.50
21 Nov 2017 to 20 Aug 2018	3.00	0.50
23 Aug 2016 to 20 Nov 2017	2.75	0.50
29 Sep 2009 to 22 Aug 2016	3.00	0.50

Corporation tax pre-pay and file

From	Under-paid %	Over-paid %
7 April 2020	2.60	0.50
30 March 2020 to 6 April 2020	2.75	0.50
21 August 2018	3.25	0.50
21 Nov 2017 to 20 Aug 2018	3.00	0.50
23 Aug 2016 to 20 Nov 2017	2.75	0.50
29 Sept 2009 to 22 Aug 2016	3.00	0.50

IHT

(IHTA 1984, s 233)

Interest period	Interest rate (%)	Interest on repayments (%)	Days
7 April 2020	2.60	0.50	–
30 March 2020 to 6 April 2020	2.75	0.50	8
21 Aug 2018 to 29 March 2020	3.25	0.50	587
21 Nov 2017 to 20 Aug 2018	3.00	0.50	273
23 Aug 2016 to 20 Nov 2017	2.75	0.50	456
29 Sept 2009 to 22 Aug 2016	3.00	0.50	2,520

Note

Earlier years – Interest rates for IHT for earlier years can be found here: tinyurl.com/ IHTinsrts.

Interest on IHT paid in yearly instalments

(IHTA 1984, ss 227, 234)

Month of death	Due date	Interest starts from
January	31 July	1 August
February	31 August	1 September
March	30 September	1 October
April	31 October	1 November
May	30 November	1 December
June	31 December	1 January
July	31 January	1 February
August	28/29 February	1 March
September	31 March	1 April
October	30 April	1 May
November	31 May	1 June
December	30 June	1 July

Note

For IHT payable by ten equal yearly instalments, the first instalment is due six months from the end of the month in which the individual died. The second instalment is due on the same day 12 months after the first payment, and subsequent instalments are due on the same day each year. The preceding table shows how to work out the due date. Interest commences from the following day.

Discovery assessments

(TMA 1970, ss 29, 34, 36; FA 1998, Sch 18, para 46)

	Time limit for assessment to be raised on:	
Circumstances	*Individual*	*Company*
Loss of tax but no careless or deliberate behaviour by taxpayer	4 years from the end of the tax year *(TMA 1970, s 34)*	4 years from the end of the accounting period (6 years for periods ending before 1 April 2010) *(FA 1998, Sch 18, para 46(1))*
Loss of tax due to careless behaviour of taxpayer or agent	6 years from the end of the tax year *(TMA 1970, s 36(1), (1B))*	6 years from the end of the accounting period *(FA 1998, Sch 18, para 46(2), (2B))*
Loss of tax due to deliberate behaviour by taxpayer or agent	20 years from the end of the tax year *(TMA 1970, s 36(1A), (1B))*	20 years from end of the accounting period *(FA 1998, Sch 18, para 46(2A)(a), (2B))*
Fraudulent or negligent conduct by taxpayer or in case of a company: someone acting on behalf of the company.	For periods before 6 April 2009: 20 years after 31 January following the tax year *(TMA 1970, s 36(1))*	For periods ending on or before: 31 March 2010: 21 years after the end of the accounting period *(SI 2009/403).*

Notes

(1) *Scope* – Separate 'discovery' assessment provisions and time limits apply in certain circumstances, such as:

- Failure to provide information about a tax avoidance scheme *(TMA 1970, s 118(2); FA 1998, Sch 18, para 46(1), (2A)(b), (c))*;

- Failure to notify liability to tax *(TMA 1970, ss 34, 36(1A), (1B), 118(2))*; and

- Discovery assessment on personal representatives of a deceased person in respect of years/periods up to the date of death *(TMA 1970, s 40(1), (2))*.

(2) *Further information* – See HMRC's Compliance Handbook for tables of assessment time limits for income tax, capital gains tax (CH56100) and for corporation tax purposes (CH56200).

Data-gathering

(FA 2011, Sch 23, Pt 4, paras 30, 31, 32)

Offence	Penalty
Failure to comply with a data-holder notice	
• Initial penalty	• £300 fixed
• Continued failure	• Up to £60 per day on which the failure continues
• Continued failure for more than 30 days after £300 penalty imposed	• Up to £1000 per day if approved by First-tier tribunal
Concealing, destroying, disposing of documents required by data-holder notice	£300 fixed
Carelessly or deliberately providing inaccurate data or information when complying with a data-holder notice.	Up to £3,000

Notes

(1)   *Data notice* – An HMRC officer may require a 'relevant data-holder' to provide 'relevant data'. Penalties can apply from 1 April 2012 to a failure by the data-holder to comply with a data-holder notice relevant to any period (ie before, on or after that date) *(FA 2011, Sch 23, para 65)*.

(2)   *Right of appeal* – Against the liability to, or amount of, the penalties listed in the table above *(FA 2011, Sch 23, para 36)*.

(3)   *Reasonable excuse* – The £300 fixed penalty, and the penalties of up to £60 per day, do not apply if there is a 'reasonable excuse' for the failure *(FA 2011, Sch 23, para 34)*.

Information and inspection

(FA 2008, s 113, Sch 36, paras 5, 39, 40, 40A, 50)

Offence	Penalty
Failure to comply with an information notice	
• Initial failure	• £300 fixed
• Continued failure after £300 penalty imposed	• Up to £60 per day on which failure or obstruction continues
• Where notice is 'identity unknown' notice and failure continues for more than 30 days	• Up to £1000 per day if approved by First-tier tribunal
• Continued failure where significant tax is at risk	• Tax related penalty of amount to be decided by the Upper Tribunal
Concealing, destroying, disposing of documents required by information notice	£300 fixed

Offence	Penalty
Deliberately obstructing an inspection approved by the tribunal	£300 fixed
• Continued deliberate obstruction	£60 per day while obstruction continues
Carelessly or deliberately providing inaccurate information or documents	Up to £3,000 for each inaccuracy

Notes

(1) *Applies to* – Information notices issued or inspections carried out from 1 April 2009 for direct tax and VAT purposes (*SI 2009/404, art 2*), and for other taxes and duties generally from 1 April 2010 (*FA 2009, s 96, Sch 48; SI 2009/3054*).

(2) *Reasonable excuse* – Penalties for the above offences do not arise if there is a 'reasonable excuse' for the failure or obstruction (*FA 2008, Sch 36, para 45*).

Anti-avoidance Notices

(*FA 2014, ss 204–229, Sch 32*)

HMRC power to issue:	Right of appeal?
Accelerated Payment Notice (APN) when there is an open enquiry or appeal relating to taxpayer's affairs, HMRC think the taxpayer has achieved a tax advantage and he has: • used a DOTAS disclosed scheme; or • received a Follower Notice; or • received a GAAR counteraction notice.	No, but taxpayer or agent can make representations to HMRC within 90 days of issue of APN.
Follower Notice (FN) when there is an open enquiry into taxpayer's affairs or open appeal and: • taxpayer has obtained a tax advantage from use of particular tax arrangements; and • HMRC believe there is a final judicial ruling relevant to those arrangements; and • FN has not been issued to that taxpayer for those tax arrangements which has not been withdrawn.	No, but can make representations to HMRC within 90 days of issue of FN that conditions for issue have not been met.
GAAR counteraction notice after the issue has been considered by the GAAR advisory panel and an opinion has been given.	Yes.

Notes:

(1) *APN tax due* – Within 90 days of the issue of the APN or within 30 days of HMRC decision regarding representations, if later. Taxpayer can ask for time to pay. Note the tax amount demanded by the APN doesn't have to be proved to be due by a Court or Tribunal.

(2) *Penalties* – Where APN tax is paid late: 5% of tax due, when 5 months late: further 5% of tax due, when 11 months late further 5% of tax due. If the APN is withdrawn any tax and the penalties paid in respect of the APN will be repaid.

(3) *Interest* – No interest is charged for late payment of APN tax, but interest is charged if underlying tax liability is found to be due and is paid late.

(4) *FN action* – When FN is received taxpayer must either amend their own tax return as requested on FN and pay tax due, or carry on fighting the case and risk receiving an APN. If no action is taken a penalty of up to 50% of the tax due may be imposed (see note 5).

(5) *Changes to FN penalties* – *Finance Bill 2021* amends *FA 2014* to reduce the rate of FN penalty to 30% of the avoided tax in most cases. The 50% rate is effectively kept in cases where the Tribunal or court deem a taxpayer was unreasonable in pursuing litigation via issuance of a new additional 20% penalty. There is limited scope to appeal against the further 20% penalty. The amendment will come into effect on the day the Act is passed (*Finance Bill 2021, cl 115*).

(6) *Further information* – Detailed guidance on Follower Notices and Accelerated Payments: tinyurl.com/fnapns and HMRC Factsheets: CC/FS24, CC/FS25a, and CC/FS26.

Tax agents: dishonest conduct

(*FA 2012, s 223, Sch 38*)

HMRC power	Right of appeal?
Obtain working papers from tax agent voluntarily or under a file access notice. Penalties apply if the notice is not complied with.	No appeal against file access notice, but can appeal against the penalties
Issue a Conduct Notice which includes evidence of the dishonest conduct	Yes, within 30 days.
Charge civil penalties of between £5,000 and £50,000, plus interest on late paid penalties (*SI 2013/280*)	Yes, against the amount of the penalty but not against the imposition of the penalty.
Disclose details of the agent's dishonest conduct to the agent's professional body	No appeal.
'Name and shame' by publishing details of the tax agent on the HMRC website, where the agent has been charged a penalty of more than £5,000	No appeal.

Notes

(1) *Who these powers apply to* – A tax agent is an individual who, in the course of business, assists other persons (ie clients) with their tax affairs. These terms are defined widely (*FA 2012, Sch 38, para 2*).

(2) *What is dishonest conduct* – An individual engages in dishonest conduct if, in the course of acting as a tax agent, the individual does something dishonest with a view to bringing about a loss of tax revenue (*FA 2012, Sch 38, para 3*).

(3) *Commencement* – The powers listed above came into force on 1 April 2013 (*SI 2013/279*).

(4) *Further information* – For a summary of the dishonest conduct powers see https://www.gov.uk/dishonest-conduct-by-tax-agents. Technical guidance is found in the HMRC Compliance Handbook at paras CH180000-186220. A factsheet is available at: www.hmrc.gov.uk/agents/strategy/tafs.pdf.

HMRC CLEARANCES

Non-Statutory Clearances

(a) *All taxpayers* – HMRC's non-statutory clearance service is available to businesses, individuals and their advisers.

(b) *What is covered* – The tax consequences of transactions for which there is material uncertainty and:

- that uncertainty arises due to interpretation of legislation within the last four Finance Acts; or

- if the point relates to legislation older than the last four Finance Acts there is material uncertainty around the tax outcome of a transaction.

(c) *When to make an application* – Clearance applications can be made both pre-transaction (where evidence is supplied that the transaction is genuinely contemplated) and post-transaction. But HMRC expect the taxpayer (or their tax adviser) to have first fully considered all the HMRC relevant guidance and/or contacted the HMRC helpline, if there is one.

(d) *Not suitable* – HMRC will not accept clearance applications that:

- ask whether the General Anti-Abuse rule (GAAR) applies;

- concern employment contracts (although applications may ask for confirmation on the tax treatment of salary sacrifice arrangements put in place);

- ask HMRC for tax or NICs planning advice;

- are minor variations of previous applications in respect of the same person and the same transaction;

- concern arrangements primarily to gain a tax or NICs advantage rather than being primarily commercially motivated;

- relate to a period for which HMRC have already opened an enquiry;

- relate to a period for which the 'enquiry window' has closed or the tax return is final;

- include questions not involving interpretations of tax law or its application (eg asset valuations or transfer pricing);

- concern tax consequences of executing trust deeds or settlements, and whether the 'settlements' anti-avoidance provisions apply (*ITTOIA 2005, Pt 5, Ch 5*).

(e)   *Contents of application* – HMRC publish three checklists (Annexes A, B & C) which list the information required in support of a clearance application. HMRC they ask that the numbering of the questions be adhered to in the clearance application. The checklists in should be used as follows:

A – for all transactions other than business investment relief and BRP;

B – for business investment relief for non-domiciled persons; and

C – for BPR for inheritance tax.

Those checklists can be downloaded here: tinyurl.com/nrpowa9

(f)   *Send it to* – Clearance applications from large business should be submitted to the Client Relationship Manager (CRM) assigned to that business. Those from other applicants should be sent to the address on the appropriate checklist.

(g)   *Further information* – See HMRC's Other Non-Statutory Clearance Guidance Manual (ONSCG).

Valuation checks for capital gains

(a)   *Checking service* – Any taxpayer can request a check of a valuation of assets or shares from HMRC in order to compute capital gains tax, or corporation tax on chargeable gains.

(b)   *When to apply* – This service can be used after a disposal, or after a deemed disposal to support a claim that an asset has become of negligible value. But the application should be made well before the related tax return is submitted. HMRC states it will take at least two months to check a valuation. If HMRC have agreed a valuation, it will not challenge the subsequent use of it in a tax return.

(c)   *Contents of application* – Form CG34 must be completed for each valuation which HMRC are asked to check, and submitted together with the information listed on the form. Copies of Form CG34 can be downloaded from: tinyurl.com/FMCG35.

(d)   *Where to send it* – Completed forms CG34 plus related documents should be submitted by post to the appropriate HMRC office shown on the form.

Statutory Clearances

Clearance applications may be submitted to HMRC by letter, fax or email, including in respect of the following:

Clearance category	Statutory reference
Demergers*	*CTA 2010, s 1091*
Demergers: Chargeable payments*	*CTA 2010, s 1092*
Purchase of own shares*	*CTA 2010, s 1044*
EIS shares: acquisition by new company*	*ITA 2007, s 247(1)(f)*
Employee share schemes	*ITEPA 2003, Schs 2, 3 & 4*
Transactions in securities*	*ITA 2007, s 701; CTA 2010, s 748*

Clearance category	Statutory reference
Share exchanges*	*TCGA 1992, s 138(1)*
Share exchanges: continuity of SEIS relief*	*ITA 2007, s 257HB(1)(f)*
Reconstructions involving the transfer of a business*	*TCGA 1992, s 139(5)*
Transfer or division of a UK business between EU member states*	*TCGA 1992, s 140B*
Transfer or division of non-UK business by a UK company to a company resident in another EU member state	*TCGA 1992, s 140D*
Company reorganisations involving intangible assets*	*CTA 2009, s 831*
Loan relationships: transfers*	*CTA 2009, s 427*
Loan relationships: mergers*	*CTA 2009, s 437*
Derivative contracts: transfers*	*CTA 2009, s 677*
Derivative contracts: mergers*	*CTA 2009, s 686*
Targeted Anti Avoidance Rule 3 (Capital Gains)*	*TCGA 1992, ss 184G–184H*
Company migrations	*TMA 1970, s 109B*
Insurance companies: Transfer of long-term business	*FA 2012, s 133*
Insurance companies: Transitional rules	*FA 2012, Sch 17, para 18*
Assignment of lease at undervalue*	*ITTOIA 2005, s 300; CTA 2009, s 237*
Transactions in land*	*ITA 2007, s 770; CTA 2010, s 831; CTA 2009, s 237; ITTOIA 2005, s 300*
Offshore funds:	*SI 2009/3001, reg 54(2)*
(a) Reporting fund status	*SI 2009/3001, reg 78*
(b) Equivalence and genuine diversity of ownership requirements	
Stamp Duty Adjudication	*SA 1891, s 12A*

* See note (2) below.

(1)   *Submission of applications* – A list of HMRC contact details in respect of each category of statutory clearance application can be found here: tinyurl.com/ SCCNTAD.

(2)   *Clearance applications* under more than one of the provisions marked * above may be submitted to HMRC as a single application, by email or letter, as follows:

HMRC Clearance and Counteraction Team
BAI Clearance
HMRC
BX9 1JL

Email: reconstructions@hmrc.gov.uk

Mark the application 'Market sensitive' or 'Non-market sensitive'.

For general enquiries to the unit: Tel 03000 589 004

Scottish and Welsh Taxes

SCOTTISH INCOME TAX (SIT)

(ITA 2007, ss 18, 19; FA 2004, ss 192, 192A; SI 2015/1810)

Non-savings and non-dividend income £	Effective rates for band %	Tax in band £	Cumulative tax £
2021/22			
0–2,097	19	398.43	398.43
2,098–12,726	20	2,126.00	2,524.43
12,727–31,092	21	3,856.23	6,380.66
31,093–150,000	41	48,751.87	55,132.53
Over 150,000	46	–	
2020/21			
0–2,085	19	396.15	396.15
2,086–12,658	20	2,114.60	2,510.75
12,659–30,930	21	3,837.12	6,347.87
30,931–150,000	41	48,818.70	55,166.57
Over 150,000	46	–	–
2019/20			
0–2,049	19	389.31	389.31
2,050–12,444	20	2,079.00	2,468.31
12,445–30,930	21	3,882.06	6,350.37
30,931–150,000	41	48,818.70	55,169.07
Over 150,000	46	–	–
2018/19			
0–2,000	19	380.00	380.00
2,001–12,150	20	2,030.00	2,410.00
12,151–31,580	21	4,080.30	6,490.30
31,581–150,000	41	48,552.20	55,042.50
Over 150,000	46	–	–

Non-savings and non-dividend income £	Effective rates for band %	Tax in band £	Cumulative tax £
2017/18			
0–31,500	20	6,300.00	6,300.00
31,501–150,000	40	47,400.00	53,700.00
Over 150,000	45	–	–
2016/17 (SRIT)			
0–32,000	20	6,400.00	6,400.00
32,001–150,000	40	47,200.00	53,600.00
Over 150,000	45	–	–

Notes

(1) *Scottish income tax (SIT)* – This applies from 6 April 2017 to 'other income' (see note 2) received by Scottish taxpayers, and all revenues from SIT flow to the Scottish Government.

(2) *SIT rates and bands apply to* – Income which is not savings income or dividend income, so broadly earned income, pensions, income from self-employed trades and property businesses. The tax bands which used to determine the rates of CGT or the personal savings allowance are those which apply in the rest of the UK (see **Chapter 1**).

(3) *Pension relief* – Tax relief at source is deducted at 20% for all Scottish taxpayers on pension contributions from 6 April 2018, and that tax is reclaimed by the pension fund. Scottish taxpayers with a higher marginal tax rate (21% or above) must claim additional tax relief by contacting HMRC or through their SA tax return (*FA 2004, s 192*).

(4) *Marriage allowance* – This transferred portion of personal allowance can only be received by taxpayers who are taxed at rates no higher than the basic rate (20%) or the Scottish intermediate rate (21%). Thus Scottish taxpayers can continue to qualify for the marriage allowance onwards even if they are taxed at 21%, see **Chapter 1** (*ITA 2007, s 55B(2)*).

(5) *SIT also affects* – The following income tax charges and reliefs are affected by the rate of SIT paid by Scottish taxpayers:

    (a) lump sum payments of the state retirement pension;

    (b) deficiency relief in respect of a life insurance policy (*ITTOIA 2005, s 539*);

    (c) annual allowance charge under *FA 2004, s 227* (see **Chapter 5**);

    (d) tax relief on Gift Aid donations.

(6) *Adminstered by* – SIT is collected through PAYE and self-assessment, adminstered by HMRC not by Revenue Scotland.

(7) *Scottish rate of income tax (SRIT)* – Applied for 2016/17 only. SRIT replaced 10% points of income tax in each rate band applicable to such 'other income' (see note 2) received by Scottish taxpayers, and the revenues from SRIT flowed to the Scottish

Government. As the SRIT was set at 10% for 2016/17 there was no effect on taxpayers for 2016/17.

(8)   *Armed Forces* – British troops who are subject to SIT receive an annual payment of up to £2,200 per year to compensate them for having to pay higher income tax (see tinyurl.com/SITcomp).

(9)   *Further information* – Guidance on; SIT: tinyurl.com/Scttxrts, Scottish taxpayer status: tinyurl.com/GSTPS, scope of SIT: https://www.gov.uk/scottish-income-tax.

LAND AND BUILDINGS TRANSACTION TAX

LBTT on freehold property in Scotland

(Land and Buildings Transaction Tax (Scotland) Act 2013; SSI 2020/215)

Wholly residential property

Purchase price	Main rate %	Temporary main rate %	ADS %	ADS %
Sales completed in:	1 April 2015 to 14 July 2020 and from 1 April 2021	15 July 2020 to 31 March 2021	1 April 2016 to 24 January 2019	From 25 January 2019
Up to £145,000	0	0	3	4
£145,001–£250,000	2	0	3	4
£250,001–£325,000	5	5	3	4
£325,001–£750,000	10	10	3	4
Over £750,000	12	12	3	4

Notes

(1)   *Applies* – From 1 April 2015 to acquisitions of property located in Scotland. There are transitional rules for contracts entered into on or before 1 May 2012 to determine if SDLT or LBTT applies.

(2)   *Temporary main rate* – Applied from 15 July 2020 to 31 March 2021 inclusive, to match the SDLT reduction in England and Northern Ireland. It was not extended to align with the SDLT 'holiday' to 30 June 2021.

(3)   *First-time buyers* – From 30 June 2018 where all the purchasers have never owned an interest in a residential property, LBTT on the first £175,000 is charged at 0% with no upper limit on the value of the property (*SSI 2018/221*).

(4)   *Additional Dwelling Supplement (ADS)* – Applies from 1 April 2016 to the whole purchase price where an additional residential property is purchased for more than £40,000. The ADS may apply to mixed-use properties where the non-residential rates apply. Rate increase on 25 January 2019 does not apply if the contract was entered into prior to 12 December 2018. The conditions for the ADS charge are not identical to those for which the SDLT supplement applies (see **Chapter 11**).

(5) *Calculation of duty* – The LBTT is calculated as a percentage of the amount of relevant consideration which lies within each appropriate band.

(6) *Payable by* – The purchaser is liable to pay the LBTT within 30 calendar days of the effective date of the transaction (normally the settlement date). Registers of Scotland will not register the buyer's title to the property until the LBTT return has been submitted and the tax has been paid.

(7) *Mixed use property* – Where the property acquired in a single transaction consists of both residential and non-residential property, the LBTT rates for non-residential property apply to the whole transaction (see below).

(8) *No flat rate* – There is no flat rate of LBTT equivalent to flat 15% rate of SDLT which may apply where a residential property is purchased by a non-natural person (see **Chapter 11**), but the ATED can apply to Scottish properties (see **Chapter 13**).

(9) *Further information* – See Revenue Scotland: www.revenue.scot/land-buildings-transaction-tax.

Non-residential

Purchase price or lease premium	Rate %	Leases NPV of rents	Rate %
From 7 February 2020			
Up to £150,000	0	Up to £150,000	0
£150,001 to £250,000	1	£150,001 to £2 million	1
Over £250,000	5	Above £2 million	2
From 25 January 2019			
Up to £150,000	0	Up to £150,000	0
£150,001 to £250,000	1	Over £150,000	1
Over £250,000	5		
From 1 April 2015			
Up to £150,000	0	Up to £150,000	0
£150,001 to £350,000	3	Over £150,000	1
Over £350,000	4.5		

Notes

(1) *Calculation* – Where the chargeable consideration includes rent, LBTT is payable on the lease premium and on the net present value (NPV) of the rent payable. The LBTT chargeable on a lease is generally subject to a three-yearly regular review on assignation or termination of the lease. LBTT calculators are available on the Revenue Scotland website in respect of both new leases and freehold transactions: (tinyurl.com/LBTTcal).

(2)   *Annual rent* – Where the annual rent for the lease of non-residential property amounts to £1,000 or more, the 0% LBTT band is unavailable in respect of any lease premium (*LBTT(S)A 2013, Sch 9*).

(3)   *Licence to occupy* – Such licences for retail shops are subject to LBTT.

(4)   *Residential leases* – No LBTT is charged on a residential lease unless the term exceeds 175 years.

(5)   *Exemptions* – There are a large number of exemptions and reliefs from LBTT such as for transactions with no chargeable consideration, sale and leaseback arrangements, incorporation of LLPs, for charities and crofting community right to buy (*LBTT(S)A 2013, Schs 3–16*).

SCOTTISH LANDFILL TAX (SLfT)

(*Landfill Tax (Scotland) Act 2014; SSI 2019/58*)

Disposals made or treated as made in year beginning:	Standard rate per tonne £	Lower rate per tonne £	Maximum credit %
1 April 2021	96.70	3.10	5.6
1 April 2020	94.15	3.00	5.6
1 April 2019	91.35	2.90	5.6
1 April 2018	88.95	2.80	5.6
1 April 2017	86.10	2.70	5.6
1 April 2016	84.40	2.65	5.6
1 April 2015	82.60	2.60	5.1

Notes

(1)   *Commencement* – Scottish landfill tax applies to disposals of waste in licensed sites in Scotland made on and after 1 April 2015.

(2)   *Applies to* – Waste disposals by way of landfill at a licensed site, unless specifically exempted. Landfill site operators are taxed on disposals of waste by reference to the weight and type of waste concerned. Unlike Landfill tax, SLfT also applies to illegal disposals of waste.

(3)   *Which rate* – The lower rate of landfill tax relates to inactive (or inert) wastes, as listed in the the *Scottish Landfill Tax (Qualifying Material) Order 2015, SSI 2015/45*. The standard rate applies to all other taxable waste.

(4)   *Further information* – see Revenue Scotland www.revenue.scot/scottish-landfill-tax.

WELSH RATE OF INCOME TAX (WRIT)

(ITA 2007, s 6B; SI 2018/1327)

2021/22	**WRIT = 10%**
Up to £37,700	10% + WRIT
£37,701-150,000	30% + WRIT
Over £150,000	35% + WRIT
2020/21	**WRIT = 10%**
Up to £37,500	10% + WRIT
£37,501-150,000	30% + WRIT
Over £150,000	35% + WRIT
2019/20	**WRIT = 10%**
Up to £37,500	10% + WRIT
£37,501-150,000	30% + WRIT
Over £150,000	35% + WRIT

Notes

(1) *Commencement* – Welsh rate of income tax (WRIT) replaces 10% points of income tax in each rate band applicable to 'other income' (see note 2) received by Welsh taxpayers on and after 6 April 2019.

(2) *Applies to* – WRIT applies to income which is not savings or dividends. It will also affect:

    (a) the 'marriage allowance' which is 10% of the personal allowance transferred between married couples on election (see **Chapter 1**);

    (b) income tax relief at source on pension contributions, and the income tax reclaimed by the pension fund;

    (c) deficiency relief in respect of a life insurance policy (*ITTOIA 2005, s 539*);

    (d) tax on state pension lump sum;

    (e) tax relief on Gift Aid donations, but not the basic rate tax reclaimed by the charity under *ITA 2007, s 520*.

(3) *Adminstered by* – WRIT is collected through PAYE and self-assessment, adminstered by HMRC not by the Welsh Revenue Authority.

(4) *Further information* – Guidance on Welsh taxpayer status: tinyurl.com/Wlshtpg.

LAND TRANSACTION TAX

LTT on residential property in Wales

(SI 2018/128, SI 2018/126, SI 2018/125)

Wholly residential property purchase price	Main Rate %	Higher rates %	Main Rate %	Higher rates %
Sales completed from:	1 April 2018 to 26 July 2020 and from 1 July 2021	1 April 2018 to 21 December 2020	27 July 2020 to 30 June 2021	22 December 2020
Up to £180,000	0	3.0	0	4.0
£180,001–£250,000	3.5	6.5	0	7.5
£250,001–£400,000	5.0	8.0	5.0	9.0
£400,001–£750,000	7.5	10.5	7.5	11.5
£750,001–£1,500,000	10.0	13.0	10.0	14.0
Over £1,500,000	12.0	15.0	12.0	16.0

Notes

(1) *Applies to* – Transactions involving residential property located in Wales from 1 April 2018.

(2) *Higher Rates* – Applies to the whole consideration for purchases of residential property for £40,000 or more, by an individual or connected individuals where the property will not be their main home, or the purchaser is a company. The thresholds for the higher rates were not changed on 27 July 2020 when the threshold for main rate was increased. The conditions under which the LTT higher rates apply are not identical to those under which the SDLT supplement applies (see **Chapter 11**).

(3) *Calculation of duty* – LTT is calculated as a percentage of the amount of relevant consideration which lies within each appropriate band, see tinyurl.com/WLTTcal.

(4) *Payable by* – The purchaser is liable to pay the LTT within 30 calendar days of the effective date of the transaction, which is normally the completion date.

(5) *Administered by* – Welsh Revenue Authority (WRA) https://gov.wales/welsh-revenue-authority.

Non-residential

(SI 2018/133)

Non-residential & mixed property purchase price	Rate for freehold purchase or lease premium %	Non-residential & mixed property purchase price	Rate for freehold purchase or lease premium %
1 April 2018 to 21 December 2020		From 22 December 2020	
Up to £150,000	0	Up to £225,000	0
£150,001 to £250,000	1	£225,000 to £250,000	1
£250,000 to £1m	5	£250,000 to £1m	5
Over £1m	6	Over £1m	6

NPV of rents threshold	Rate %	NPV of rents threshold	Rate %
1 April 2018 to 21 December 2020		From 22 December 2020	
Up to £150,000	0	Up to £225,000	0
£150,000 to £2 million	1	£225,000 to £2 million	1
Over £2 million	2	Over £2 million	2

Notes

(1) *Applies to* – Leases of commercial property located in Wales entered into on or after 1 April 2018.

(2) *Specified rent* – If the annual rent is more than £9,000 (inc VAT), the 0–£150,000 band is removed for the lease premium, so that the first amount £250,000 of the premium falls within the 1% band. This minimum annual rent increased to £13,500 in February 2021.

(3) *Calculation of duty* – Use WRA calculator: https://gov.wales/land-transaction-tax-calculator.

WELSH LANDFILL DISPOSALS TAX (LDT)

(Landfill Disposals Tax (Wales) Act 2017)

Disposals made or treated as made in year beginning:	Standard rate per tonne £	Lower rate per tonne £	Unauthorised disposals per tonne £
1 April 2021	96.70	3.10	145.05
1 April 2020	94.15	3.00	141.20
1 April 2019	91.35	2.90	137.00
1 April 2018	88.95	2.80	133.45

Notes

(1)   *Commencement* – LDT applies to disposals of waste in licensed sites in Wales made on and after 1 April 2018.

(2)   *Applies to* – Waste disposals by way of landfill at a licensed site, unless specifically exempted. Landfill site operators are taxed on disposals of waste by reference to the weight and type of waste concerned.

(3)   *Further information* – see https://gov.wales/landfill-disposals-tax-landfill-site-operators.

DISTRIBUTION OF INTESTATE ESTATES

Prior rights of surviving spouse or civil partner in Scotland: threshold limits

(Succession (Scotland) Act 1964, ss 8, 9; Prior Rights of Surviving Spouse And Civil Partner (Scotland) Order 2011, SSI 2011/436)

Prior rights	From 1 February 2013 £	1 June 2005 to 31 Jan 2013 £
Interest of spouse in dwelling house where surviving spouse or civil partner lived	473,000	300,000
Entitlement to furniture and plenishings in that dwelling house	29,000	24,000
Entitlement out of the estate:		
If the deceased left children	50,000	42,000
If there are no children	89,000	75,000

Notes

(1)   *General* – The prior rights of a surviving spouse or civil partner take precedence over all other rights of succession in a fully or partially intestate estate.

(2)   *Further information* – For a table of prior rights for previous periods, see HMRC's Inheritance Tax Manual at IHTM12212.

Scotland – Legal rights*

Survivors	Surviving spouse or civil partner	Children (Legitim)	Dead's part
Spouse or civil partner and children	One-third	One-third	One-third
Spouse or civil partner but no children	One-half	None	One-half
Children but no spouse or civil partner	None	One-half	One-half
No spouse, civil partner or children	None	None	Whole moveable estate

* *Source* – HMRC's Inheritance Tax Manual at IHTM12221.

Notes

(1) *General* – Legal rights apply whether the estate is testate or intestate, and can be claimed only from the moveable estate of the deceased person. A surviving spouse or civil partner is entitled to both prior rights and legal rights.

(2) *Dead's part* – The balance of the estate which the deceased was free to dispose of by will, or which passes under the laws of intestacy, is called the dead's part.

(3) *Further guidance* – See HMRC's Inheritance Tax Manual at IHTM12141-12156.

Remainder of estate

(Succession (Scotland) Act 1964, s 2)

After the prior and legal rights have been satisfied, the rest of the estate broadly devolves in the following order of succession:

- children;
- parents and brothers or sisters (and children) – one-half each;
- brother and sisters (and children) if no surviving parents;
- parents if no surviving brothers or sisters;
- spouse or civil partner;
- uncles and aunts;
- grandparents;
- brothers or sisters of grandparents;
- other ancestors (eg great grandparents);
- The Crown.

International issues

DIVERTED PROFITS TAX (DPT)

(FA 2015, Pt 3)

Period	Main rate	Special rate
From 1 April 2015	25%	55%

Notes

(1) *Objective* – To counteract contrived arrangements by international groups of companies to avoid paying corporation tax on profits generated by activities carried on in the UK.

(2) *Applies to* – Taxable diverted profits arising on and after 1 April 2015. Profits of accounting periods that straddle that date are apportioned (*FA 2015, ss 88–91*).

(3) *Payable by* – UK resident companies that enter into transactions which lack economic substance, and non-resident companies carrying on a trade through a permanent establishment in the UK with UK-related sales revenue of at least £10 million or UK-related expenses of at least £1 million for the accounting period. There are exceptions for small and medium sized companies, and provisions to catch companies that avoid a UK taxable presence (*FA 2015, ss 86, 87*).

(4) *Paid when* – HMRC issue a charging notice to the company specifying the amount of taxable diverted profits (*FA 2015, ss 79(1), 95*).

(5) *Special rate* – This applies to diverted ring fence profits from the oil and gas industry (*FA 2015, s 79(3)*).

(6) *Requirement to notify* – A company which is potentially liable to pay DPT must notify HMRC in writing within three months of the end of the accounting period to which the DPT charge relates. There is no requirement to notify if it is reasonable to conclude no charge to DPT will arise in the period, or HMRC has confirmed the company does not have to notify (*FA 2015, s 92*).

(7) *Off-set* – The DPT is not a deduction for income tax or corporation tax purposes, but the DPT paid may be given as a credit against certain UK or foreign taxes in defined circumstances (*FA 2015, s 100*).

(8) *Future increase – Finance Bill 2021* provides for an increase in the rate of DPT to 31% from 1 April 2023 (*Finance Bill 2021, cl 8*).

(9) *Further information* – HMRC technical note: tinyurl.com/ppxyusp and HMRC Compliance Manual CH155481.

DIGITAL SERVICES TAX (DST)

(FA 2020, ss 39-72, Sch 8)

Period	Rate	Global revenue threshold	UK revenue threshold	UK revenue allowance
From 1 April 2020	2%	£500 million	£25 million	£25 million

Notes

(1) *Objective* –To ensure that the amount of tax paid in the UK by international groups who receive digital services revenues from online marketplaces, online advertising or any other digital services including social media and internet search engines, is reflective of the value derived from UK users.

(2) *Applies to* – Group revenues earned from 1 April 2020 derived from UK users of digital services activity. The group revenues from the relevant digital activities must exceed the annual thresholds above. The DST is calculated at group level, so revenues from all members of the group contribute to these thresholds. It is irrelevant where the component companies in the group are located. However, the DST arises on the individual companies which recognise the revenue from UK users in their accounts.

(3) *Annual allowance* – The DST does not apply to the first £25 million of digital revenues attributable to UK users per year.

(4) *Alternative basis* – The group may elect to pay the DST on the basis of its UK operating margin for the digital services activity instead of the turnover.

(5) *Deductible* – In most cases DST will be a deductible expense for corporation tax purposes as it is wholly and exclusively incurred for the purposes of the trade.

(6) *Registration* – A responsible member of the group should register with HMRC for DST on behalf of the group. This will be the ultimate parent company if no other company is nominated.

(7) *Returns* – The responsible member must submit a DST return online within 12 months of the end of the first accounting period for which DST arises, and for every subsequent accounting period even if there is no DST liability, unless HMRC agree no return is required.

(8) *Further information* – See HMRC Digital Services Tax manual tinyurl.com/ DSTmanual.

FOREIGN EXCHANGE RATES

| Average for the year to 31 December 2020 | | Country/Currency | | Average for the year to 31 March 2021 | |
Sterling value of Currency Unit £	Currency Units per £1	Country	Unit of Currency	Sterling value of Currency Unit £	Currency Units per £1
0.8858	1.128925	European Community	Euro	0.897	1.114767
0.2133	4.68905	Abu Dhabi	Dirham	0.2105	4.751333
0.0072	139.3108	Albania	Lek	0.0072	137.9708
0.0062	160.5908	Algeria	Dinar	0.006	166.8867
0.0014	719.3033	Angola	Readj Kwanza	0.0013	785.9833
0.2901	3.447167	Antigua	E Caribbean Dollar	0.2863	3.492542
0.0113	88.14175	Argentina	Peso	0.0102	97.95342
0.0016	619.2425	Armenia	Dram	0.0016	642.7075
0.4376	2.285333	Aruba	Florin	0.4319	2.315417
0.5339	1.873142	Australia	Dollar	0.5446	1.836092
0.4614	2.167325	Azerbaijan	New Manat	0.4552	2.196692
0.7832	1.276733	Bahamas	Dollar	0.7731	1.293542
2.0802	0.480725	Bahrain	Dinar	2.0531	0.487058
0.0092	108.3958	Bangladesh	Taka	0.0091	109.7183
0.3916	2.553458	Barbados	Dollar	0.3865	2.587067
0.3273	3.055558	Belarus	Rouble	0.3093	3.232717
0.3916	2.553458	Belize	Dollar	0.3865	2.587067
0.0014	740.5308	Benin	CFA Franc	0.0014	731.2375
0.7832	1.276733	Bermuda	Dollar (US)	0.7731	1.293542
0.0106	94.38583	Bhutan	Ngultrum	0.0104	96.1967
0.1134	8.822192	Bolivia	Boliviano	0.1119	8.938317
0.4544	2.200517	Bosnia-Herzegovinia	Marka	0.4587	2.180308

	Average for the year to 31 December 2020	Country/Currency			Average for the year to 31 March 2021	
	Sterling value of Currency Unit £	Currency Units per £1	Country	Unit of Currency	Sterling value of Currency Unit £	Currency Units per £1
	0.0685	14.59167	Botswana	Pula	0.0676	14.79667
	0.154	6.491583	Brazil	Real	0.144	6.94205
	0.5669	1.764075	Brunei	Dollar	0.564	1.773183
	0.4529	2.208083	Bulgaria	Lev	0.4586	2.180367
	0.0014	740.5308	Burkina Faso	CFA Franc	0.0014	731.2375
	0.0004	2440.218	Burundi	Franc	0.0004	2495.95
	0.0002	5207.862	Cambodia	Riel	0.0002	5272.73
	0.0014	740.5308	Cameroon Republic	CFA Franc	0.0014	731.2375
	0.5819	1.718633	Canada	Dollar	0.5801	1.723967
	0.0071	140.0775	Cape Verde Islands	Escudo	0.0072	138.5233
	0.9552	1.046908	Cayman Islands	Dollar	0.9428	1.060692
	0.0014	740.5308	Central African	CFA Franc	0.0014	731.2375
	0.0014	740.5308	Chad	CFA Franc	0.0014	731.2375
	0.001	1011.878	Chile	Peso	0.001	1007.135
	0.1132	8.83605	China	Yuan	0.1138	8.789867
	0.0002	4728.159	Colombia	Peso	0.0002	4833.27
	0.0018	555.3967	Comoros	Franc	0.0018	548.4258
	0.0014	740.5308	Congo (Brazaville)	CFA Franc	0.0014	731.2375
	0.0004	2337.635	Congo (DemRep)	Congo Fr	0.0004	2463.205
	0.0013	741.5783	Costa Rica	Colon	0.0013	765.1583
	0.0014	740.5308	Cote d'Ivoire	CFA Franc	0.0014	731.2375
	0.1177	8.498333	Croatia	Kuna	0.1187	8.423958
	0.7832	1.276733	Cuba	Peso	0.7731	1.293542

continued

237

Average for the year to 31 December 2020		Country/Currency		Average for the year to 31 March 2021	
Sterling value of Currency Unit £	Currency Units per £1	Country	Unit of Currency	Sterling value of Currency Unit £	Currency Units per £1
0.0335	29.85	Czech Republic	Koruna	0.0336	29.73917
0.1188	8.418783	Denmark	Krone	0.1204	8.3037
0.0044	226.8967	Djibouti	Franc	0.0044	229.8833
0.2901	3.447167	Dominica	E Caribbean Dollar	0.2863	3.492542
0.0139	71.73333	Dominican Republic	Peso	0.0135	74.26333
0.2133	4.68905	Dubai	Dirham	0.2105	4.751333
0.7832	1.276733	Ecuador	Dollar	0.7731	1.293542
0.0495	20.20417	Egypt	Pound	0.0489	20.43083
0.0895	11.17	El Salvador	Colon	0.0884	11.3175
0.0014	740.5308	Equatorial Guinea	CFA Franc	0.0014	731.2375
0.0522	19.14667	Eritrea	Nakfa	0.0516	19.39833
0.0227	44.01583	Ethiopia	Birr	0.0212	47.11167
0.3596	2.780583	Fiji Islands	Dollar	0.3614	2.767367
0.0074	134.7142	Fr. Polynesia	CFP Franc	0.0075	133.0233
0.0014	740.5308	Gabon	CFA Franc	0.0014	731.2375
0.0152	66.00482	Gambia	Dalasi	0.0149	66.93232
0.2541	3.935558	Georgia	Lari	0.2423	4.127825
0.1368	7.308	Ghana	Cedi	0.1336	7.4869
0.2901	3.447167	Grenada	E Caribbean Dollar	0.2863	3.492542
0.1016	9.838883	Guatemala	Quetzal	0.1	10.00193
0.0014	740.5308	Guinea Bissau	CFA Franc	0.0014	731.2375

Average for the year to 31 December 2020		Country/Currency		Average for the year to 31 March 2021	
Sterling value of Currency Unit £	Currency Units per £1	Country	Unit of Currency	Sterling value of Currency Unit £	Currency Units per £1
0.0001	12279.96	Guinea Republic	Franc	0.0001	12628.36
0.0037	266.8233	Guyana	Dollar	0.0037	270.5058
0.0083	120.1592	Haiti	Gourde	0.0087	114.69
0.0318	31.4225	Honduras	Lempira	0.0316	31.6475
0.101	9.904692	Hong Kong	Dollar	0.0997	10.02654
0.0025	394.4542	Hungary	Forint	0.0025	396.1217
0.0058	172.7783	Iceland	Krona	0.0057	175.9592
0.0106	94.38583	India	Rupee	0.0104	96.1967
0.0001	18468.68	Indonesia	Rupiah	0.0001	18809.99
0.0007	1520.055	Iraq	Dinar	0.0006	1602.636
0.2259	4.426167	Israel	Shekel	0.2265	4.415492
0.0055	181.42	Jamaica	Dollar	0.0054	186.8
0.0073	136.9667	Japan	Yen	0.0073	136.7317
1.1047	0.9052	Jordan	Dinar	1.0904	0.917108
0.0019	526.415	Kazakhstan	Tenge	0.0018	546.3242
0.0074	135.2292	Kenya	Schilling	0.0071	140.16
2.5534	0.391633	Kuwait	Dinar	2.5222	0.396475
0.0103	97.18917	Kyrgyz Republic	Som	0.0097	103.2792
0.0001	11536.41	Lao People's Dem Rep	Kip	0.0001	11834.26
0.0005	1930.905	Lebanon	Pound	0.0005	1958.484
0.0478	20.92333	Lesotho	Loti	0.047	21.26667
0.7832	1.276733	Liberia	Dollar (US)	0.7731	1.293542
0.5633	1.775383	Libya	Dinar	0.4004	2.497567

continued

239

Average for the year to 31 December 2020		Country/Currency		Average for the year to 31 March 2021	
Sterling value of Currency Unit £	Currency Units per £1	Country	Unit of Currency	Sterling value of Currency Unit £	Currency Units per £1
0.098	10.20106	Macao	Pataca	0.0968	10.32773
0.0144	69.51917	Macedonia	Denar	0.0146	68.64583
0.0002	4863.433	Madagascar	Malagasy Ariary	0.0002	4948.669
0.0011	947.64	Malawi	Kwacha	0.001	972.155
0.1861	5.374058	Malaysia	Ringgit	0.1846	5.417408
0.0508	19.6875	Maldive Islands	Rufiyaa	0.0502	19.9325
0.0014	740.5308	Mali Republic	CFA Franc	0.0014	731.2375
0.0212	47.225	Mauritania	Ouguiya	0.0211	47.43917
0.02	49.93833	Mauritius	Rupee	0.0194	51.45
0.0365	27.36	Mexico	Mexican Peso	0.0355	28.14083
0.0452	22.1275	Moldova	Leu	0.0447	22.35667
0.0003	3580.108	Mongolia	Tugrik	0.0003	3663.994
0.2901	3.447167	Montserrat	E Caribbean Dollar	0.2863	3.492542
0.0823	12.15083	Morocco	Dirham	0.0829	12.065
0.0114	87.615	Mozambique	Metical	0.0108	92.47833
0.0006	1782.799	Myanmar	Kyat	0.0006	1771.008
0.0066	151.0208	Nepal	Rupee	0.0065	153.92
0.0074	134.7142	New Caledonia	CFP Franc	0.0075	133.0233
0.5044	1.982358	New Zealand	Dollar	0.5104	1.959167
0.0229	43.7525	Nicaragua	Gold Cordoba	0.0224	44.655
0.0014	740.5308	Niger Republic	CFA Franc	0.0014	731.2375
0.0021	483.495	Nigeria	Naira	0.002	501.5642
0.0825	12.11667	Norway	Norwegian Krone	0.0827	12.08667

Average for the year to 31 December 2020		Country/Currency		Average for the year to 31 March 2021	
Sterling value of Currency Unit £	Currency Units per £	Country	Unit of Currency	Sterling value of Currency Unit £	Currency Units per £
2.0342	0.4916	Oman	Rial	2.0078	0.498067
0.0049	205.5642	Pakistan	Rupee	0.0048	209.9408
0.7832	1.276733	Panama	Balboa	0.7731	1.293542
0.2267	4.410667	Papua New Guinea	Kina	0.2219	4.505708
0.0001	8614.232	Paraguay	Guarani	0.0001	8832.771
0.2257	4.430742	Peru	New Sol	0.2183	4.581367
0.0157	63.58583	Philippines	Peso	0.0157	63.60083
0.1998	5.003908	Poland	Zloty	0.1997	5.0079
0.2151	4.648642	Qatar	Riyal	0.2123	4.709917
0.1833	5.455892	Romania	New Leu	0.1847	5.4152
0.011	91.295	Russia	Rouble	0.0103	96.965
0.0008	1213.142	Rwanda	Franc	0.0008	1244.74
0	27989.93	Saotome & Principe	Dobra	0	27681.02
0.2088	4.789858	Saudi Arabia	Riyal	0.2061	4.852992
0.0014	740.5308	Senegal	CFA Franc	0.0014	731.2375
0.0075	132.73	Serbia	Dinar	0.0076	131.0725
0.0461	21.7075	Seychelles	Rupee	0.0409	24.44917
0.0001	12664.01	Sierra Leone	Leone	0.0001	12957
0.5669	1.764075	Singapore	Dollar	0.564	1.773183
0.0953	10.488	Solomon Islands	Dollar	0.0948	10.553
0.0013	743.9658	Somali Republic	Schilling	0.0013	754.2633
0.0478	20.92542	South Africa	Rand	0.047	21.26875
0.0007	1511.498	South Korea	Won	0.0007	1506.368
0.0042	236.4675	Sri Lanka	Rupee	0.0041	243.1075

continued

Average for the year to 31 December 2020		Country/Currency		Average for the year to 31 March 2021	
Sterling value of Currency Unit £	Currency Units per £1	Country	Unit of Currency	Sterling value of Currency Unit £	Currency Units per £1
0.2901	3.447167	St Kitts & Nevis	E Caribbean Dollar	0.2863	3.492542
0.2901	3.447167	St Lucia	E Caribbean Dollar	0.2863	3.492542
0.2901	3.447167	St Vincent	E Caribbean Dollar	0.2863	3.492542
0.0147	68.125	Sudan Republic	Pound	0.014	71.515
0.0854	11.70961	Surinam	Dollar	0.0708	14.13147
0.0478	20.92333	Swaziland	Lilangeni	0.047	21.26667
0.0842	11.87083	Sweden	Krona	0.0862	11.605
0.827	1.209258	Switzerland	Franc	0.8363	1.195758
0.0265	37.76833	Taiwan	Dollar	0.0266	37.55917
0.0003	2953.545	Tanzania	Schilling	0.0003	2997.417
0.025	39.9225	Thailand	Baht	0.0249	40.24
0.0014	740.5308	Togo Republic	CFA Franc	0.0014	731.2375
0.5339	1.873142	Tonga Islands	Pa'anga (AUS)	0.5446	1.836092
0.116	8.620492	Trinidad/Tobago	Dollar	0.1145	8.735967
0.2778	3.599142	Tunisia	Dinar	0.278	3.5974
0.1141	8.765433	Turkey	Turkish Lira	0.1068	9.361358
0.2234	4.476125	Turkmenistan	New Manat	0.2206	4.5339
0.2133	4.68905	UAE	Dirham	0.2105	4.751333
0.0002	4744.463	Uganda	Schilling	0.0002	4806.03
0.0294	34.065	Ukraine	Hryvnia	0.0279	35.80333
0.0188	53.31	Uruguay	Peso	0.018	55.61333

Average for the year to 31 December 2020		Country/Currency		Average for the year to 31 March 2021	
Sterling value of Currency Unit £	Currency Units per £1	Country	Unit of Currency	Sterling value of Currency Unit £	Currency Units per £1
0.7832	1.276733	USA	Dollar	0.7731	1.293542
0.0001	12779.25	Uzbekistan	Sum	0.0001	13272.06
0.0067	149.0783	Vanuatu	Vatu	0.0067	148.3033
0	312878.4	Venezuela	Bolivar Fuerte	0	310877.3
0	29649.39	Vietnam	Dong	0	29998.28
0.0074	134.7142	Wallis & Futuna Islands	CFP Franc	0.0075	133.0233
0.2943	3.397967	Western Samoa	Tala	0.2945	3.3955
0.0031	319.2808	Yemen (Rep of)	Rial	0.0031	323.9842
0.044	22.72167	Zambia	Kwacha	0.0395	25.29583
0.0022	462.0433	Zimbabwe	Dollar	0.0021	468.1242

Note

This table is reproduced from information provided by HMRC (tinyurl.com/ExrYrASpt) and is Crown copyright.

Table of spot rates on 31 December 2020 and 31 March 2021					
31 December 2020		**Country/Currency**		**31 March 2021**	
Sterling value of Currency Unit £	**Currency Units per £1**	**Country**	**Unit of currency**	**Sterling value of Currency Unit £**	**Currency Units per £1**
0.5647	1.7709	Australia	AUD Dollar	0.5542	1.8043
0.5759	1.7363	Canada	CAD Dollar	0.5775	1.7316
0.1215	8.2306	Denmark	DKK Krone	0.1150	8.6959
0.9038	1.1064	European Community	EUR Euro	0.8553	1.1692
0.0948	10.5506	Hong Kong	HKD Dollar	0.0938	10.6597
0.0071	140.5114	Japan	JPY Yen	0.0066	151.2457
0.0861	11.6191	Norway	NOK Krone	0.0853	11.7222
0.0503	19.8767	South Africa	ZAR Rand	0.0489	20.4492
0.0898	11.14	Sweden	SEK Krona	0.0834	11.9964
0.8322	1.2016	Switzerland	CHF Franc	0.7733	1.2932
0.7348	1.361	USA	USD Dollar	0.7293	1.3712

Note

This table is reproduced from information provided by HMRC (tinyurl.com/ExrYrASpt) and is Crown copyright.

RECOGNISED STOCK EXCHANGES

(ITA 2007, s 1005; CTA 2010, s 1137)

A 'recognised stock exchange' is one which is either:

- A recognised investment exchange designated as a recognised stock exchange by an order of the Commissioners for HMRC; or

- Any designated market outside the UK.

A recognised stock exchange within *ITA 2007, s 1005* is also treated as such for corporation tax purposes *(CTA 2010, s 1137(1))*.

Stock exchanges designated as recognised stock exchanges

Stock exchange	Date of recognition
Aquis Stock Exchange (AQSE) formerly NEX	25 April 2013
Astana International Exchange (AIX)	25 January 2019
The Athens Stock Exchange	14 June 1993
The Australian Stock Exchange ASX	22 September 1988
National Stock Exchange of Australia	19 June 2014
Bahamas International Securities Exchange (BISX)	19 April 2010
The Barbados Stock Exchange	2 April 2019
The Bermuda Stock Exchange	4 December 2007
The Botswana Stock Exchange	8 October 2018
The Cayman Islands Stock Exchange	4 March 2004
Cboe Europe Limited	1 July 2020
The Colombo Stock Exchange	21 February 1972
The Copenhagen Stock Exchange	22 October 1970
The Cyprus Stock Exchange	22 June 2009
The Dutch Caribbean Securities Exchange	8 December 2014
European Wholesale Securities market	17 January 2013
Euronext London	4 February 2015
Global Board of Trade	30 July 2013
Gibraltar (GSX Ltd)	16 August 2016
GXG Official List	16 May 2013
GXG Main Quote	23 September 2013
The Helsinki Stock Exchange	22 October 1970
The Iceland Stock Exchange	31 March 2006
IPSX UK Limited	25 January 2019
The Johannesburg Stock Exchange	22 October 1970
The Korea Stock Exchange (KRX)	10 October 1994
The Kuala Lumpur Stock Exchange	10 October 1994
LIFFE Administration and Management (LIFFE A&M)	26 September 2011
The London Stock Exchange	19 July 2007
The Malta Stock Exchange	29 December 2005
The Mexico Stock Exchange	10 October 1994
The Stock Exchange of Mauritius	31 January 2011
MERJ Exchange Limited	28 September 2020
The MICEX Stock Exchange	5 January 2011
NASDAQ OMX Tallinn (except its First North market)	5 May 2010
NASDAQ OMX Vilnius (except securities quoted solely on its First North market)	12 March 2012
NASDAQ Riga	8 January 2019
The New Zealand Stock Exchange	22 September 1988

continued

Stock exchange	Date of recognition
The Rio De Janeiro Stock Exchange	17 August 1995
The Sao Paulo Stock Exchange	11 December 1995
The Singapore Stock Exchange	30 June 1977
Singapore Exchange Securities (SGX)	7 October 2014
SIX Swiss Stock Exchange	12 May 1997
The Bond Exchange of South Africa	16 April 2008
The Stockholm Stock Exchange	16 July 1985
The Tel-Aviv Stock Exchange	8 January 2019
The Stock Exchange of Thailand	10 October 1994
The Warsaw Stock Exchange	25 February 2010

Recognised stock exchange countries

The following are countries where any stock exchange in that country that is a stock exchange within the law of that country is a recognised stock exchange.

Stock exchange	Date of recognition
Austria	22 October 1970
Belgium	22 October 1970
Canada	22 October 1970
France	22 October 1970
Germany	5 August 1971
Guernsey	20 December 2013 (note 2)
Hong Kong	26 February 1971
Ireland (Republic of)	22 October 1970
Italy	3 May 1972
Japan	22 October 1970
Luxembourg	21 February 1972
Netherlands	22 October 1970
Norway	22 October 1970
Portugal	21 February 1972
Spain	5 August 1971
USA	22 October 1970 (note 1)

Notes

(1)   *USA* – A stock exchange in the USA is a recognised stock exchange for UK tax purposes if it meets the following criteria:

> 'Any exchange registered with the Securities and Exchange Commission of the United States (SEC) as a national securities exchange under Section 6 of the Securities Exchange Act of 1934 is a recognised stock exchange for UK tax purposes.'

(2)   *Channel Islands* – The Channel Islands Stock Exchange restructured on 20 December 2013 with the business of the exchange being transferred to The Channel Islands Securities Exchange Authority Limited.

Alternative finance investment bonds

(ITA 2007 s 564G)

The following is a list of recognised stock exchanges designated solely for the purposes of *ITA 2007, s 564G* (alternative finance arrangements: investment bonds). The date of recognition in all cases is 1 April 2007:

- Abu Dhabi Securities Market

- Bahrain Stock Exchange

- Dubai Financial Market

- NASDAQ Dubai (formerly Dubai International Financial Exchange)

- Labuan International Financial Exchange

- Saudi Stock Exchange (Tadawul)

- Surabaya Stock Exchange

Recognised futures exchanges

(TCGA 1992, s 288(6))

Tax year of recognition	Exchange
1985/86	ICE Futures (formerly: International Petroleum Exchange London)
	The London Metal Exchange (IME)
	The London Rubber Market
	The London Gold Market
	The London Silver Market
1986/87	The Chicago Mercantile Exchange
	The Philadelphia Board of Trade
	The New York Mercantile Exchange
1987/88	The Chicago Board of Trade
	The Montreal Exchange
	The Mid America Commodity Exchange
	The Hong Kong Futures Exchange
	The New York Board of Trade (NYBOT)
1988/89	The Commodity Exchange, Inc (COMEX)
	The Citrus Associates of the New York Cotton Exchange, Inc
	The New York Cotton Exchange
	The Sydney Futures Exchange Ltd
1991/92	London International Financial Futures and Options Exchange (LIFFE)
	OM London
	OM Stockholm AB
2014/15	Eurex Deutschland

Notes

(1)   Recognised futures exchange means the London International Financial Futures Exchange and any other futures exchange which is designated (for the purposes of *TCGA 1992*) by order of the Board.

(2)   The above exchanges are accepted as recognised futures exchanges for the tax year of recognition onwards (CG56120).

Recognised investment exchanges

(*ITEPA 2003, s 702*)

Date of recognition	Exchange
22 November 2001	ICE Futures Europe
11 July 2013	Cboe Europe Limited (formerly BATS trading)
2 June 2014	Euronext London Limited
19 July 2007	Aquis Stock Exchange Limited (formerly NEX Exchange/ICAP Securities & Derivatives Exchange Limited)
22 November 2001	London Stock Exchange plc
22 November 2001	The London Metal Exchange Limited
8 January 2019	IPSX UK Limited

Recognised overseas investment exchanges

(*ITEPA 2003, s 702*)

Date of recognition	Exchange
30 January 2002	Australian Securities Exchange Limited
23 November 2001	Chicago Board of Trade [CBOT]
21 February 2019	EUREX Frankfurt AG
23 November 2001	National Association of Securities Dealers Automated Quotations (NASDAQ)
23 November 2001	New York Mercantile Exchange Inc. [NYMEX Inc.]
23 November 2001	SIX Swiss Exchange AG
23 November 2001	The Chicago Mercantile Exchange [CME]

Notes for recognised investment and overseas investment exchanges

(1)   Source: The Financial Services Register: (www.fsa.gov.uk/register/exchanges.do).

(2)   The definition of 'readily convertible asset' (*ITEPA 2003, s 702*) includes an asset capable of being sold or otherwise realised on a recognised investment exchange, within the meaning of the *Financial Services and Markets Act 2000*. The Financial Conduct Authority recognises and supervises a number of recognised overseas investment exchanges.

DOUBLE TAXATION AGREEMENTS

(TIOPA 2010, Pt 2, Ch 1)

Countries with a Double Taxation Agreement with the UK

Country	Authority	Coverage
Albania	SI 2013/3145	C
Algeria	SI 2015/1888	ATP
		C
Antigua & Barbuda	SRO 1947/2865	C
	Amended by SI 1968/1096	
Argentina	SI 1997/1777	C
	Amended by Protocol of 3 January 1996	
Armenia	SI 2011/2722	C
Australia	SI 2003/3199	C
Austria	SI 1970/1947	C
	Amended by Protocols SI 1979/117, SI 1994/768	
	SI 2010/2688, and SI 2019/255	
Azerbaijan	SI 1995/762	C
Bahrain	SI 2012/3075	C
Bangladesh	SI 1980/708	C
Barbados	SI 2012/3076	C
Belarus	SI 1974/1269 replaced by:	C
	SI 2018/778	C
Belgium	SI 1987/2053	C
	Amended by Protocol SI 2010/2979	
Belize	SRO 1947/2866	C
	Amended by Protocols SI 1968/573 and SI	
	1973/2097	
Bolivia	SI 1995/2707	C
Bosnia- Herzegovina	SI 1981/1815	C
Botswana	SI 2006/1925	C
Brazil	SI 1968/572	S, ATP
British Virgin Islands	SI 2009/3013	IT
Brunei Darussalam	SI 1950/1977	C
	Amended by Protocols SI 1968/306 and SI	
	1973/2098 brought into effect by SI 2013/3146	
Bulgaria	SI 1987/2054	C
	SI 2015/1890	
Cameroon	SI 1982/1841	ATP
Canada	SI 1980/709	C
	Amended by Protocols SI 1980/1528, SI	
	1985/1996 and SI 2003/2619	
	SI 2015/2011	

continued

Country	Authority	Coverage
Cayman Islands	SI 2010/2973	IT
Chile	SI 2003/3200	C
China	SI 1981/1119 (not superseded)	ATP
	SI 2011/2724	C
	Amended by Protocol, SI 2013/3142	
Colombia	SI 2018/377	C
Croatia	SI 1981/1815	C
	SI 2015/1889	
Cyprus	SI 1975/425	C
	Replaced by: SI 2018/839	
Czech Republic	SI 1991/2876	C
Denmark	SI 1980/1960	C
	Amended by Protocols SI 1991/2877 and SI 1996/3165	
Egypt	SI 1980/1091	C
Estonia	SI 1994/3207	C
Ethiopia	SI 2011/2725	C
Falkland Islands	SI 1997/2985	C
Faroes	SI 2007/3469	C
Fiji	SI 1976/1342	C
Finland	SI 1970/153	C
	Amended by Protocols SI 1973/1327, SI 1980/710, SI 1985/1997, 1991/2878 and 1996/3166	
France	SI 2009/226	C
	SI 2012/458	B
Gambia	SI 1980/1963	C
Georgia	SI 2004/3325	C
	Amended by Protocol SI 2010/2972	
Germany	SI 2010/2975	C
	SI 2012/459	B
	Amended by Protocol SI 2014/1874	
Ghana	SI 1993/1800	C
Gibraltar	SI 2020/275	C
Greece	SI 1954/142	C
Grenada	SI 1949/361	C
	Amended by Protocol SI 1968/1867	
Guernsey	SI 1952/1215	C
	Amended by Protocols in: 1994, 2009/3011,SI 2015/2008, SI 2016/750	
	New agreement: SI 2018/1345	
Guyana	SI 1992/3207	C
Hong Kong	SI 2010/2974 including Protocol	C
Hungary	SI 2011/2726	C

250

Country	Authority	Coverage
Iceland	SI 2014/1879	C
India	SI 1993/1801 plus Protocol SI 2013/3147	C
Indonesia	SI 1994/769	C
Iran	SI 1960/2419	ATP
Ireland	SI 1976/2151 Amended by Protocols SI 1976/2152, SI 1995/764 and SI 1998/3151	C
Isle of Man	SI 1955/1205 Amended by Supplementary Arrangements SI 1991/2880, SI 1994/3208, SI 2009/228 and SI 2016/749 and exchange of letters in 2013	C
Israel	SI 1963/616 Amended by Protocols SI 1971/391, SI 2019/1111	C
Italy	SI 1990/2590	C
Ivory Coast	SI 1987/169	C
Jamaica	SI 1973/1329	C
Japan	SI 2006/1924	C
Jersey	SI 1952/1216 Amended by Arrangements SI 1994/3210 and SI 2009/3012, SI 2015/2009 and SI 2016/752	C
Jordan	SI 2001/3924	C
Kazakhstan	SI 1994/3211 Amended by Protocol SI 1998/2567	C
Kenya	SI 1977/1299	C
Kiribati	SI 1950/750 Amended by Arrangements SI 1968/309 and SI 1974/1271	C
Korea (Republic of)	SI 1996/3168	C
Kosovo	SI 2015/2007	C
Kuwait	SI 1999/2036	C
Latvia	SI 1996/3167	C
Lebanon	SI 1964/278	S, ATP
Lesotho	SI 1997/2986 SI 2018/376	C
Libya	SI 2010/243	C
Liechtenstein	SI 2012/3077	C
Lithuania	SI 2001/3925 Amended by Protocol SI 2002/2847	C
Luxembourg	SI 1968/1100 Amended by Protocols SI 1980/567, SI 1984/364 and SI 2010/237	C
Macedonia	SI 2007/2127	C

continued

Country	Authority	Coverage
Malawi	SI 1956/619 Amended by Protocols SI 1964/1401, SI 1968/1101 and SI 1979/302	C
Malaysia	SI 1997/2987, SI 2010/2971	C
Malta	SI 1995/763	C
Mauritius	SI 1981/1121 replaced by SI 2018/840	C
Mexico	SI 1994/3212 Amended by Protocol SI 2010/2686	C
Moldova	SI 2008/1795	C
Mongolia	SI 1996/2598	C
Montenegro	SI 1981/1815	C
Montserrat	SRO 1947/2869 Amended by Protocol SI 1968/576 SI 2011/1083	C
Morocco	SI 1991/2881	C
Myanmar (Burma)	SI 1952/751 including Protocol	C
Namibia	SI 1962/2352 Extended by SI 1962/2788 – Amended by Protocol SI 1967/1489 as extended by SI 1967/1490	C
Netherlands	SI 2009/227 amended by Protocol SI 2013/3143 SI 2015/344 Bank Levy double taxation	C
New Zealand	SI 1984/365 Amended by Protocols SI 2004/1274, SI 2008/1973	C
Nigeria	SI 1987/2057	C
Norway	SI 2013/3144	C
Oman	SI 1998/2568 Amended by Protocol SI 2010/2687	C
Pakistan	SI 1987/2058	C
Panama	SI 2013/3149	C
Papua New Guinea	SI 1991/2882	C
Philippines	SI 1978/184	C
Poland	SI 2006/3323	C
Portugal	SI 1969/599	C
Qatar	SI 2010/241, SI 2011/1684	C
Romania	SI 1977/57	C
Russia	SI 1994/3213	C
St. Christopher (St. Kitts) and Nevis	SRO 1947/2872	C
Saudi Arabia	SI 1994/767 (not superseded) SI 2008/1770 including Protocol	ATP C

Country	Authority	Coverage
Senegal	SI 2015/1892	C
Serbia	SI 1981/1815	C
Sierra Leone	SRO 1947/2873 Amended by Protocol SI 1968/1104	C
Singapore	SI 1997/2988 Amended by Protocols SI 2010/2685 and SI 2012/3078	C
Slovak Republic	SI 1991/2876	C
Slovenia	SI 2008/1796	C
Solomon Islands	SI 1950/748 Amended by Arrangements SI 1968/574 and SI 1974/1270	C
South Africa	SI 2002/3138 Amended by Protocol SI 2011/2441	C
Spain	SI 2013/3152	C
Sri Lanka	SI 1980/713	C
Sudan	SI 1977/1719	C
Swaziland	SI 1969/380	C
Sweden	SI 2015/1891	C
Switzerland	SI 1978/1408 Amended by Protocols SI 1982/714, SI 1994/3215, SI 2007/3465, SI 2010/2689 and exchange of letters from 19 December 2012. SI 2018/627	C
Taiwan	SI 2002/3137	C
Tajikistan	SI 2014/3275	ATP C
Thailand	SI 1981/1546	C
Trinidad and Tobago	SI 1983/1903	C
Tunisia	SI 1984/133	C
Turkey	SI 1988/932	C
Turkmenistan	SI 1986/224 SI 2016/1217	ATP C
Tuvalu	SI 1950/750 Amended by SI 1968/309 and SI 1974/1271	C
UAE	SI 2016/754	C
Uganda	SI 1993/1802	C
Ukraine	SI 1993/1803, SI 2018/779	C
Uruguay	SI 2016/753	C
USA	SI 2002/2848 including Protocol and Exchange of Notes	C

continued

Country	Authority	Coverage
Uzbekistan	SI 1994/770 replaced by: SI 2018/628	C
Venezuela	SI 1996/2599	C
Vietnam	SI 1994/3216	C
Zaire	SI 1977/1298	S, ATP
Zambia	SI 2014/1876	C
Zimbabwe	SI 1982/1842	C

Notes

(1) Key to coverage of agreements:

ATP Air Transport Profits

B Bank Levy

C Comprehensive

S Shipping Profits

IT Income taxes only

(2) *Multilateral Instrument (MLI)* – This was signed on 7 July 2017 and will have effect for UK tax treaties from:

- 1 January 2019 for taxes withheld at source;

- 1 April 2019 for corporation tax; and

- 6 April 2019 for income tax and capital gains tax.

The date which individual UK tax treaties are modified by the MLI depends on the date the treaty partner deposits their own instruments of ratification, acceptance or approval.

(3) *Further information* – Full collection of Double Taxation Treaties: www.gov.uk/government/collections/tax-treaties, MLI: tinyurl.com/y79h46tr, and HMRC's Double Taxation Relief Manual DT2140 et seq.

DTAs signed but not in force

(1) *Anguilla* – Exchange of letters were signed on 20 December 2013.

(2) *Belgium* – Second Protocol to the Double Taxation Convention was signed on 14 March 2014.

(3) *Germany* – The 2021 Protocol to the 2010 Double Taxation Convention was signed in London on 12 January 2021.

(4) *Kyrgyzstan* – Double Taxation Relief and International Tax Enforcement

(5) *Sweden* – The 2021 Protocol to the 2015 Double Taxation Convention was signed in London on 23 February 2021.

Double Taxation Conventions (DTCs): Inheritance Tax

(*IHTA 1984, s 158*; IHTM 27161 et seq)

Country	Authority
France	SI 1963/1319
India	SI 1956/998
Ireland	SI 1978/1107
Italy	SI 1968/304
Netherlands	SI 1980/706 Amended by Protocol SI 1996/730
Pakistan	SI 1957/1522
South Africa	SI 1979/576
Sweden	SI 1981/840 Amended by Protocol SI 1989/986
Switzerland	SI 1994/3214 including Protocol
USA	SI 1979/1454

Note

The UK Government may enter into a DTC with the Government of any territory outside the UK. Where the deceased was domiciled in a DTC territory or owned property situated in one of those territories, the terms of the relevant DTC should be considered in relation to IHT and any tax imposed by the laws of that territory which is of a similar character or is chargeable by reference to death or gifts made *inter vivos* (*IHTA 1984, s 158;* IHTM27161).

Tax Information Exchange Agreements (TIEAs)

TIEAs in force

An updated list of TIEAs in force is available at: tinyurl.com/TIEAIF.

Country	Authority	Scope
Anguilla	SI 2010/2677 SI 2014/1357	B NR
Antigua and Barbuda	SI 2011/1075	B
Aruba	SI 2011/2435	R
Bahamas	SI 2010/2684	B
Bermuda	SI 2018/518	B
Belize	SI 2011/1685	B
British Virgin Islands	SI 2005/1457 SI 2009/3013	R B
Cayman Islands	Agreement effective 16 April 2005	NR

continued

Country	Authority	Scope
Curaçao, Sint Maarten and BES Islands	SI 2011/2433	B
Dominica	SI 2011/1686	B
Gibraltar	SI 2006/1453	R
	SI 2010/2680	B
Grenada	SI 2011/1687	B
Guernsey	SI 2009/3011	B
Isle of Man	SI 2005/1263	R
	SI 2009/228	B
Jersey	SI 2009/3012	B
Liberia	SI 2011/2434	B
Liechtenstein	SI 2010/2678	B
Montserrat	SI 2005/1459	R
Monaco	SI 2015/804	B
Netherlands Antilles	SI 2005/1460	B
San Marino	SI 2011/1688	B
St Christopher (St Kitts) and Nevis	SI 2011/1077	B
St Lucia	SI 2011/1076	B
St Vincent and the Grenadines	SI 2011/1078	B
Turks and Caicos Islands	SI 2010/2679	B
		NR
Uruguay	SI 2014/1358	B

Notes

Key to scope of TIEAs:

B   Bilateral agreements for co-operation in tax matters through exchange of information

NR   Non-reciprocal Agreements relating to the EU Directive on taxation of savings income in the form of interest payments

R   Reciprocal Agreements relating to the EU Directive on taxation of savings income in the form of interest payments

TIEAs signed/not in force

Country	Signed
Turks & Caicos Islands	26 November 2013
British Virgin Islands	28 November 2013
Marshall Islands	17 September and 26 October 2012
Brazil	2012

Index